CHILDREN FOR HIRE

CHILDREN FOR HIRE

The Perils of Child Labor in the United States

Marvin J. Levine

Westport, Connecticut
London

Library of Congress Cataloging-in-Publication Data

Levine, Marvin J., 1930–
Children for hire : the perils of child labor in the United States / Marvin J. Levine.
p. cm.
Includes bibliographical references and index.
ISBN 1–56720–433–3 (alk. paper)
1. Child labor—United States. 2. Youth—Employment—United States. 3. Children—Health and hygiene—United States. 4. Youth—Health and hygiene—United States. 5. Industrial safety—United States. 6. Agricultural laborers—United States. 7. Working class—Education—United States. I. Title.
HD6250.U6 L48 2003
331.3′1′0973—dc21 2002029767

British Library Cataloguing in Publication Data is available.

Library of Congress Catalog Card Number: 2002029767
ISBN: 1–56720–433–3

First published in 2003

Praeger Publishers, 88 Post Road West, Westport, CT 06881
An imprint of Greenwood Publishing Group, Inc.
www.praeger.com

Printed in the United States of America

The paper used in this book complies with the Permanent Paper Standard issued by the National Information Standards Organization (Z39.48–1984).

10 9 8 7 6 5 4 3 2 1

To my grandchildren, Jonathan (Yoni) and Rachel. We love and cherish you and hope that your lives will be filled with health, happiness, and good fortune.

To Batya Harari. Your life has served as an example to all of selflessness and enduring humanity.

Contents

Preface

My involvement in writing this book came about indirectly. I intended to pursue a project dealing with global child labor, and in the course of investigating prior research on this topic, discovered that the Bureau of International Labor Affairs of the U.S. Department of Labor had recently published two volumes covering child labor throughout the world. However, I noted that the United States was not included; hence my decision to concentrate on the child labor situation in this country.

This book will focus on a number of areas that directly impact the safety and health of children and adolescent workers. The legal background is important in that American youths are regulated by legislation enacted more than six decades ago that, consequently, is in need of revision in important areas, particularly agricultural employment. Occupational employment in retail trade, especially restaurant and fast-food enterprises, poses serious safety and health risks for young workers and is an area discussed in detail. Young people working on farms, whether they be children on small family farms, hired farm labor, or children of migrant farm workers, are treated differently under the law, and in my estimation, without justification.

For that matter, the health risks to children and adolescents created by agricultural chemicals is a present-day reminder of the warnings voiced by Rachel Carson in her seminal book forty years ago. This is an important public policy topic that deserves closer examination because of the latent effects that presently plague farm adults from exposure years earlier and will threaten the lives of youth in years to come. Also, the inordinately long and intensive work performed by farm children and adolescents, which negatively affects their educational achievement, is worthy of closer examination.

One of the most egregious examples of exploitative child labor involves under-age immigrant children toiling under extremely dangerous working conditions in garment industry sweatshops located in urban centers, primarily on the east and west coasts. This brings into play the efforts being undertaken by American manufacturers, both domestically and abroad, to monitor the operations of their contractors and subcontractors to ensure that minimum wage and child labor laws are not being violated. Voluntary corporate codes of conduct, implemented in a haphazard fashion, and subjected to cursory audits by less than independent internal monitoring, leave much to be desired in terms of protecting child workers from abusive treatment.

One of the most important, and frustrating, challenges lies in the relationship between student employment and academic performance. How much work is too much? Does intensive employment beyond a set number of hours per week exacerbate the problem of school dropouts?

Is this work a valuable experience leading to productive, rewarding careers, or does it promote aimlessness, exposure to poor role models, and delinquent, sometimes criminal, behavior?

Another important inquiry is directed toward the seemingly insoluble problem of accurate statistical data depicting the quantitative scope of child labor in our nation. Serious problems exist here, with the federal government consistently undercounting child laborers, due to minimum age limitations and inadequate description of the characteristics of work accidents, which hamper the implementation of effective safety programs and preventive measures. Tens of thousands of children remain as invisible statistics because of lack of coordination between federal, state, and local data-gathering efforts.

I hope this book will contribute to a much-needed public awareness of a serious societal problem affecting millions of children and lead to more effective remedial measures by both private and public sector organizations.

I would like to thank the following persons for their assistance in the preparation of this book: Barbara Chipman, the Robert H. Smith School of Business, University of Maryland, College Park; Lynn Goldman, National Institute for Occupational Safety and Health, Washington, D.C.; John R. Myers, Public Health Service, Department of Health & Human Services, Morgantown, West Virginia; Ayn Lowry, Farmworker Justice Fund, Washington, D.C.; Consuelo Holguin, World Resources Institute, Washington, D.C.: Dawn Castillo, Centers for Disease Control and Prevention, National Institute for Occupational Safety and Health, Morgantown, West Virginia; Jillian Hopewell, Migrant Clinicians Network, Austin, Texas; Julie Herlands, Council for Citizenship Education, Russell Sage College, Troy, New York; Fred Blosser, NIOSH Public Affairs, Washington, D.C.; Nancy Davidson, The Brookings Institution, Washington, D.C.; Cindy Schneider, Migrant Legal Program, Washington, D.C.; Mark Taylor, U.S. Department of Education, Washington, D.C.; Barbara Lee, National Farm Medicine Center, Marshfield, Wisconsin; Shari Burgus, Farm Safety 4 Just Kids, Earlham, Iowa; Gail McCallion, Congressional Research Service, Library of Congress, Washington, D.C.; Jayne Bertovich, Bureau of Primary Health Care, Department of Health & Human Services, Washington, D.C.; and E. Lynn Jenkins, Office of the Director, NIOSH, Washington, D.C.

I would also like to send special thanks to James R. Dunton, Consulting Editor for Praeger Publishers, for his seemingly limitless patience and assistance in the preparation of the manuscript.

Last, but not least, as the author, I take full responsibility for any errors of omission or commission.

1

The Scope of the Problem

The role of work in the lives of our children is an issue that has been long neglected in the United States. Workers, especially children, have always been expendable. As a society, we have allowed ourselves to think that work, almost any work, is a positive influence in the lives of young people. The troubles that make the lives of many young people—drugs, gangs, pregnancy, among many others—seem more serious than employment practices. But make no mistake about it, work has an adverse effect in the lives of American youth, as this book will reveal.

OVERVIEW

"The most beautiful sight that we see is the child at labor. As early as he may get at labor the beautiful, the more useful does his life get to be."

That was the opinion of Asa G. Candler, founder of the Coca-Cola Co., around the turn of the century. But the view from below, on the factory floor, was less pretty, as one woman testified after finding children as young as 5 years old amid the looms of South Carolina's textile mills:

> It is over eight o'clock when the children reach their homes—later if the millwork is behind-hand and they are kept over hours. They are usually beyond speech. They fall asleep at the table, on the stairs; they are carried to bed and there laid down as they are, unwashed, undressed; and the inanimate bundles of rags so lie until the mill summons them with its imperious cry before sunrise, while they are still in stupid sleep.

This excerpt comes from Milton Meltzer's *Bread and Roses,* a history of American labor. It is the kind of scene that shocked Americans of the past and triggered movements to abolish child labor. Now, the pictures are coming back to haunt Americans, not in history books, but in the present reality of global economics.

The corporations and unions that manufacture goods in the United States and Europe often complain about the unfair competition from factories in the underdeveloped world that employ children and pay low wages. These groups are responsible for much of the political pressure against child labor in overseas factories. However, as the following quote indicates, present-day business leaders still resent what is considered to be intrusive regulation of child labor in this country:

> We do not condone one instance of illegal employment of children—on the farm or in the city. But we are more than tired of pieces of emotional and undocumented prose pleading child labor abuse as a reason to unionize farm workers, or to change our economic structure, or to impose restrictive new pesticide standards on agriculture.[1]

As do most Americans, the majority of business leaders strongly oppose child-labor violations. But some suggest the problem is not nearly as pervasive as child welfare advocates imply. Moreover, executives in industries buffeted by the demands of the international marketplace and the changing demographics of the labor force contend that child-labor laws are often outdated and enforced mostly for publicity.

For instance, advocates of increased reliance on teenagers working legally insist that the vast majority of American firms do not violate child-labor laws and argue that bagging burgers at a local fast-food place is far different from working in an urban sweatshop. They also point out that most parents believe in the value of children developing good work habits at an early age. In fact, a widely held opinion is that children may be better off working under substandard labor conditions than in the streets selling drugs. That complaint has been often expressed in the past few years. Labor enforcement officials admit its veracity but, nevertheless, maintain it cannot excuse broken laws and dangerous industrial practices.

A presidential task force has called for a worldwide ban on child-labor and sweatshop conditions in overseas factories operated by American companies in the apparel industry. However, Western critics forget that child labor was common in the United States and Europe at the turn of the twentieth century. For example, the U.S. Census Bureau reports that in 1890 more than 1.5 million children between the ages of 10 and 14 were gainfully employed, despite the reluctance of parents to admit to the census takers at that time that they were violating laws against child labor in many states.

Regulations of child labor has been motivated by diverse concerns: economic, humane, and more broadly, social. In the nineteenth and early twentieth centuries, child workers were viewed as an alternative source of cheap labor who competed with their parents and other adults for employment at the cost of their own health and education. Products of child labor vied with goods produced by adults, exerting a downward pressure on wages and living standards. Aside from health and safety hazards, inadequate rest, it was argued, left children ill-suited for educational activities and, in turn, as adults, ill-prepared for employment and for support of their own children, thus extending the cycle of poverty and adding to social welfare costs.

Despite the common belief that the problem of illegal child labor was remedied long ago, the practice has persisted in the United States and appears to be on the rise. Today, more than four million children and adolescents are legally employed. A generally unknown fact is that the United States has more of its children in the workforce than any other developed country.

Child labor has a long history that complicates attempts to limit or control it. Serious efforts to protect children are hampered by deep-seated cultural values. Many Americans hold ambivalent views toward child labor. They view work as redemptive and as a morally legitimate method of self-improvement. Within this context, exploited children are those forced into premature adulthood due to long hours of work at substandard wages under circumstances that threaten their physical and mental health. They may be separated from the security, protection, and guidance of their families. Their hopes for a better life are compromised by the absence of meaningful educational and training opportunities. They are found working illegally in textile, jewelry, and machine shops in New York and New Jersey; operating meat-cutting machines and paper-box bailers in supermarkets in the Southeast; selling candy door-to-door in Washington state; and in farming operations throughout the country.

A majority of teenagers are employed in the growing service sector, an industry that has become increasingly dependent on youth labor, particularly in regions with strong economies. In many families, economic pressures force children to work to replace family income that has disappeared because of diminished earnings of primary bread winners. This decline in income has placed limits on the ability of adults to support real or imagined needs important in the lives of their children: clothes, food, transportation, educational expenses, entertainment, and so forth. Complicating this scenario are insidious advertising and peer group pressures that create the perception of need and exacerbate the need to earn more disposable income.

Meanwhile, employers are necessarily motivated by traditional business objectives. All businesses must be profitable in order to operate, and for most companies, there is an imperative to find employees willing to work at the lowest possible cost. For too many firms, especially those in the burgeoning service area, and even more so in the fast-food industry, hiring consequently is focused on luring teenagers into employment. The documentation of abuses is pervasive and has been the subject of congressional oversight hearings, comprehensive regulatory and enforcement actions, and federal legislation to increase child-labor penalties.

Yet, despite incontrovertible evidence of child-labor excesses, government regulation has drawn pejorative criticism, as this comment by an American Farm Bureau Federation official illustrates: "The words 'government efficiency' tend to register in my mind as an oxymoron, perhaps equivalent to other classics: 'child labor' and 'Army intelligence.'"[2]

THE LEGAL CONTEXT

As defined, child labor generally refers to any economic activity performed by a person under the age of 18. Not all work performed by children is detrimental or exploitative. Child labor does not usually refer to light work after school or legitimate apprenticeship opportunities for youth. Nor does it refer to young people helping out in the family business. Instead, the child labor open to critique is generally employment that prevents effective school attendance and that is often performed under conditions hazardous to the physical and mental health of children.

Since 1938, child labor in the United States has been regulated under the federal Fair Labor Standards Act (FLSA). This law prohibits employment in any hazardous nonagricultural occupation for all children under 18. No child under 18 may work in mining, logging, construction, on a motor vehicle, or with power-driven machinery. The Act imposes additional restrictions on the employment of children under age 16 and sets limits on the number of hours a child may work on school days (no more than three hours per day for 14- and 15-year-olds). In agriculture, where legal restrictions are much less stringent, work with power-driven equipment and hazardous pesticides is prohibited only until age 16, while all work on family farms with less than 11 employees is exempt from legal protection.

The FLSA limits the employment of minors in agriculture according to age and occupational activity. Children 14 to 15 years old may work on farms outside school hours in nonhazardous farm occupations. Children aged 12 to 13 may work after school in any nonhazardous farm job with written parental consent or on the same farm where their parents are employed. Children 10 to 11 years of age may work outside school hours in any nonhazardous farm job, with written parental consent only on farms where none of the employees are legally entitled to the federal minimum wage, but a special waiver may be obtained from the Department of Labor. Children of farm owners and operators may be employed by their parents at any time and in any occupation on a farm owned or operated by their parents.

Unfortunately, since 1981, there has been a relaxation in enforcement of federal child-labor law provisions limiting maximum permissible hours of work and prohibiting use of dangerous machinery. Repeal of the ban on industrial homework, which was created fifty years ago to protect women and children from industrial exploitation in piecework industries, has further undermined the FLSA. The spread of industrial homework has resulted in children being exposed in their homes to solvents (in electronic assembly), to lead and cadmium (in costume jewelry manufacture), to repetitive motion injury, and to power-driven equipment (in the garment trades).

Furthermore, illegal child labor is widespread and apparently has increased in frequency over the past decade. No exact figures are available, but the number has been estimated at over two million. Evidence from a variety of sources—the Labor Department's strike force, the General Accounting Office (GAO), states' investigations, and emergency room records—suggests that children work illegally in the fields, in the garment industry, in fast-food restaurants, on construction sites, and in mines, sawmills, and gas stations.

On the job, they suffer amputations, burns, deep cuts, and electrocutions. At least several hundred a year are killed, according to investigators at the National Institute for Occupational Safety and Health. Other children work late on school nights, in violation of state and federal laws, and often fall asleep in class.

Also compounding the weak and ineffective enforcement system is an ambivalent attitude vis-à-vis enforcement and penalties. In opposing the Child Labor Amendments of 1991, an acting assistant secretary of labor for employment standards opposed criminal sanctions of up to ten years in prison for violations that result in a minor's death or serious bodily injury. Asserting that it is "inadvisable to legislate again so soon," he argued for a year's delay to assess whether the increase in civil penalties from $1,000 to $10,000 for willful violations had a dampening effect on compliance. He suggested that employers may be less willing to cooperate with Labor Department investigations in light of the higher penalties and seemingly overlooked the high death and injury rates of illegally employed minors.[3]

Another serious problem, the widespread employment of children in sweatshops (establishments that repeatedly violate fair labor as well as occupational health and safety standards) has been documented. Also, tens of thousands of children are employed in illegal farm labor.

In this regard, the problem of permissive standards for children working in agriculture is exemplified by a North Carolina study that determined loopholes in federal labor contribute to dozens of childhood deaths and injuries each year. The study revealed that 86 percent of workplace deaths among those under eighteen were "in situations that appear to have violated the federal Fair Labor Standards Act, or at least its intent." A majority of the deaths were caused by farm equipment, especially tractors, which under the FLSA, may be used by child workers along with other hazardous equipment on family farms excepted from FLSA coverage.[4]

Illegal child labor may be seriously understated, and the statistics gathered so far may be only the "tip of the iceberg" because there is no systematic data collection, and many injuries and even death are not reported. The GAO, an investigative arm of Congress, for instance, reported that Labor Department data indicated that the number of illegally employed minors had almost tripled during the 1983–1991 period from 9,200 to 27,500, but these figures may grossly underestimate the problem because they were derived from woefully inadequate surveillance and reporting systems.

An example of underreporting surfaced when a search of 1988 census data revealed that at least 166,000 15-year-old children were working too many hours or in occupations like construction, that are prohibited for children that young. More than half were working in prohibited jobs.[5]

One problem is simply discovering violators, given the relatively few inspectors the federal government employs for that purpose. For example, the National Institute for Occupational Safety and Health (NIOSH) has 2,000 inspectors, and the Labor Department has another 1,000 wage-and-hour division employees, who attempt to uncover illegal child labor as well as violations involving adults. That combined force equals only a quarter of the 12,000 inspectors who work for the Fish and Wildlife Service. One could characterize this as a case of misplaced priorities with the investigators spread thin: 816 of them for 113 million workers, of whom, an estimated 20 million are under the age of eighteen.

Child labor is included as part of an overall investigation of a company's wage and time records. With their focus on time cards, personnel records, and employee interviews, investigators admit that they seldom witness minor workers involved in hazardous tasks. The most common violations found by investigators are young employees working later hours or more hours than those allowed by the law.

Not all children are protected by federal law from working in hazardous conditions. For the most part, agriculture is exempt from federal and state laws governing the working hours and conditions of child labor and federal restrictions on hazardous jobs for minors. As previously noted, there really is not much enforcement presence on either a federal or state level. Probably the only time an employer would be targeted for an investigation of child-labor law violations would be if a complaint were received or an accident involving a minor reported. As is the case with many violators of occupational health and safety laws, the most frequent excuse given by employers for child-labor law violations is ignorance. OSHA has so few inspectors that it would take eighty-four years to get around to inspecting all the workplaces for which it is responsible; it would take twenty-five years just to visit every high-hazard workplace for a surprise inspection. With such inadequate resources, we are fighting, to put it mildly, an uphill battle.

The problem is exacerbated by the dilemma of children who must work to support their families and those for whom work is a real part of their preparation for assuming the responsibilities of adulthood. Although work can encourage the development of discipline by teaching a child the value of money and providing valuable role models, employment during childhood and adolescence carries significant risks. These risks are magnified greatly when employment is illegal or exploitative.

OCCUPATIONAL HEALTH AND SAFETY RISKS

There were approximately 2.6 million working adolescents aged 16 to 17 in the United States in 1995. Younger workers are at increased risk of work-related injury because they often have limited job knowledge, training, and skills. Private industry reported in 1993 that more than 95,000 illnesses and injuries that involved days away from work occurred among workers ages 16 to 19. The most serious of these injuries were burns occurring in the food service industry and sprains and strains due to overexertion. In addition, the number of children under 16 who are working and the illnesses and injuries they experience are not well documented. The best documented examples are childhood traumatic injuries to children illegally employed in various manufacturing settings.

Disregard for the law, especially those provisions covering hazardous jobs, has led to a litany of serious injuries suffered by underage workers. Such injuries do not just occur in sweatshops or on farms. Department of Labor news releases read like a Dickens tale:

> In Millstadt, Illinois, two 12-year-old boys were injured when the blade of a forklift fell off and hit them. Their employment was illegal for several reasons: they were under 14 years of age; employed in manufacturing; and tending a hoisting apparatus or power-driven machinery. The same employer was also cited because a 16-year-old was operating a forklift, another violation of child-labor regulations.
>
> A forklift driven by a 14-year-old Florida boy flipped and crushed his right arm and leg, requiring him to spend several weeks in the hospital and several months in physical therapy.
>
> A 17-year-old was severely injured while using a power-driven circular saw at a construction site in Wisconsin.
>
> A minor working at a company in Snohomish, Washington, was injured operating power-driven equipment at an electrical supply company.[6]

Child-labor laws are more than sixty years old, yet children at workplaces all across the country are being killed and injured at rates much higher than those of their adult counterparts. The hazardous orders provisions of child labor laws, which we will detail later, cover eighteen jobs which are forbidden to workers under the age of 18, but which are disregarded by employers and underage workers every day. In addition, the Department of Labor does not track illness, injury or fatality rates for workers less than 16 years of age. Injuries probably occur at least as frequently for those workers as they do for older workers. Furthermore, with many of the younger workers, there is not even a consideration that an injury might be work-related when it is being treated, with the result that injuries are definitely being underreported. Also, reported injuries do not include those children who are treated by a family doctor or who do not seek treatment. In this regard, a serious and perhaps the number-one problem facing foes of illegal child labor is the lack of a national database targeted at workers under 18 (especially under the age of 16) which could provide information about the numbers employed, the jobs they perform, and the number and causes of injuries and deaths.

NIOSH has found that 41 percent of occupational injury fatalities investigated by the Occupational Health and Safety Administration (OSHA) occurred while the child was engaged in work prohibited by federal child-labor laws. It is clear that many deaths resulted from violations of laws, such as the FSLA and state child labor laws, intended to protect young workers. Reducing the number of work-related injuries suffered by minors has always been difficult, since most Wage and Hour (a division of the Department of Labor charged with enforcing minimum wage and child labor requirements) offices have no access to specific information regarding these injuries. Consequently, child labor enforcement efforts usually take place only after an injury has occurred, and only then, when the accident is directly reported to the Labor Department.

And what jobs do these young workers typically perform? The Bureau of Labor Statistics of the Department of Labor reports that almost four out of five young workers aged 16 through 19 are concentrated in just three types of employment: in retail sales and service work (particularly in food service), as administrative support staff, and as laborers and handlers.

And are these jobs wholesome, safe activities for developing youngsters? Occupationally related accidents and injuries have been soaring in the past few years. NIOSH estimates that each year over 64,000 teens are treated in emergency rooms for their occupational injuries, exclusive of agricultural injuries. However, studies have shown that only 36 percent of work-related injuries are treated in emergency departments. Moreover, in a study of workplace deaths, NIOSH revealed that 670 16- and 17-year olds died at work in the ten-year period, 1980–1989.

In fact, adolescents suffer an estimated occupational injury rate of up to 16 per 100 full-time employees, compared to the adult rate of less than 9 per 100 full-time workers. Cuts and lacerations, usually of the hands and fingers, are the most common youth employment injuries, followed by bruises and contusions, and strains and sprains. These injuries arise from the inexperience of younger workers, not their age or developmental level. An extremely large proportion of workplace injuries, some 40 percent, occur to workers in their first year of work, regardless of their age.

Little information is available on the incidence or severity of work-related illness caused by poisons. Children, however, experience a variety of toxic exposures at work. These include formaldehyde and dyes in the garment industry, solvents in paint shops, pesticides in agriculture plant nursery, field and lawn work, asbestos in building abatement, and benzene in pumping unleaded gasoline.

Exposure in childhood and adolescence may result in serious disease in adulthood. Given the wide range of exposure to toxins, some cases of adolescent asthma might be related to occupational exposures to dusts or formaldehyde; some instances of neurological dysfunction or behavioral impediment may be due to occupational exposure to solvents and pesticides; and some leukemias or lymphomas may result from occupational exposure to benzene.

In addition, physical and psychosocial factors may also place young workers at increased risk of injury in the workplace, and children and adolescents may have increased or different susceptibilities to chemical exposure than adult workers.

Tragically, many of these younger workers have fallen through the cracks in the system, designed to collect occupational data for adult workers, at a time when adolescent employment is at the highest level it has ever been. The number is expected to peak in 2010 with 21.6 million minors in the workforce. When that growth is coupled with reduced enforcement activity, it may be a recipe for disaster.[7]

HEALTH RISKS OF AGRICULTURAL CHILD LABOR

Life on a working farm is not all pastoral serenity. Fatigue, time pressures, and malfunctioning equipment plague farmers during planting and harvest seasons and are often factors in accidents. Children usually help with the farm work and care of animals and often play near hazardous equipment, so they may be involved in accidents with machinery or livestock. Farm machinery, especially the older equipment that does not have the latest safety devices, causes most of the serious and fatal injuries to children. And while there are federal laws regulating farm safety and child labor, nearly every one exempts farm children, young people hired by farm families, and the children of migrant workers. Estimates are that about 100,000 young people are injured, and 100 killed annually, in a wide range of agriculture-related activities.

Ironically, the image of farmers as independent and responsible individuals and of agriculture as a special occupation has contributed to the exclusion of most of the farm population from OSHA, the major federal occupational safety program. As a result, most American farms lie outside OSHA coverage, which helps explain the continued high rate of injuries and deaths to farm owners and employees. The government has no jurisdiction over the vast majority of the nation's 1.1 million farms since most are small family operations. Congress prohibits OSHA from spending money to inspect farms with eleven or fewer employees.

Several factors contributed to the granting of the agricultural exemption. The OSHA law was very unpopular with many businessmen and conservatives, who were willing to use any means to attack it. Exempting any occupation (such as agriculture), they recognized, could later set a helpful precedent for exempting their own businesses or occupations. Moreover, by implying that the heavy and unthankful hand of government was trying to quash the spirit of independent family farmers, who had sacrificed and suffered to make America strong, OSHA's opponents used the myth to frame the debate in especially potent and emotional terms. This enabled them to draw attention away from their vested interest and political maneuvering and to vote against the regulations without appearing to be uncaring or anti-labor. Consequently, the need to prevent injuries in one of the country's most dangerous occupations was slighted.[8]

All this has made farming a virtually unregulated industry made up of proudly independent families that is more deadly than traditionally dangerous occupations, particularly for children who routinely work on farms but are rarely observed in more dangerous jobs. Unlike other workers, many of these farmers and their children die from survivable injuries because they are isolated in the fields far from other family members or live many miles from the nearest physician.[9]

Many farmworkers are driven by economic necessity, the piece-rate system that characterizes much of corporate agriculture in America. The least protected of them are children in the fields working side by side with their parents. Though the health and safety standards do not adequately protect children, they work in the fields to help families make a living. Children of migrant and seasonal farmworkers are caught in a life of poverty and backbreaking work, whose moves from place to place leave them lacking in self-confidence and lagging behind in school. At sunrise, many can be found in the fields, where they are exposed to dangerous pesticides as they work. At day's end, exhausted, they return home to substandard shacks.

For that matter, pesticide poisoning is a primary reason that agriculture is ranked as the second most dangerous occupation in the United States. Because the majority of agricultural workers in the Southwest are of Mexican origin, and because they are among the most poorly paid and least protected in the U.S. workforce today, many workers and their families live in conditions that chronically expose them to toxic agrochemicals. Children of farm laborers are particularly vulnerable to the health effects of pesticides because of their living circumstances (e.g., substandard housing in close proximity to pesticide applications), participation in family activities (e.g., accompanying parents into the crop fields because of the lack of child care facilities), and physiological characteristics (e.g., high metabolic rates and developing organs).

At present, little is known about the exact risk to these children, although various studies have been published regarding children's health problems associated with pesticides. In order to accurately compute risks for a given population, accurate estimates of pollutant exposure (human contact) and intake dose (penetration into the body) are necessary. Because exposure and dose depend on complex human activity patterns, such as what contaminated objects children touch and the duration of contact, and because previous studies to determine where and how people spend their time have relied on questionnaires and diary recall, no tools currently exist to accurately determine exposure and dose through all three pathways: inhalation, ingestion, and dermal absorption. Without such tools, public policy makers cannot effectively assess and manage health risks posed by pesticides and other pollutants to sensitive populations.

CHILD LABOR IN THE APPAREL SECTOR

Illegal employment of children occurs in all industries and often under "sweatshop" conditions. A sweatshop is defined as an establishment that violates wage, hour, and child-labor laws, as well as the laws protecting occupational safety and health. Traditionally, these shops have been considered fringe establishments, and have been concentrated in the garment and meatpacking industries. Increasingly, however, restaurants, fast-food outlets, retail shops, and grocery stores are violating child labor and occupational-health laws and fulfilling the definition of sweatshops.

Health and safety conditions in sweatshops are often dangerous. Fire hazards may be created by blocked exit doors, accumulations of combustible materials, and inadequate lighting and ventilation. Electrocution hazards result from overloaded electrical connections, work stations located close to exposed wires, and bare fuse boxes. Large numbers of recent fire code violations suggest that sweatshop workers, including children, are at high risk of dying by fire if these conditions are not corrected.

The abuses uncovered in the garment districts are pervasive. The garment industry offers employment to America's immigrants, individuals who come with a dream of a better life but little or no knowledge of labor laws. For them, the abuses they suffer in this nation's garment districts are routinely accepted in their home countries. Children are often found in cramped and horrendous conditions, sewing and stitching the nation's clothes, typically for less than the minimum wage.

New York state, which has some of the toughest laws restricting child labor, also has the nation's only state task force to look for labor-law violations in garment industry sweatshops. However, there are only fifteen inspectors assigned to inspect New York City's estimated 4,000 to 6,000 factories where small contractors hire workers to sew clothing. And the inspectors report that when they enter a building, owners on one floor quickly warn others in the structure, and children are hastily sent away. Unfortunately, other state governments are even less attentive to garment employers in their large urban centers.[10]

CORPORATE CODES OF CONDUCT

In a recent development, corporate codes of conduct and other business guidelines prohibiting the use of child labor are becoming more common, as consumers, as well as religious, labor, and human rights groups, are increasingly calling upon companies to take responsibility for the conditions under which the goods they sell are being manufactured. Many U.S. firms that import apparel have adopted codes of conduct that prohibit the use of child labor and promote other labor standards. For the purposes of our book, the term "codes of conduct" is used generically to refer to various types of corporate policies and standards on child labor and other working conditions. These instruments take different forms: statements of company policy in the form of letters to suppliers, provisions in purchase orders or letters of credit, and/or compliance certificates.

Codes of conduct for suppliers represent a significant expansion of what should be included in evaluating whether a corporation is socially responsible. Codes for suppliers establish the fundamental principle that retailers can and should be held accountable for the working conditions and basic rights of workers who produce the goods they sell and that the companies cannot escape responsibility by contracting and outsourcing their production.

Codes of conduct for suppliers are new, the first having been adopted by Levi Strauss in 1992, and evolving. True, most came in response to negative news media stories reporting child labor and abusive conditions at work sites in Third World countries. The next step is to hold these companies accountable for enforcing the commitments they have in their codes. A critical breakthrough was accomplished when The Gap became the first apparel firm to agree to independent monitoring of its code of conduct after the National Labor Committee reported abuses at a Gap-producing factory in El Salvador.

A glaring weakness in code enforcement exists because companies that have codes of conduct for their suppliers, which seek to set acceptable standards with respect to working conditions and wages for their suppliers' workers, do not, at this point, systematically monitor and enforce their codes.

HAZARDS TO EDUCATION AND DEVELOPMENT

Another serious consequence of child labor is interference with school attendance and performance. Employed children risk not having enough time for homework and being tired on school days. Teachers of children in areas where child labor is common and industrial homework is escalating have reported declines in the academic performance of previously good students. Child labor also interferes with the normal, necessary play of children, with negative developmental consequences. Child labor can also expose children to undesirable role models and to adverse habits such as smoking, drinking, and drug abuse.

Young people attending school have the advantage of being able to choose among opportunities, in work as well as education. However, many immigrant children may not be able to leave the work environment long enough to complete an education, and their school dropout rates are very high. These young people are being denied an education because they may not have a choice. If they are given an opportunity to learn, they will realize that their potential may exceed that of a sewing machine operator or garment trimmer.

Child labor laws were not written to prevent young people from working, but to prevent them from sacrificing their education for a future limited in job opportunities, career goals, and personal growth potential. It is not enough, therefore, to merely punish employers for exploiting children or for robbing young people of the means to achieve in future years. Adolescents attracted by the idea of earning wages, perhaps for the first time in their lives, should be informed of how the law affects them and protects them. At the risk of assuming the role of devil's advocate, it may be that child labor laws might be anomalous in that they do not significantly influence adolescent employment behavior from what would occur without legal restrictions. Second, they are ineffective due to inadequate enforcement.

Unfortunately, ignorance blinds rational discussion of the contemporary child labor experience and its adverse effects on student workers, especially those who work in the service sector. That ignorance, of course, serves to perpetuate the problem as children unwittingly accept employment prospects that may diminish their capacity in ways that will be felt for decades. This is especially true since the late-night employment associated with the rapidly growing service sector reduces precious study time for academic work, especially in math and science, that comprises the intellectual foundation for engineering, computer science, and many of the highly skilled jobs that are essential to America's future.

The evidence suggests that children are an exploited minority, doing poorly paid work, often illegally, in conditions that are potentially harmful to their health and safety. However, the case for allowing school-age children to work is often expressed in terms of the benefits they may gain from the experience. Equally, the costs to the child who works also need to be examined.

AREAS OF INQUIRY

This book will address a number of key issues involved in the child labor area, including the following:

- How can child labor law enforcement be strengthened?
- What should be the role of physicians who treat young person for problems that may be work-related?
- How can the problem of school dropouts caused by child labor be ameliorated?
- What measures are needed to prevent workplace injuries and deaths among young people?
- How can data collection by federal, state and local agencies be improved to more efficiently define the extent and severity of the problem of child labor and its associated injuries and illnesses?
- What are the characteristics of farm life and children that may contribute to agricultural injuries?
- In what manner can the effectiveness of agricultural injury programs be enhanced?

FUTURE PROSPECTS

Changing demographics will make the problems addressed in this book much more acute if left unmet. Yet the demand for child labor shows no signs of abating as the service sector, especially the fast-food industry, continues to grow. Teenagers, particularly from middle-class families, are caught in a vise, the pressure of work competing against the demands of school, family, and community. Many adolescents have difficulty coping with the circumstances they face, and the institutions that are designed to help, child labor regulators and the schools, are largely unaware of these new circumstances and the difficulties they pose for students during their crucial adolescent years.

The destructive quality of work in the lives of American youth has not come as an intended consequence from any segment of society. Rather, this problem has been evolutionary. In earlier generations, much of the childhood work experience was seasonal farm labor. It did not involve late night hours, whereas the convenience sector has extended the commercial life of even small towns well after midnight. Previously, jobs were typically challenging, with diverse and varied job chores. They involved mentoring and supervision, whereas today's teenage workers in fast-food establishments are often supervised by other teenagers. Given these changes, researchers have suggested that today's work experience is of significantly lower quality then that of previous generations of student workers.

The role of work in the lives of our young people will only grow more serious as the demand for young workers increases while the supply remains relatively stable. There is now a window of opportunity to catapult this neglected issue onto the national agenda. In recent years, the United States has spent millions on educational reform and remedial education. There is a growing consensus for change to improve educational opportunities for America's youth. There is a need for a more educated and skilled workforce to fill society's new entry-level jobs as the twenty-first century begins. If we are to meet this challenge, we must begin the process to reform our approach on child labor and abusive employment practices.

Through a combination of lax enforcement, underfunding, society apathy, and an influx of immigration, child-labor abuse is as bad as, and in some areas worse than, it was in the 1920s. We will reexamine this problem in light of the recent rise in child-labor abuse and the toll that this abuse has taken on children, as well as the detriment it imposes to the future productivity of our nation. There are no easy answers. If we are to succeed in controlling this problem, it will require a combination of legislative reform, political support, intergovernmental cooperation, and education of the public. By allowing thousands of children to be employed by abusive employers in our fields, restaurants, and sweatshops, our society contributes to their illnesses, injuries, and deaths. We must distinguish between the productive employment of children and the abusive use of child labor, and take the necessary steps to ensure that thousands of our children are not victimized by abusive child labor.

Unless the situation is addressed as a serious public policy problem, abuses will grow as the pool of available teenage labor declines and the service sector enlarges. As we will see, the myths and realities of work are miles apart. Our children are the workforce of the future. How they prepare for that future will depend on our choices today.

NOTES

1. Comments of Jack Angell, Farm Labor Specialist, American Farm Bureau Federation, Park Ridge, Ill., 14 July 1981, reported in "Feeble Exposé of Farmers' Child Labor Abuse," *New York Times,* 31 July 1981, A22.

2. Ibid.

3. Todd Olson, "Robbed of a Childhood," *Scholastic Update,* 25 January 1991, 17.

4. Douglas A. Levy, "Study: Child Labor Laws Ineffective," United Press International, 11 October 1993, 1.

5. Gina Kolata, "More Children Are Employed, Often Perilously," *New York Times,* 21 June 1992, 1.

6. S.L. Smith, "In Harm's Way: Child Labor in the 90s," *Occupational Hazards* (November 1995): 23.

7. Brian Dumaine, "Illegal Child Labor Comes Back," *Fortune,* 5 April 1993, 86; Michael Powell, "Illegal Labor Flourishes Again: Children Working in Many Sweatshops," *Newsday,* 8 January 1989, 3.

8. Timothy W. Kelsey, "The Agrarian Myth and Policy Responses to Farm Safety," *American Journal of Public Health,* 84 (July 1994): 1175–1176.

9. Isabel Wilkerson, "Farms Deadliest Workplace, Taking the Lives of Children," *New York Times,* 26 September 1988, A1.

10. Kolata, "More Children Are Employed."

2

The Historical Record

"When my mother died I was very young, And my father sold me while yet my tongue could scarcely cry weep weep weep. So your chimneys I sweep and in soot I sleep."[1]

Children have always taken part, and continue to take part, in social and economic activities as members of the groups to which they belong. Today's economically developed countries took for granted, in the past, that children would work alongside their parents, learning to gather food, hunt, cultivate crops, tend cattle, and help in the household. The child's work was seen as a process of socialization and apprenticeship. The family, not the individual, was the unit of social activity.

The notion that child labor is a social problem came to the fore during the industrial revolution when paid child labor became common. The old family-based production system was replaced by the factory system. Without family supervision, it became common for children to work in abysmal working conditions for long hours with almost no means of protection against the risk of accidents. Neither the institutions nor the legislation was adequate to meet the new circumstances.

Today it is easy to become complacent about labor standards in the United States. We take for granted long-established laws and prohibitions against children working in coal mines and factories. The good sense and fairness of these laws seems so obvious that it is hard to imagine a time when they were not followed. But that time existed, and a nightmarish era it was.

THE COLONIAL PERIOD

Child labor has a long history. In the Middle Ages, children worked in agriculture and as apprentices to artisans. In Colonial America, children who helped out on their own farms and households were commonly hired out to perform similar tasks at neighboring farms and households (a practice that has continued in rural areas almost without change). The contractual relationship that existed between employer and child was one that was supposed to recognize the responsibility of each to the other, and although this did not (and does not) always preclude exploitation, proximity and social interrelationships provided some degree of protection.

No such protection existed for children of the same era who were brought to the colonies as indentured servants. Such children were often impoverished inhabitants of the streets of English cities. Gathered up by the hundreds and bonded for five to seven years of work in Virginia and other states, they were packed tightly into ships. Those who profited enormously from this system were not concerned about travel conditions; if the ocean crossing took too long due to bad weather, the food ran out. On one such trip thirty-two children died of hunger and disease and were thrown overboard. Of those who survived to reach America, many more died of disease within a few months.

The early European colonists in America took it for granted that children should work. They had little choice because laborers were few and far between in the 1600s. But child labor was more than a necessity; it was seen as a blessing. Religious settlers were convinced that hard work kept children out of trouble. An early Virginia law promoted child labor "to avoid sloth and idleness wherewith young children are easily corrupted."[2]

In the eighteenth century, Americans were not legally adults until they turned 21, but they did important work on farms when they were only seven or eight years of age. When they were physically grown, at only 13 or 16, they had virtually the same jobs as any other adult. For instance, in the 1790s the United States' first factories, textile mills in Pawtucket, Rhode Island, started operation with only nine workers, all of them under 12. In 1820, half the country's textile workers were under 10 years old and toiling twelve hours a day. Still, few observers found anything amiss. According to Alexander Hamilton, the first Secretary of the Treasury, "Children are rendered more useful by manufacturing establishments than they otherwise would be."[3] The only complaint heard was that children missed school. The first child labor law, Connecticut's in 1813, merely required that factories teach their young workers how to read, write, and add. In those days, education was irregular at best, but each child had his or her own vocational guidance teacher: the family. So, the transition to adulthood was handled through a long apprenticeship, on the farm or in a craft, by people who could point out a direct social path to adulthood.

Industrialization changed all that. In the nineteenth century, mills and factories replaced farms, and cities replaced the countryside. Children didn't automatically follow their parents' occupations, and so family relations became less important for job training than something called "school." In that century, the need for child labor on farms diminished, and the horrors of industrial child labor, as chronicled by Charles Dickens in *Hard Times* and Francis Trollope in *The Life and Times of Michael Armstrong, the Factory Boy,* became widespread. Drawings of children being beaten in the cotton mills, lowered on ropes into the coal mines, and carrying fifty-pound rocks on their backs up mine ladders sparked great popular revulsion against the worst abuses of child labor, but still these continued.

THE EARLY SWEATSHOPS

Boys and girls were pressed into service across the industrializing economy in the decades after the Civil War. At the turn of the century, many industries relied on child labor. The 1900 census found more than 1,750,000 children between the ages of 10 and 16 were working for wages in the United States—almost one out of every five persons in this age bracket. This figure excludes at least a quarter million workers under the age of 10. Due to extensive falsification of age records and the simple absence of data, the precise number and age distribution of laboring boys and girls in the late nineteenth and early twentieth centuries is unknown. Contemporary observations suggest that many entered the workplace at tender ages. Where urban immigrant families assembled clothing, toys, or novelties in their own homes under the sweatshop system, they sometimes employed household members younger than 5 years of age.[4]

> As soon as a little child can be of the least possible help, it must add to the family income by taking a share in the family toil. A child 3 years old can straighten out tobacco leaves or stick the rims which form the stamens of artificial flowers through the petals. He can put the covers on paper boxes at four years. He can do some of the pasting of paper boxes, although as a rule this requires a child of 6 to 8 years. But from 4 to 6 years he can sew on buttons and pull basting threads. A girl from 8 to 12 can finish trousers as well as her mother. After she is 12, if of good size, she can earn more money in a factory. The boys do practically the same work as the girls, except that they leave the home earlier, and enter street work, as peddlers, bootblacks, and newsboys. I have seen but two children under 3 years of age working in tenements, one a boy 2-years-old who assisted the mother and 4 other children under 12 years in making artificial flowers. The other, an extraordinary case of a child of 1 years, who assisted at a kind of passementerie.[5]

After the Civil War, industries in the United States rapidly mechanized, and the production of manufactured goods increased by a factor of 20. The shift to a high-output factory system encouraged more employers to draw children into industrial occupations. The South, particularly, was faced with rebuilding its industries and a generation of men who had died in the war. That further encouraged industrialists to hire youths, in part because of their agility and speed. Another factor encouraging children to work was that many families placed no value on formal education for children.[6] Economic necessity dictated the employment of children. As a South Carolina cotton manufacturer contended: "We cannot possibly gravitate from agriculturalism to industrialism without the employment of minors. Take a family on the farm who is living in absolute poverty. If the family moves to the cotton-mill town and you say that the father only can work, he cannot make enough to support the family."[7]

THE NATIONAL CHILD LABOR COMMITTEE AND LEWIS HINE

A reform movement had swept the country at the turn of the century, and a coalition of social workers, politicians, and labor leaders formed the National Child Labor Committee in New York City. In Indiana, examples of the egregious exploitation of children fueled a fledgling national movement to rid the workplace of abusive child labor. In December 1904, the newly formed Child Labor Committee investigated child labor conditions in Indiana. Revealed were a large number of children working at night, laws setting age limits disregarded, and lax enforcement because there were too few government inspectors.

Children 14 and younger went to work on night shifts at 5 P.M., sometimes working twelve hours or longer in hellish conditions. During one such night shift at the Inland Steel Plant in East Chicago, 13-year-old John Yedinak fell asleep after working eleven hours, and his legs were crushed by a carload of iron. It was hardly an isolated incident.

Yet Indiana's glass factories, not the steel mills, drew the attention of progressive reformers. News accounts of the era describe the situation:

> Many boys of all ages from 8 up are employed in the Indiana glass factories, and at night. From a small boy who works in a glass factory during the school vacation, it was learned that a number of boys, all under 14 years of age, work regularly in glass factories in Marion during part of the night and attend school during the day. . . . One of the boys said his parents made him work. Not one of them was an orphan, although the father of two had deserted their families.[8]

The ovens were kept constantly fired at several thousand degrees, filling the work area with fumes. Glass shards were strewn everywhere. The work typically continued around the clock, feeding the ovens.

There were no records kept of injury rates, but, glassblowing was among the most dangerous occupations. In 1908, the committee hired photographer Lewis Hine to travel to Indiana and other areas to begin documenting the need for reform. Hine, a sociologist by training, became an investigative reporter with a camera, risking physical assault and resorting to deception at times to bring attention to the deplorable conditions. He took more than 100 photographs in Indianapolis, Anderson, Marion, Peru, Muncie, South Bend, and Hammond, capturing haunting images of exploitation.

Although there were few inspectors, the monetary penalties were severe, compared with penalties today. A $50 fine in 1906 for child-labor violations would be the equivalent of an $826 fine today, adjusting for inflation. By comparison, a $50 fine today amounted to a $3 penalty then. Hine's photographs were used to illustrate pamphlets promoting child labor law reforms in Indiana.

Efforts to improve conditions were rejected by the legislature in 1909, but reformers persisted, and the laws were revised in 1911.

The National Child Labor Committee published *THE SURVEY*, a weekly magazine that frequently featured Hine's photographs and articles, for Hine was also adept at painting pictures with words. Describing child labor in the hard coal mines of Pennsylvania, he wrote, "Then the pieces rattled down though long chutes at which the breaker boys sat. These boys picked out the pieces of slate and stone that cannot burn. It's like sitting in a coal bin all day long, except that the coal is always moving and clattering and cuts the fingers."[9]

His work appeared in numerous magazines, local newspapers, and on posters that spooned the public a heavy dose of guilt. If his child-labor photographs were not enough to ignite the most frigid social conscience, his written data could surely be counted on to spark the flame of revulsion. He took copious notes on small pads of paper he hid in his pocket and often transcribed his notes at night in his hotel room on a portable typewriter. Here is a sampling:

> Fairmont, W. Virginia, Oct. 1908. 5 p.m. Boys going home from Monogai Glass Works. A native remarked, "De place is lousy wid kids [*sic*]."
>
> Mississippi. 4-year old and her sisters shuck oysters.
>
> Nightshift in North Carolina factory. Two of the smaller girls with three other sisters work on the night shift and support a big, lazy father who complains that he is not well enough to work. He loafs around the country store.[10]

When his critics shouted, "Fake," Hine was able to set them straight with his combined visual and written data.

Farms also employed children. Unfortunately, the children who worked on farms were usually the sons or daughters of migrant farm workers. They were not boys and girls just helping out on their parents' farm. Working on a farm was also dangerous, for sharp tools were used to harvest and cut the crops.

MINES, MILLS, AND CANNERIES

In the hard coal industry, fathers brought their sons to the breakers as early as age 6, although more often at ages 8, 9, or 10. In 1902, the Reverend James Moore, a Methodist minister in Avoca, Pennsylvania, reported: "I have seen boys going to the breaker that did not seem really able to carry their dinner pail."[11]

The younger boys who worked at the mines were called breaker boys. They did not actually work in the mine itself. They sat on benches while coal flowed along beneath their feet, and they picked out the bits of rock from the coal. These children worked in the picking room, a crowded, high-ceilinged vault, crisscrossed with rickety catwalks and crooked stairs, lit only by a wall of grime-choked windows.

The breaker boys sat astride six metal chutes, four to each, slowing down the steady stream of coal with their feet. Here they picked out slate and "bony," which was half coal, half rock, as well as sulfur balls and any other foreign objects and dropped them into the "rock box" below. These places were poorly lit, and the boys had constant coughs because of the dust. The moving coal would often cut their fingers, and they could hardly stand up straight because of leaning over the coal for seemingly interminable hours each day. Also, boys would sometimes fall and get smothered or crushed in the huge piles of coal. Worse yet, when the boys turned 12, they would be sent down into the mines where there was a constant threat of cave-ins and explosions.

It was a Dickensian world of almost unimaginable poverty and brutality, not so far distant in our country's past. The United Mine Workers Union was just beginning to unionize the Welsh and Polish laborers in the anthracite mines of Pennsylvania.

Less than a hundred years ago, many American children, the sons and daughters of wealthy families, would probably spend their days at school. However, the sons or daughters of poor parents or immigrants worked in a mill, mine, canning shed, or field for many hours each day for very little. Many worked in mills because they were small, light, and had nimble fingers. They would change the bobbins of thread while standing on top of the machines themselves, for they were too short to reach them from the floor. This was very dangerous, for children would slip and lose a finger or foot. Also, some little girls would be scalped when their hair got entangled in the machinery.

Canning sheds were poorly lit places where children of an even younger age worked alongside their parents shucking oysters or peeling fruits or vegetables. In 1889, thirty-six Baltimore canneries each employed, on average, 362 women and children, 19 percent of whom were under eighteen. There were 152 rural canneries, each employing an average of forty-two women and children, 42 percent of whom were under 18. Not only were there proportionately more children in the rural canneries but also the ratio of boys to girls was roughly even, 48 to 52 percent, which suggests a workforce of brothers and sisters. In the city canneries, the ratio of boys to girls was 39 to 71 percent, suggesting that child workers were not primarily from within family groups. In the seafood-processing plants on the Gulf of Mexico, children often went to work by the age of 8.[12]

THE ADVENT OF REFORM

Only at relatively rare moments, mostly in this century, has there been any serious questioning of the role of children's participation in the world of work. Around 1900, an influential group of progressive reformers began to reformulate our ideas, seeking to bring to public attention a greater awareness of the exploitation of children in factories. For the first time, less than one hundred years ago, the idea of children toiling in mines and mills, fields, and factories was portrayed in the popular press and professional literature as a repugnant and extreme example of the exploitation of the innocent. Images of Dickensian suffering among an exploited group whose childhood had been stolen from them became a rallying cry for reformers in the early part of this century.

While reformers such as the National Child Labor Committee attacked urban factory labor and sweatshops, work as an ideal, and labor as an indicator of moral and social worth, still left their imprint on reformers' attitudes and actions toward children. Even during the height of child-labor reform activities in the early twentieth century, most political activity was aimed at regulating child labor in order to protect children only from the worst type of exploitation, not to free children from the employer, the field, or the factory.

At the same time that unorganized and unskilled workers found themselves and their children forced to accept horrendous conditions in mines and mills, unionized workers found themselves in alliance with reformers whose protectionist programs forced women and children out of industries where their labor posed a threat to unionized labor. In foundries, for example, children, and women as well, were excluded from relatively high-paying and skilled positions by a joining of reform and labor interest in the teens and 1920s. Reformers in the early twentieth century only rarely noted the bitter irony of their alliance with portions of the adult laboring community at the expense of other families who desperately depended on children's income. "It is perhaps unnecessary to mention the obvious fact that the child worker is in competition with the adult and drags down his wages," Lillian Wald noted in passing in her book *The House on Henry Street* in 1915.[13]

CHILD LABOR IN AGRICULTURE

Much of the reform rhetoric that marked the early movements to control the industrial workplace romanticized the rural environment and its supposedly healthful impact on families, parent-child relationships, and work routines. In the full swing of the industrial revolution, many states met the dangers of the new workplace by passing child labor legislation but did not include agricultural labor in this coverage. In fact, as other industries became increasingly regulated, an exodus of children from the sweatshops of the city to the country occurred.

The attention of the public was fully focused on the atrocities taking place in the mines, factories, and mills. The need for protection of the children working on farms was beyond their concern. Moreover, the financial success of farm employers increased the demand for inexpensive child labor and spurred their opposition toward reform efforts. The potential costs that would be incurred by extending federal legislation to agricultural laborers was viewed as undermining the supply of cheap labor, and consequently, farm laborers were not included in the definition of "employee" in legislation such as the National Labor Relations Act and its progeny.

Cheap labor was perceived to be a necessity, and powerful agricultural lobbying groups curbed legislative efforts to protect the social and economic welfare of farm laborers. As a result, children lacked protection, as did all agricultural workers. At the time, this lack of legislation was present in almost all industries. Not only were minors subject to unsafe conditions, but that they were not afforded a minimum wage through such legislation exacerbated the child's lot.[14]

In addition, the evils of agricultural employment were disguised by a general perception that work on a farm was free from the moral turpitude of city sweatshops and that farm labor for a child was a divine occupation, strengthening the moral constitution of the child.

While the dangers of nonagricultural employment were acknowledged at the turn of the twentieth century, such was not the case for child labor in agricultural settings. New York and Georgia, for example, enacted legislation that represented many states' attempts to address child-labor problems in nonagricultural industries.

Regarding his proposed national child-labor bill in 1910, Senator Albert Beveridge pointed out that it did "not strike at the employment of children engaged in agriculture." He stated, "I do not pretend . . . that working children on the farm is bad for them."[15]

Securing protective legislation in the states also was opposed by rural representatives holding the balance of power in badly proportioned state legislatures. Occupying a position where the stories of bucolic child labor defrayed the cost of finding more expensive labor elsewhere, such economic concerns became explicit at the federal level with Congress needing the support of agricultural interests for the passage of important labor legislation in the New Deal. Opposition to child labor legislation in agriculture was also voiced by parents and teachers, who, while in a position to require school attendance, believed that the harvesting of crops was more important than regulation. The difficulties of regulating the labor of children in agriculture was summed up in a 1930 report of the National Child Labor Committee: "Improved state laws and the federal child labor statute, which reduced the openings for children in industry, seemed to drive more boys and girls into unregulated agriculture."[16]

An additional factor that prevented the acknowledgment of the dangers of child labor on farms was the fact that it occurred in the country or fields, away from the centrality of the city, making any imagined attempt at regulation impractical to implement and police. The regions that had the most need for cheap labor, and the most influence in Congress to block agricultural coverage, were in the South and West where large agricultural employers depended upon a cheap supply of minority labor, much as they had depended upon slave labor before 1865.

Powerful agricultural lobbyists such as the Grange, the Cooperative Council, and the Farm Bureau Federation were instrumental in excluding agriculture from coverage. In this regard, since 1938, when a Senate panel exempted agriculture from the main provisions of the Fair Labor Standards Act, Congress has continued a tradition of giving farming special treatment in social legislation. W.S. Campfield of the Virginia State Horticulture Society, defended child farm labor at a Senate hearing: "I have seen them come down, the father and mother and boy and girl. They pick a large number of apples a day and are satisfied. They are anxious for work—they always come back."[17]

Two decades later, in the mid-1950s, when congressional committees considered erasing the agricultural exemption under the FLSA, the American Farm Bureau Federation advised against it, claiming that already burdened farmers would have a hard time coping with new paperwork requirements. Convinced, the lawmakers did nothing.

When the House Labor and Public Works Committee went to California for a field hearing on the subject in November 1957, its members heard again about the benefits of child labor from a California Farmers Inc. spokesman: "Many a teenager is surprised into saying, 'Gee, all this money, it's just like finding it. I'd have been playing if I had not been here, and this is just as much fun.' These checks are the greatest builders of American character in existence."[18]

In 1961 a Michigan lawmaker again tried to narrow agriculture's loophole. He proposed outlawing farm labor by children younger than 14, except for those working with their parents' written permission, and banning all children younger than 18 from hazardous farm work. Another legislator demurred: "I sincerely believe that an honest day's work by a youngster, no matter how tender his age, is the greatest character builder a child can have. I am telling you that the greatest deterrent to juvenile delinquency is the honor and privilege of doing an honest day's work."[19]

The bill went nowhere.

A decade later, the same Michigan lawmaker proposed banning interstate shipment of farm goods produced with oppressive child labor. But few votes were swayed, and the legislators again refused to act.

In 1974 Congress finally modified the double standard exempting agriculture. It prohibited agricultural employment for those younger than 12, except on family farms; children younger than 14 needed parental permission and could not work during school hours. In 1977 Congress decided to allow children younger than 12 to work up to thirteen weeks a year doing hand harvesting, with a waiver from the Department of Labor. The solons who supported the provision used the arguments often heard in the debate. Representative Al Ullman, a liberal Democrat from Oregon, maintained, "It has involved creative and meaningful work during the summertime for thousands and tens of thousands of young people in a very clean, healthy environment."[20]

These sentiments expressed over the years either indicated a lack of concern for the safety and health hazards confronting children in agricultural labor or general ignorance of its risks.

CHILD-LABOR LAWS AND COMPULSORY SCHOOL ATTENDANCE

Fierce legal battles over child-labor laws occurred in many states throughout the 1880–1920 period. Although legal restrictions on the use of child labor increased during these decades, they did so unevenly across states and, in some cases, across counties within states. In 1879 only seven states restricted the age of children in manufacturing, and, among them, the average minimum age was eleven. By 1909, forty-three states had legal limits on the minimum age for work in manufacturing, and the average minimum age was 14. In addition to age limits, restrictions on the use of child labor in manufacturing included maximum limits on daily and weekly hours of work and proscription of child employment in specific occupations regarded as immoral or dangerous. In 1915 Alabama approved a child-labor law that forbade the employment of children under 16 in mines, quarries, coal breakers, and coal ovens. Furthermore, increased activity at state legislatures resulted in the passage of compulsory schooling laws requiring that children be able to read and write and attend school up to a certain age or grade level before they were allowed to work.

The growth of child-labor laws and of state legislation making school attendance compulsory worked hand in hand to transform children from laborers to students. Massachusetts enacted the first child labor and compulsory school attendance statutes in 1836 and 1952, respectively. Most states followed suit during the late nineteenth and the early twentieth centuries, but these laws were riddled with exceptions, and enforcement was minimal. Reflecting the prevalence of child labor, the decennial census included 18-year-olds in its count of gainfully employed persons until 1940. Some 43 percent of 14- and 15-year-old boys worked at the turn of the century, dropping to 23 percent two decades later. However, these figures may have understated the true extent of child labor because, before 1930, fewer than half of all teenagers were enrolled in high school.[21]

In the late 1800s, society addressed the need for educating children with laws making education compulsory. At the turn of the century, increasingly stringent child-labor laws made it more difficult to hire children in factory, farm, and craft jobs. Students instead began to work in restaurants and shops and other service-related jobs, in part because of the flexible hours and the availability of part-time positions. In 1879, seven states had compulsory school attendance laws for children below an average age of twelve. By 1909, twenty-eight states had compulsory schooling laws that applied, on average, to children below the age of 16.

Predictably, the political alliances for and against education and labor laws tended to be similar. Progressive reformers viewed child-labor legislation and compulsory education laws as integral parts in a unified campaign to improve the lot of children. Likewise, organized labor strongly supported both child-labor laws and compulsory school laws as keys to an increased living wage for working-class parents and equal opportunity for working-class children. Among the most active opponents of the Child Labor Amendment, and of expansion of compulsory education in general, were many leading Catholic organizations, churchmen, and laymen. Mainstream Catholics viewed the amendment with alarm, believing it posed a danger to parochial education and transferred to the state powers that ought to belong to parents.

The economics of price competition, however, placed those states that enacted stricter reforms at a disadvantage. Nationwide uniformity was essential. During the first two decades of the century, reform-minded Progressives, in coalition with the so-called child-savers, trade unionists, and religious leaders, made enormous strides on a state-by-state basis toward raising the ages and reducing the hours of child workers. Yet their goal of enacting uniform protective laws in every state was frustrated by opposition from the South, where low wages were deemed essential to the revitalization of the textile industry, and in the conservative business community of the North, where distrust of any federal economic regulation was widespread.

Business also had cause to oppose both compulsory education and child-labor regulation. Although business promoted education, and especially vocational training, as necessary to create competent workers, businessmen were often arrayed against reformers when it came to passing the taxes to support expanded common schooling. Likewise, employers benefited from using children as workers. Not only were they cheap labor, but their contributions to family income meant adults would earn less than a living wage. Moreover, children who went to work at an early age provided a future docile workforce. Parents were divided between the two camps. Many middle-class parents embraced the new notions of childhood, but conservative or traditional parents, particularly immigrant parents who depended on children's wages for survival, felt that compulsory education infringed upon their rights in their children.[22]

LEGAL SETBACKS AND ULTIMATE PROGRESS

Despite federal and state legislation, child labor continued to be a major problem during the first third of the twentieth century. Inadequate enforcement of existing statutes contributed to this persistence. The need for enforcement was tragically demonstrated by the Triangle Shirtwaist fire in New York City in 1911. Late in the afternoon on one Saturday in March, a fire broke out on the eighth floor of a building that housed the Triangle Shirtwaist Company. Having recently lost their strike for a forty-hour week, 500 women and children on the seventh, eighth, and ninth floors of the building were still laboring, as part of their 59-hour workweek. Since "the factory doors were locked each day to keep the (workers) in and the union organizers out" and the interior doors opened inward, fire escapes seemed the only recourse, but they broke under the weight of the desperate child labor workers. The fire-engine ladders reached only to the sixth floor. Ultimately, 146 young women lost their lives that day, only eight years after the passage of landmark child-labor legislation and fire protection laws in New York. Many of those killed were the sole providers for their widowed mothers and siblings.[23]

This tragedy reinforced the arguments of the child-labor reformers for legislative reform. However, as the legal noose tightened around child labor, legal loopholes developed that particularly favored agricultural interests. In 1909, seventeen of the twenty-eight states with age restrictions on child labor in manufacturing, based on compulsory schooling laws, exempted school vacation periods. Seven had exemptions for rural areas and small cities, and four exempted industries with perishable products. Laws also varied in the penalties they imposed, in their enforcement and compliance characteristics, and in their definitions of factories and manufacturing establishments. Rural areas often benefited from agricultural exemptions and lax enforcement.

Despite these obstacles, the use of child labor in the United States declined drastically between 1880 and 1920. During that time, the proportion of workers under the age of 16 in manufacturing fell from 7 to 1 percent. Both contemporary observers and historians of the Progressive Era have generally interpreted this phenomenon to be the result of the widespread adoption of laws restricting child labor and mandating school attendance. Recently, however, economic historians have argued that the decline in child labor was primarily the result of long-term economic forces. In their view, the supply of child labor declined as family incomes rose, and the demand for child labor decreased as technological progress required a better-trained, more skilled, and more reliable labor force.

Until 1906, states were given control over laws regulating the employment of children. This practice resulted in extensive differences in child-labor laws among the states. States with more stringent laws, however, found their effect diluted by competition from other states. If one state had stricter child labor laws than its neighbors, children were often "imported" by the lower-standard states. Predictably, differentials in labor costs that arose from differences in state laws made it attractive for firms to move from high-regulation to low-regulation states. Competitive forces acted to harmonize standards downward. Congress sought ways to reverse this trend by taking child labor out of competition.

Between 1916 and 1930, three major pieces of child labor legislation were enacted but struck down by the courts. After years of debate and several commissioned studies, Congress passed the Keating-Owen bill in 1916, which used powers granted under the Commerce Clause in the U.S. Constitution to prohibit interstate and international trade in many goods produced with child labor. The passage of the Keating-Owen bill quickly led to legal challenges that Congress had overstepped its constitutional authority by prohibiting such trade. In *Hammer v. Dagenhart* 247 U.S. 251 (1918), an anti-labor Supreme Court prohibited Congress from restricting the interstate transport of goods produced by child labor. The logic of the ruling was that the evil was in the employment of children, not in interstate trade.

Reuben Dagenhart, the 14-year-old boy who won the "right" to work in *Hammer v. Dagenhart,* summed up the need for child-labor standards years after the decision. As a grown man and father, Dagenhart said he would have been "a lot better off" if his employer had won the suit because he sorely needed "the education I didn't get."[24]

After its defeat in the Dagenhart case, Congress quickly changed strategies and sought to limit the use of child labor by utilizing its taxing authority. As part of the Revenue Act of 1919, Congress levied a 10 percent profit tax on milling, manufacturing, and mining establishments that employed child labor in violation of federal standards. Again, in *Bailey v. Drexel Furniture Co.* U.S. 20 (1922), the high court ruled that this was an unconstitutional infringement on states' rights in regulating child labor.

In the wake of the Drexel case, Samuel Gompers met at the American Federation of Labor (AFL) headquarters with Florence Kelly of the National Consumers League, representatives of the National Child Labor Committee, and others. After extended weighing of options, the group developed a proposal for a constitutional amendment that would grant Congress the right "to limit, regulate, and prohibit the labor of persons under 18 years of age." In the late spring of 1924, Congress accepted the amendment, and the critics of child labor set out to secure approval by the requisite number of state legislatures. The amendment remained unratified in 1937 when Congress began consideration of the Fair Labor Standards Act.

The issue of federal regulation of child labor did not disappear, largely because of the marked deterioration of state child-labor laws after the federal laws were overturned by the Supreme Court. The support of minimal federal standards allowed states to strengthen their own standards as well, but once this support was removed, state standards were again relaxed.

After the failed attempt to pass a child-labor amendment to the Constitution, Congress passed the Fair Labor Standards Act (FLSA) in 1938. This act finally provided direct provisions that set minimum ages for employment in both manufacturing and nonmanufacturing industries and set minimum standards for the employment of youths in producing goods for interstate and foreign trade. President Roosevelt commented that goods produced under conditions that did not meet a rudimentary standard of decency should be regarded as contraband and ought not to be allowed to "pollute the channels of interstate commerce."[25] In an era of a more liberal court, the constitutionality of the Fair Labor Standards Act was unanimously upheld in *United States v. Darby* 312 U.S. 100 (1941).

CHILD LABOR AND INDUSTRIAL HOMEWORK

Long before enactment of the FLSA, reformers spoke of the twin evils of child labor and industrial homework. By the nature of sweatshop production, the two were closely linked, and that linkage rendered labor standards compliance difficult.

The FLSA addressed the issue of child labor, but it did not deal directly with industrial homework. Federal wage and hour requirements were easily avoided in home production where employers had no direct supervision of their workforce, which often was not even regarded as their own employees. In this setting, in 1939, the Department of Labor complained that entire families, including young children, might work on material given to one member of the family. As late as 1944, the department tried to regulate homework, but, it found that substandard wages were being paid, long and irregular hours were being worked, and children were still helping with the work of home production. Convinced that regulation would never be sufficient, the federal government imposed a total ban on industrial homework in certain garment-related fields (e.g., knitted outerwear, women's apparel, gloves and mittens, buttons and buckles, embroidery, jewelry, and handkerchiefs) where wage/hour and child labor abuses were most prevalent. Recognizing the problems home production imposed for labor standard compliance, the Supreme Court sustained the government's position in 1945 in *GEMSCO, Inc. v. Walling,* 324 U.S. 244 (1945).[26]

WORLD WAR II AND ITS AFTERMATH

During World War II, another shift in economic conditions occurred, and with it, as might be expected, came a shift in child-labor regulation. Workers were desperately needed, and the resulting economic bargaining power enabled them to insist upon improved working conditions. Hence, many of the extremely dangerous working conditions that had led to the popular outcry against child labor were eliminated. Fairly safe jobs were available for young people, and their labor was needed in defense plants. Courts adjusted to the changed conditions by narrowly interpreting or even ignoring the child-labor laws. After the war, an increasing number of groups and individuals that once had supported restrictions on child labor expressed doubts about the appropriateness in a modern economy of the restrictions that had been adopted in earlier years.[27]

During the 1960s and 1970s a general expansion of civil rights led to a great improvement in the status of children under the law. The struggles for equality waged by minorities, women, the poor, and other deprived segments of society promoted efforts to extend and broaden the rights of youth. Supreme Court decisions of the 1960s affirmed the rights of young people and clarified the fact that children are persons under the Constitution.

In view of this increasing awareness of the rights of children, it was not unexpected that legislation limiting children's right to work would be criticized. Critics of child-labor regulation contended that youths in America are "no longer weak," but are "brighter, stronger, healthier, bigger than ever before," and that it follows that so-called protection, in the guise of exclusion from the world of work, is a denial of children's right to participate responsibly in meaningful activities.

This trend toward relaxation of child-labor standards was exemplified when the issue of industrial homework reemerged in the early 1980s as the Reagan Administration sought to lift the ban on home production. The issue was fought out in the courts and before committees of the Congress. At the decade's end, regulation had replaced the ban in several industries, except for production of women's apparel, where the ban remained. But, what impact would the return of industrial homework have for labor standards, especially for child labor? Early in the Bush Administration, a Labor Department spokesperson admitted to "significant concern" about the potential for illegal use of child labor once homework was permitted. He remarked that labor officials were "not so naïve" as to think that child-labor abuses would not occur.[28]

RECENT DEVELOPMENTS

From a historical viewpoint, present-day concerns about child labor appear in stark contrast to the literature of fifty to one hundred years ago. The older picture tended to view youth employment as a blight on American society. Child-labor reformers were concerned primarily with keeping young people out of the labor market. Of course, initially, reformers were concerned with children at age levels substantially below the mid-teen years. They regarded premature employment as harmful to the health of children and as depriving them of education and proper vocational training. There were other motives as well. For example, concerns were raised about the competition between young people and adults in the labor market and the effects this might have on adult wages. However, until the 1980s, as the result of strong enforcement of the FLSA and generally favorable economic conditions, child labor outside of agriculture was not a widespread problem in the United States. In the past decade, however, a combination of economic and social factors has been responsible for a resurgence of child labor.

One important variable has been increased child poverty. More American children live below the poverty level today than did so twenty years ago. Another development has been a marked increase in immigration. Unstable world conditions, particularly war and poverty, have led to increasing numbers of immigrants, both documented and undocumented, into the United States. In the past decade there has been more immigration to the United States than in any other ten-year period since 1900–1910. Immigrants, particularly those who are undocumented, and their children are highly vulnerable to exploitation in the workplace. Also, since 1980, the federal government has substantially relaxed administration of the FLSA. Fewer inspectors are in the field. Regulations limiting the maximum number of hours of work and prohibitions against the use of dangerous machinery have not been adequately enforced.

Today, while some children still work in migrant labor and factories in the United States, they also are employed in fast-food outlets and retail stores. Child advocates estimate that five and one-half to six million youths between the ages of 12 and 17 are working. Teens are twice as likely to work as they were in 1950. The change has been fueled by the rapid growth of the service sector after World War II, the rise of the fast-food industry in the 1960s and 1970s, and an increase in the number of women entering the labor force.

So, the scourge of child labor continues. Employers claim today, as they did at the turn of the century, that work keeps children off the streets. If you can earn money at Burger King, the argument runs, you don't need to sell drugs. But for most young people, child labor is a dead end, cutting into their schooling and their hope for a better life. Years of government neglect of child-labor issues and a lust for cheap labor has put the lives, health, and futures of hundred of thousands of working children at risk.

As the twenty-first century begins, child-labor laws and regulations should continue to meet the societal expectation of protecting children in the workplace. Changes in existing standards should be approached with extreme caution. The current standards need to be studied, reviewed, and updated. However, in modifying the standards, legislators and administrative agencies should not compromise the traditional goals of child labor protection.

NOTES

1. William Blake, "The Chimney Sweeper," in Mary L. Johnson and John F. Grant (eds.) *Poetry and Designs* (New York: W.W. Norton, 1979).

2. Thomas Postal, "Child Labor in the United States: Its Growth and Abolition," *American Educator,* 13, 2 (1989): 30, 31.

3. J. McPhee, *The Craftsman and the Laird* (New York: Farrar, Straus & Giroux, 1970).

4. Alan Derickson, "Making Human Junk: Child Labor as an Issue in the Progressive Era." *American Journal of Public Health* 82 (September 1992): 1280.

5. Annie S. Daniel, "The Wreck of the Home: How Wearing Apparel is Fashioned in the Tenements," *Charities,* 14 (1 April 1905): 624–29.

6. Joan M. Clay and Elvis C. Stephens, "Child-Labor Laws and the Hospitality Industry," *Cornell Hotel & Restaurant Administration Quarterly,* 37 (December 1996): 20.

7. A.J. McKelway, "Child Labor and Social Progress," *Charities and the Commons* 20 (April 18, 1908): 4.

8. Ernie Slone, "Echoes from Past; Childhood Labor is Old Dilemma," *Indianapolis Post,* 25 October 1994, C1.

9. Ibid.

10. Walter I. Trattner, *Crusade for the Children: A History of the National Child Labor Committee and Child Labor Reform in America* (Chicago: Quadrangle Books, 1970).

11. Derickson, "Making Human Junk."

12. Martin Brown, Jens Christiansen, and Peter Philips, "The Decline of Child Labor in the U.S. Fruit and Vegetable Canning Industry: Law or Economics?" *Business History Review,* 66 (December 1992): 723.

13. Lillian Wald, *The House on Henry Street* (New York: Holt, Rinehart and Winston, Dover Edition, 1915, 1971) 146.

14. David Rosner, "Youth, Race, and Labor: Working Kids and Historical Ambivalence in Twentieth Century America," *American Journal of Industrial Medicine,* 24 (March 1993): 275–281.

15. Trattner, *Crusade for the Children.*

16. Ibid.

17. Michael Doyle, "Legislators Leave Teens Loopholes for Farm Work," *Orange County Register,* 3 January 1993, A30.

18. Ibid.

19. Ibid.

20. Ibid.

21. Sar A. Levitan and Frank Gallo, "Work and Family: The Impact of Legislation: The American Family During the 20th Century," *Monthly Labor Review,* 113 (March 1990): 34.

22. Barbara Bennett Wodehouse, "Who Owns The Child?: Meyer and Pierce And The Child As Property," *William and Mary Law Review,* 33 (Summer 1992): 995.

23. Ibid.

24. Thomas A. Coens, "Child Labor Laws: A Viable Legacy for the 1980s," *Labor Law Journal,* 10 (October 1982): 669.

25. Holly Sklar, "Raise the Floor: A Job Should Keep You Out of Poverty, Not In It," *UAW-A+ Issue,* (5 March 2002): 4.

26. Bruce Elmslie & William Milberg, "Free Trade and Social Dumping: Lessons from the Regulation of U.S. Interstate Commerce," *Challenge,* 3 (May 1996): 46.

27. Terry Collingsworth, J. William Goold, and Pharis J. Harvey, "Labor and Free Trade," *Foreign Affairs,* 1 (January–February 1994): 8.

28. "Homework," *Daily Labor Report,* 6 March 1989, A10, A11.

3

The Legal Context

> Teenagers "have become victims, not of child labor, but of child-labor laws. They are victims of a government . . . that is protecting them out of the opportunities for learning and earning."[1]

These sentiments expressed by the Republican Senator from Utah, Orrin Hatch, linking an antigovernment mindset with opposition to child labor laws, make it apparent that prospects for amendment of the New Deal-era statute, the Fair Labor Standards Act (FLSA), are quite remote for the foreseeable future. Consequently, it is important that we understand how this sixty-five-year-old law regulates child labor in the United States at a time when employment activity for young people is at high levels.

THE FAIR LABOR STANDARDS ACT

In the previous chapter, we learned that, because of the involvement of children in the labor force in the 1800s and early part of the 1900s, the incidence of abuse and exploitation of child labor became the subject of extensive regulation by both state and federal government. Prior to the passage of the FLSA, during its legislative history, and in the six decades since, employment questions concerning children have constantly arisen.

Consider the following typical child labor issues: May a contractor building single-dwelling homes hire a 12-year-old this summer to mow lawns on the houses that have been built and are for sale? Should a 16-year-old be allowed to operate a forklift truck? Must one pay minimum wages to children? Can the manager of the fast-food restaurant down the street really ask a 14-year-old to come to work at six in the morning and stay until midnight? A 17-year-old was injured on the job. Is he covered by workers' compensation? Can a farmer hire a neighbor's 15-year-old son to drive a farm tractor while the farmer works in the fields? Are 10- and 11-year-old children of migratory farmers allowed to work in the fields? Can children be used in the cast of a theatrical production if the play will be presented in the evening during a normal school semester?

Today, both state and federal laws substantially regulate the use of child labor in both the agricultural and nonagricultural sectors of the American economy and protect young workers from employment that might interfere with their educational opportunities or be detrimental to their health or well-being. The FLSA applies to most of the workers in the United States. It covers all workers who are engaged in or producing goods for interstate commerce or who are employed in certain enterprises. Employers whose products never leave a state and whose sales amount to less than $500,000 annually are exempt. Employers involved in interstate commerce can also be held responsible under federal "hot goods" statutes, which are part of the FLSA. For example, a tomato harvested by an underage child can taint a batch of pasta sauce all the way to the manufacturer or retailer. "Hot goods" shipped across state lines can be seized pursuant to a court order.

Under the FLSA's federal regulatory structure, "oppressive child labor" is defined as "employment of a minor in an occupation for which he does not meet the minimum age standards of the Act as set forth in Section 570.2. . . ." In general, in nonagricultural employment, the minimum age for employment of children is 16. Children between 14 and 16 years old may be employed in certain specified industries that the Secretary of Labor determines will not interfere with their education or health and well-being. Eighteen years of age is the minimum for all occupations that the Secretary of Labor has declared hazardous. In agriculture, there are numerous specific regulations, but in general, 16 is the minimum age for full employment, and 14 is the minimum age for employment outside of school hours, and in occupations not declared hazardous by the Secretary. Twelve- and 13-year- olds may be employed under specific restrictions with parental consent, and the 1979 amendment to the Act allows work to be performed, under very stringent standards, for 10- and 11-year-olds as hand harvesters in special short season crop activities.[2]

SPECIFIC PROVISIONS

After more than sixty years of revisions, federal child labor statutes are comprehensive in scope, prohibiting 16-year-olds from using blowtorches to burn hair from animal carcasses in slaughterhouses, but allowing them to work as "headskinners."[3] Other provisions of the FLSA, as amended, also include the following: Children under 12 are barred from nearly all employment but may work on their parents' farms. They also may work on small farms that are exempt from federal minimum wage rules, but only with parental consent. There are four exempted jobs in which children may work with little restriction: acting, wreath-making, delivering newspapers, and sports-related jobs such as baseball batboys.

However, seventeen types of jobs are considered "hazardous" for 16- and 17-year-olds, including work involving explosives, driving cars and trucks, mining, logging, and slaughtering. There are more such restrictions for younger children under the so-called hazardous orders, many of which have not been altered for many decades and wherein the most recent revisions occurred thirty years ago. As a result, federal labor law officials have begun reviewing existing hazardous labor orders and have revised them where necessary. Older orders restricted child labor in industries that no longer exist or that have changed radically over the years. Some new industries that have recently emerged are not regulated at all.[4]

STATE LAWS

Each of the fifty states has enacted laws prohibiting the employment of children in hazardous occupations within its borders. These state statutes are remedial in nature and are directed at the employer, both in his obligations and his liability. The FLSA provides a minimum level of protection unless a stricter law applies. For that matter, throughout the section of the federal regulations pertaining to the FLSA is the reminder that the federal law governing child labor standards does not in any way restrain the application of laws that establish a higher standard. The federal law's relationship with state law has been described by one observer in this manner:

> One unique aspect of the child labor act is that if the individual state where the child is employed has a stricter child labor code and standard of employment, the federal law, under section 218 of the Act, will adopt and apply the state's stricter standard. In effect, the federal law becomes the stricter state standard.[5]

This relationship with other laws is consistent with the FLSA's objective of abolishing oppressive child labor.

All states have some laws restricting the employment of children or minors. Generally, there are restrictions in two areas: (1) the type of occupation, and (2) the hours of employment. In addition, many states provide for the issuance of employment certificates or work permits as a prerequisite to employment.

By law, regulation, or both, all states list hazardous occupations in which minors below a specific age cannot be employed. Many times, there are separate lists for minors under 18, minors under 16, and minors under 14. A substantial number of states prohibit most employment for all minors under 14. Usual exceptions include newspaper deliveries, family businesses, and agricultural work.

Almost all states restrict the hours of employment for minors under the age of 16. Several also have hour restrictions for 16- and 17-year-olds. Employment may be restricted to a specified number of hours a day or week and to daytime or early evening hours. In addition, permissible hours of work usually are reduced even more for school-age minors while school is in session. Restrictions may be liberalized for vacation periods.

Child labor provisions are divided into two categories: agricultural and non-agricultural labor. Minors working in agriculture are less protected from exploitation and more exposed to hazardous employment that threatens their health, safety, education, and well-being. Seventy-six percent of the states set a minimum age for nonagricultural employment at 14 years. In agricultural employment, 27 percent of the states set a minimum age below 14 years and 49 percent have no minimum age for employment. For child agricultural workers, the maximum hours of work while school is in session is either greatly extended, or no maximum is set at all: 57 percent of the states do not set maximum hours for 14- and 15-year-olds, and 78 percent do not set maximum hours for 16- and 17-year-olds. For the states that do set maximum hours of work, they are as high as 60 hours a week, even when school is in session.

Nearly all states have adopted standards similar to the federal standards for 14- and 15-year-olds, although the restrictions vary significantly. With regard to nonagricultural child labor, most states limit the number of hours that may be worked in a day when school is not in session to eight hours; only three states allow more than eight hours of work in a day when school is not in session. Most states limit the number of hours that may be worked in a week when school is not in session to forty hours; fifteen states, however, permit work in excess of forty hours when school is not in session, with the number of hours allowed ranging from forty-four to fifty-six. With respect to the number of hours that may be worked in a week when school is in session, a large number of the states do not have any specific restrictions. Eighteen states restrict work to no more than eighteen hours; two states restrict work to sixteen and fifteen hours, respectively; two states restrict work hours to eighteen hours, but allow more hours when school is not in session for a full week; and seven other states have provisions that allow work in excess of twenty hours a week when school is in session.

Of the states that restrict daily work hours, twenty provide for a three-hour limitation on a school day, whether or not the following day is a school day; one state sets a three-hour limit on days followed by a school day; and one state permits longer hours on Saturdays and Sundays. A daily limit of four hours is allowed by seven states, with one of those states permitting additional hours on Fridays and on a school day preceding a day when school is not in session.

In twenty-eight states, work beyond 7 P.M. is prohibited except during the summer, on a holiday, or on a day preceding a day when school is not in session, when work until 9 P.M. is allowed in twenty-six of these states, and until 10 P.M. in the other two states. Two additional states prohibit work after 7 P.M. at all times. An additional nineteen states allow work at least until 8 P.M.; another five states permit work until 10 P.M.[6]

AGRICULTURAL EMPLOYMENT IS DIFFERENT

Federal child labor regulations allow children to work in agriculture at a younger age than in other industries, in more hazardous occupations, and for longer periods of time than their peers in other industries. The minimum age at which children can work in hazardous occupations, such as mining and logging, is 18. But 16-year-olds are allowed to do hazardous farm work, such as operating a tractor, hay bailer, or grain combine. Furthermore, on farms either owned or operated by their parents, children of any age can do hazardous farm work. Minimum age standards differ between agriculture and other industries, in part to exclude family farms from federal regulation.

Federal child labor regulations for non-hazardous work also specify lower age restrictions for children in agriculture than for those in other occupations. The minimum age at which minors can work in nonhazardous occupations other than agriculture is 14 or 16. Children younger than 14, however, can do nonhazardous farm work under certain conditions. Minors at the age of 12 or 13 can work in agriculture outside school hours with parental consent. Children of any age can work on family farms.

According to the U.S. Department of Labor, the following specific regulations pertain to child labor on a farm:

- 14- and 15-year-olds may work outside school hours in nonhazardous jobs. In addition, a 14- or 15-year-old may perform some hazardous farm work if he or she is enrolled in a vocational agricultural program, if there is a written training agreement with the employer, and the student is closely supervised. They may also operate machinery if they have completed a 4-H or other approved tractor- or machine-operation program.
- 12- and 13-year-olds may work outside school hours in jobs not declared hazardous with either written consent from their parents or on the same farm where their parents are employed.
- Children 12 years of age and younger are banned from working on farms employing workers covered by the minimum wage regulations. On all other farms, they may work in nonhazardous jobs outside school hours with written parental consent.
- 10- and 11-year-olds may hand-harvest crops outside school hours for no more than eight weeks between June 1 and October 15 if their employers obtain special waivers.

The Secretary of Labor determines which farm jobs are declared hazardous. These jobs include operating equipment driven by a PTO (power take-off such as a corn picker, grain combine, or hay mower); working from a ladder or scaffold more than twenty feet high; or transporting, transferring or applying anhydrous ammonia. According to the child labor laws outlined in the FLSA, an employer can face fines of up to $1,000 for each child labor violation. The employer may also face civil penalties of up to $10,000. However, as noted earlier, there is an exception to these regulations. Youths of any age may work on a farm owned or operated by their parents. They are not excluded from any job or restricted to certain hours. Consequently, under federal law, a 13-year-old cannot do paid clerical work in an air-conditioned office. But the same youngster can pick strawberries all day under the blazing summer sun.

Agricultural employers need to be aware of how the child labor laws apply to farming and know the stiff penalties levied if they violate these regulations. The most common violation occurs when the employer, uninformed of the regulations, hires a juvenile to work with chemicals or machinery. The employer's biggest mistake is simply not being familiar with the laws. Compounding the situation, government agencies responsible for enforcement have devoted a relatively low level of resources to policing child workers in agriculture.[7]

MINIMUM WAGES, OVERTIME COMPENSATION, AND EQUAL PAY

Both federal and individual state laws provide for minimum wages and overtime compensation for employees. In order to determine whether a child is covered under the federal or state system, the individual statutes need to be consulted. The FLSA exempts from the minimum-wage provision children who are engaged in the delivery of newspapers to consumers. State minimum wage laws either provide for the application of a state minimum wage to minors or provide for a separate subminimum wage for child workers. As under the federal regulatory scheme, the state statutory structure provides very limited exceptions to the minimum wage provisions, usually, again applying to the delivery of newspapers by children or employment in the agriculture sector.

The principle of equal pay for equal work, unaffected by considerations of gender, is equally applicable to the employment of children. Under the federal Equal Pay Act of 1967, and in those states which have adopted equal pay legislation, gender, and not minority of the employee, is the basic criterion.

UNEMPLOYMENT COMPENSATION

General entitlement to unemployment compensation is regulated by each individual state. The nature of employment, term of occupation, and manner of termination of work govern eligibility for unemployment benefits. The age of the employee is normally not a factor; rather, the only consideration is whether the employee has qualified under the terms of a particular unemployment statute.

SOCIAL SECURITY COVERAGE

An employee's entitlement to social security coverage, particularly death or disability benefits, is set forth by the federal social security laws, which are primarily concerned with the nature and duration of employment and not the age of the employee. If a child has filed six of the last thirteen quarters under social security, and is injured or dies, the child employee is entitled to all the normal benefits of the social security system as an adult employee under similar circumstances.

WORKERS' COMPENSATION

Whether a child employee is employed legally under the child labor laws or illegally in violation of the federal or state statutes, the question of injury to child employees constantly arises. Workers' compensation coverage is determined by each individual state's workers' compensation laws. In general, most states' compensation laws provide workers' compensation benefits to injured child employees, whether the contract of employment is within or without the purview of the child labor statutes. Some states' compensation laws even mandate double compensation for the injured child if the child worked in violation of the child labor laws, as a penalty to the employer.

Workers' compensation laws guarantee that the injured employee will receive monetary benefits, but in return, the employee generally loses the right to file a lawsuit against the employer. However, if for some reason, it is determined that the child employee was not eligible for workers' compensation coverage, then the child has the common law right to sue for the injury. Some statutes even provide an option to the child to sue under the workers' compensation statute or under the old common law action. In some instances, even the defense of contributory negligence of the minor is not available to the employer. Benefits are not uniform throughout the states, with critics contending that they are still too low for children injured doing illegal work, although payments are higher in some states. The fact that benefit amounts are tied to the occupation held by the child at the time of a fatal work injury drew the ire of Dorianne Beyer, general counsel for the National Child Labor Committee, who maintained that "[a] 14-year-old hay baler who loses his life in a mechanical accident is compensated as if he were going to be a hay baler all his life. Is that fair?" In contrast, Peter Eide, manager for labor law policy at the U.S. Chamber of Commerce, thought that the remedy was equitable.[8]

OSHA SURVEILLANCE

Virtually all workers, including minors, are protected by safety and health standards set by the Occupational Safety and Health Administration (OSHA), under the provisions of the OSHA law enacted in 1970. These standards cover fire and electrical safety, chemical hazards, machine guarding, and many other on-the-job risks. Employers with ten or more workers in more hazardous industries must keep records of injuries and illnesses that occur at their sites. All employers must report to OSHA incidents in which one or more workers are killed or three or more are hospitalized. OSHA enforces its standards through inspections targeted toward high-hazard industries or conducted in response to worker complaints. Penalties can range up to $7,000 for serious violations or $70,000 for willful violations of safety and health standards. Penalties follow the criteria set by the 1970 statute, which determines fines based on two criteria that have remained unchanged during the past three decades: the severity of the violation, and the size, good faith, and history of the employer. The gravity of the problem determines the base amount of the fine; the other factors determine reductions in the amount assessed.

Critics contend that OSHA investigates industries that employ large numbers of children only when there is a fatality or an incident of multiple injuries. Also, routine health and safety audits are scheduled only on industries that are considered to be especially dangerous. Furthermore, OSHA is continually underfunded. There are only 1800 federal and state inspectors and a small administrative staff to oversee the safety and health of 90 million workers in 6 million workplaces under its jurisdiction. At its current strength, the agency is able to inspect individual workplaces about once every eighty-seven years.

WORK PERMITS

There is no federal requirement that minors have a work permit or certificate of age in order to work. The FLSA requires employers to be able to prove, upon request, that minors are working in compliance with federal hours and hazardous occupation restrictions. The Department of Labor, charged with enforcement, accepts work permits and age certificates issued in most states as proof of age for the purposes of the act. In states without a work permit program that meets standards set forth in federal regulations, the Department issues age certificates upon request. These "age certificates" have features similar to work permits while also providing proof of age. For example, they are specific to a given employer. A large majority of states (forty-two, plus the District of Columbia) require either a work permit or certificate of age, but these requirements vary considerably from one state to another.

Permits are issued to children by state and local school systems. School authorities may exercise discretion in issuing work permits, based on a student's academic standing. Also, in most states, a physician's signature is required on the work permit certifying that the child is fit for work. Unfortunately, school systems seldom exercise discretionary authority in issuing work permits. Children and adolescents receive little or no counseling and education on the hazards of work. In most states there is also a lack of centralized data collection that records the number of work permits issued or the industries in which children are employed.[9]

A lack of uniformity characterizes the state systems of work permits. For instance, in North Carolina, anyone under 18 years of age who wants to work in a nonagricultural setting is required to get a permit. As part of the permit process, an employer is required to write out what a teen's responsibilities will be, and a parent must sign the form. Some 120,000 work permits are issued annually. However, probably the most common child labor law violation in

North Carolina is employers hiring minors without permits.[10] In New York state, there are twelve kinds of employment certificates for students who are residents. On the other hand, Connecticut issues only one kind of employment certificate for minors; it allows 16- and 17-year-olds to work up to nine hours a day, or up to forty-eight hours a week in most food service, recreation and office jobs, with stricter rules on work in retail stores. New Jersey labor regulations for minors are complex. Employment certificates for 14- and 15-year-olds carry severe restrictions; 16- and 17-year-olds may work up to eight hours a day, or up to forty hours over a 5-day period.[11] Massachusetts law prohibits "mercantile establishments," including restaurants, from employing children less than 16 years of age, unless the child has an employment permit. A child over 14 can only get an employment permit after the superintendent of schools determines the child's welfare is better served by granting the work permit. An employer hiring anyone under age 16 must first obtain the permit from the employee and keep it on file. The Workers' Compensation Act further states that employment of a child known to be under 16 and without a permit constitutes serious and willful misconduct. A workplace injury resulting from such misconduct entitles the employee to double compensation.

A Massachusetts case involving that state's Department of Industrial Accidents (DIA) illustrates the importance to employers of demanding work permits of young job seekers before hiring them. A DIA judge ruled that a doughnut shop committed "serious and willful misconduct" by employing an individual who was under age 16 and without a work permit. As a result, the employee was entitled to twice her normal workers' compensation benefits after sustaining an on-the-job injury.

The 15-year-old employee suffered severe burns on her ankle after a hot coffeepot she was holding burst. She had been hired by the doughnut shop several months earlier to perform duties that included making and serving coffee. At the time she was hired, the employer knew the girl was under age 16 and that she did not have an employment permit. The employer's insurer tried to convince the judge that an employee could only get double benefits if there was a close and causal connection between the employer's violation and the injury. Because this accident would have occurred regardless of whether the employer was in possession of an employment permit, the insurer argued that the employer had not engaged in serious and willful misconduct.

The DIA judge rejected the argument, stating that the employment of a minor without the requisite permit was "in fact criminal in nature." The judge conceded that one Supreme Judicial Court case left open the possibility that double compensation might be denied if no connection between the violation and injury were shown. The judge relied on a number of other high court decisions, however, in ruling that the mere employment of a minor without a permit as serious and willful misconduct. The Supreme Judicial Court of Massachusetts has taken the position that the employer (or its insurer) can avoid the strict effects of the law easily enough by insisting that employees under age 16 produce the necessary employment permits before starting work.

A great many firms have employees under the age of 16 and yet do not insist on obtaining proper permits before employment. Employers often complain that they cannot find nonminor employees who will work for the wages the employers want to pay. An employer might also take offense at the notion that a criminal act has been committed simply by offering a minor a job. Nevertheless, the reality is, that regardless of the rationale for hiring a minor unlawfully, a violation can bring serious consequences. Besides the double workers' compensation statute, Massachusetts and federal law also provide for civil penalties, criminal fines, and even imprisonment for illegal employment of minors.[12]

FEDERAL ENFORCEMENT PROCEDURES

The Department of Labor's Wage and Hour Division (WHD), headquartered in Washington, D.C., within the Employment Standards Administration, is responsible for administering and enforcing FLSA child labor provisions. WHD compliance officers undertake two types of compliance actions: conciliations and investigations.

Conciliations are typically initiated as a result of a complaint, involve only one employee, and generally take only a few hours to complete. When conducting a conciliation, the compliance officer does not visit the employer's premises or review the worker's records.

Investigations are more detailed than conciliations and take an average of twenty hours to complete. They may be initiated by WHD as a part of its annual work plan or as a result of a complaint and will include an on-site visit by a compliance officer who reviews employer records, interviews employees, and computes back wages and penalties due, as appropriate.

Approximately 76 percent of WHD's FLSA compliance actions are initiated as a result of complaints. Child labor case complaints often come from parents or one of the employing firms' customers, but rarely from the minor employee. Other compliance actions, called "directed investigations," are initiated by WHD. In some instances, WHD identifies violations at one establishment as a result of a complaint and then investigates other enterprises owned by the same company. In other situations, WHD may target a particular type of industry for investigation and, regardless of the reason for the investigation, a check of compliance with the child labor provisions is always included.

Several remedies are available against employers who violate FLSA. Using FLSA civil sanctions, Labor may (1) sue employers for back wages due employees, including minors, for violation of the minimum wage and overtime requirements and an equal amount in liquidated damages on behalf of employees; or (2) seek an injunction against future FLSA violations and recovery of back wages; or (3) file an action combining both remedies.

Labor also has the authority to assess civil money penalties under the child labor provisions of FLSA. The Secretary of Labor may assess penalties of up to $10,000 for each violation of the child labor provisions. Employers may appeal the penalties within fifteen days of the assessment to WHD. WHD refers the appeal to Labor's Chief Administrative Law Judge, who assigns it to an administrative law judge for formal hearing and final decision in the administrative process. Labor's Office of the Solicitor is responsible for initiating civil actions against employers or settling cases that are not resolved by WHD. Criminal actions may be brought against employers by the Department of Justice, on the recommendation of Labor's Solicitor, for violations of the act, including those related to child labor provisions.

In June, 1994, attempting to institute heavier penalties on offenders, the Labor Department began to enforce heavier fines for child work safety law violations. Since then, employers are subject to a $10,000 assessment for each violation that results in the death of or serious injury to an underage worker. Under the old interpretation of FLSA, fines were levied, based on the number of minors injured in a workplace accident.

For example, presently, a warehouse owner could face $20,000 in fines if a 15-year-old worker were killed while operating a forklift—$10,000 for operating the forklift and another $10,000 for violating the prohibition against 15-year-olds working in a warehouse.[13]

"Serious injury" is defined as any of the following on-the-job injuries that are directly or indirectly caused by a child labor violation:

- any permanent anatomical or physiological injury to any body system (e.g., neurological, musculoskeletal, special sense organs, cardiovascular) or any permanent psychological injury; or
- any injury requiring five days under medical care following the injury; or
- any injury requiring five days off work following the injury as confirmed by appropriate medical certification.

Death, as used in this new penalty structure, refers to any on-the-job fatality directly or indirectly caused by a child labor violation. Whether these more stringent penalties will prompt employers to hire fewer children is uncertain. When companies need certain types of workers, such as those who will work part-time without benefits, they may have no choice but to hire minors.

ILLEGAL CHILD LABOR IN AGRICULTURE

Detecting illegal employment in agriculture is very dependent on targeting investigations to those locations, Labor Department officials have acknowledged. Farming has been a priority for many of their directed task forces, as it was one of the primary industries targeted for investigation during three of the task forces conducted during Operation Child Watch in 1990. In addition,

Labor made agriculture one of the targeting priorities for the strike forces conducted during fiscal years 1991 and 1992. Detecting illegal employment in agriculture is a relatively small part of total detected illegal employment, as indicated in Table 3.1. For instance, in fiscal year 1991, only 1 percent of the 27,528 children who were working illegally worked in agriculture. For that matter, child labor advocates maintain that the amount of illegal child labor in agriculture is substantial and far larger than the number detected by WHD. The National Child Labor committee estimates that up to 100,000 children may be illegally employed in agriculture.[14]

During the 1993–1997 period, about 15 percent of WHD inspections were devoted to agriculture, which meant that less than 6 percent of the division's total enforcement resources were concentrated on illegal child labor in farming. A General Accounting Office report revealed that another federal agency, Occupational Safety and Health Administration (OSHA), devoted less than 3 percent of its inspections during the same time frame to agriculture, even though many analysts consider this to be one of the most hazardous industries. The report estimated that 155,000 children ages 15 to 17 may be working in agriculture, based on the government's Current Population Survey, which is the work of census-takers. No estimate was made of how many of these youngsters worked illegally.[15]

While the Omnibus Budget Reconciliation Act of 1990 increased the maximum civil penalty for each child labor violation from $1,000 to $10,000, the law required that the fines collected for child labor violations be deposited in the general fund of the U.S. Treasury. Prior to that, money collected for child

Table 3.1
Number of Illegally Employed Child Laborers Detected in Agriculture, 1983–1991

Fiscal year	Total number of illegally employed minors detected	Number of illegally employed minors in agriculture	Percent of total detected in agriculture
1983	9,243	414	4.4%
1984	8,860	516	5.8%
1985	9,937	635	6.4%
1986	12,689	296	2.3%
1987	19,081	436	2.3%
1988	21,857	487	2.2%
1989	22,502	266	1.2%
1990	38,697	649	1.7%
1991	27,528	264	1.0%

Source: Child Labor: Information on Federal Enforcement Efforts (Washington, D.C.: GAO, June 1992), p. 15.

labor penalties went to WHD and was used for child labor enforcement activities. These were funds sorely needed by the underfunded and undermanned federal agency.

THE UPWARD TREND IN VIOLATIONS

Even with these protective laws in place, the number of child labor violations increased nearly 150 percent between 1983 and 1990. The increase covered violations in all types of child labor standards: hours, minimum age, and hazardous occupations. The greatest percentage of violations were work-hour violations; however, the minimum age and hazardous occupation violations had doubled. Table 3.2 demonstrates that the restaurant industry was the largest percentage violator where illegally employed children suffered the highest percentage of workplace injuries.

Between 1983 and 1990, child labor violations had increased from approximately 10,000 to almost 25,000.[16] In November 1990 civil and criminal penalties increased tenfold, but it turned out that the federal government was not meting out the maximum penalties available. A review of the fines imposed in the first phase of Operation Child Watch in April and May revealed that of twenty-four businesses charged with seriously harming minors, only three were assessed the maximum penalty.

For example, Exquisite Builders, a general contractor in Chalfont, Pennsylvania, was fined $2,000 for three violations, one that resulted in serious injury and two that allowed a 17-year-old to use hazardous machines. A fast-food restaurant in Collins, Colo., that employed three minors illegally, one of whom was seriously injured, was fined $1,450, less than half the maximum. Two statements by labor officials illustrates the somewhat ambivalent attitude toward enforcement of child labor legal requirements. An assistant secretary stated, "We must apply effective sanctions against offenders, and fine flagrant offenders severely, without discouraging other employers from legally hiring

Table 3.2
Federal Child Labor Violations Resulting in Injury, by Industry

Industry	Violations resulting in injury	Illegally employed children with workplace injuries
Restaurants	55%	38%
Grocery stores	23%	15%
Service & other	18%	21%
Manufacturing	3%	17%
Construction	1%	10%

Source: GAO, 1991.

youngsters." The other official maintained that employers would be deterred by the new department policy that doubled the average penalty from $165 to $345. "Three hundred and forty-five dollars is significant for some small businesses," he said. At the same time, the Child Labor Advisory Committee issued over fifty recommendations aimed at strengthening child labor laws. It also urged that more occupations be included in the hazardous category, including poultry and seafood processing.[17]

In 1992 twice as many child labor offenses were reported as in 1980. To address this issue, the Senate Labor Committee toughened the child-labor laws, increased penalties for violations, and broadened the list of jobs to be considered hazardous for 16- and 17-year-olds. A computer analysis of Labor Department records for fiscal years 1993–1997 showed that more than 22,000 workers under age 18 were victims of child labor law violations. The most common violation involving 14- and 15-year-olds was making them work later than the law allows, while the most common violation involving 16- and 17-year-olds was placing them in dangerous jobs, such as meatpacking or operating bakery machines. More than 50 percent of the violations were in restaurants and grocery stores, most of the time in companies employing fewer than 50 people.

Many experts argue that these numbers understate the magnitude of child labor violations, in part because no one seems to know how many youthful workers there are. The Child Labor Coalition, an organization supporting stronger child labor laws, estimates 5.5 million youths, or more than one quarter of the population of 12- to 17-year-olds, are employed. The Labor Department has no estimates of the number of people working between ages 12 and 17.

In fiscal years 1993–1997, WHD assessed fines of $42.3 million for child labor violations. However, even when a penalty is assessed, the full sum is rarely collected because firms negotiate with the government to reduce the amount. Due to these circumstances, the average collection rate between 1993–1997 was 63.1 percent. Furthermore, when employers hire large numbers of adolescent workers, notably in the fast-food industry, federal labor law violations can be chronic. Based on complaint data, estimates are that only 40 percent of fast-food companies are in full compliance with wage and hour law requirements. In the final analysis, apparently, no matter what measures individual companies utilize or how effective the governmental compliance machinery becomes, many children in the workplace will continue to be the victims of violations. As Jeffrey Newman of the National Child Labor Committee observed recently: "Child labor violations are at their highest since the 1930s. . . . The irony of child labor is it tends to peak when the economy is at its worst, when there is a demand for cheap labor, or at its best, when companies use child labor because regular laborers are hard to find."[18]

THE STATE CHILD LABOR SURVEY

In 1998 the Child Labor Coalition conducted a survey of state labor departments and garnered a forty-six-state response, a 92 percent response rate. Nonrespondents were Florida, Ohio, Pennsylvania, Vermont, and the District of Columbia. This survey demonstrated weaknesses in child labor laws and enforcement and portrayed thousands of youth illegally employed throughout the country. Limited resources and action by states translate into fewer violations found through investigation and little incentive for employers to comply with child labor laws (see Table 3.3). The following are highlights.

The state labor departments reported a total number of only 815 compliance officers for investigating child labor compliance/violations exclusively in forty-six states. For most states, child labor law enforcement is only one of the many responsibilities of their investigators and, as such, twenty-six of the responding states have a total number of ten or fewer compliance officers who are responsible for enforcing labor laws in the state. Only eight of the states that re-

Table 3.3
State Survey on Child Labor Enforcement

	1998	1996	1994	1992
No. of compliance officers responsible for child labor enforcement only	22 (42 states)	8.5 (46 states)	40 (41 states)	36.5 (37 states)
No. of compliance officers responsible for enforcing all labor standards, including child labor	642 (42 states)	811 (45 states)	571 (41 states)	562 (37 states)
Total inspections of workplaces where child labor compliance was a component	49,288 (41 states)	48,414 (36 states)	48,918 (37 states)	N/A
Total inspections of workplaces discovering child labor violations	9,776 (39 states)	7,322 (37 states)	9,148 (38 states)	16,410 (37 states)
No. of minors found to be illegally employed	16,535 (33 states)	7,577 (29 states)	12,959 (28 states)	8,537 (28 states)
No. of employers found to be in violation of child labor laws	4,795 (36 states)	6,229 (33 states)	8,409 (34 states)	N/A
Total amount of money assessed for violations	$2,005,886 (35 states)	$2,469,016 (45 states)	$2,615,061 (29 states)	$981,468* (40 states)

* Only reflects total amount of civil money penalties assessed.

Source: National Consumers League, 1999.

sponded have a total number of twenty-five or more compliance officers to enforce the state's labor laws.

Reflecting the decreased staff and increased workload, the breakdown on the number of inspections conducted by states in 1996 in which child labor compliance was a component was the following:

- Three states conducted 0 inspections.
- Twelve states conducted 100 and fewer inspections.
- Twenty-four states conducted more than 100 inspections.
- Ten states conducted more than 1000 inspections.
- Twenty-eight states reported restrictions for occupational driving for 16- and 17-year-olds.
- Twenty-two states reported companies specializing in door-to-door sales by children (candy, magazine subscriptions, etc.) active in their state during 1996.
- Thirteen states (59 percent) of the twenty-two states who reported door-to-door companies at work took action against the companies in 1996.
- Four states instituted new child labor regulations or passed child labor laws in 1996.

According to the survey, 16 percent of the inspections resulted in uncovering child labor violations. A total of 6,229 employers were found to be in violation of child labor laws in thirty-three states and 7,577 minors were found to be illegally employed in twenty-nine states. States assessed $2,469,016 for child labor violations in 1996.[19]

MIGRANT AND SEASONAL FARM WORK

Children working as migrant and seasonal agricultural workers are among the least protected minors in the workplace. The lack of attention to this population of working children is staggering, given that reputable sources have estimated the number of child-migrant and seasonal farmworkers at 800,000 in the United States. With this in mind, the state survey showed that only seven of thirty-eight respondents conducted inspections in 1996 in which child labor compliance in agriculture was targeted. Only three of the seven conducted a significant number of inspections. Altogether, thirty-one employers were found to be in violation of child labor laws and ninety-one children were found illegally employed. Eighteen of the states have no minimum age for children who work as migrant and seasonal farmworkers, while sixteen states have minimum age limits for children between 9 and 12 years of age.[20] In April 1998 a Labor Department strike force conducted a two-week sweep in Texas's Rio Grande Valley, which resulted in a court order against a large grower in Hidalgo County. The judicial action required future compliance with federal child labor requirements and the grower's agreement to a compliance-monitoring agreement. The agricultural initiative revealed that Pemelton Farms Co. had illegally employed ten children, ages 6 to 11, to pick onions. A district court issued a judgment requiring Pemelton to pay civil money penalties of $9,600 and to comply with the child labor requirements of the FLSA. In addition, Pemelton signed an agreement to institute a monitoring program to prevent future violations. The Labor Department planned fifty more enforcement sweeps nationwide in 1998 targeting "salad bowl" commodities including onions, garlic, lettuce, cucumbers and tomatoes with a special emphasis on child labor compliance in agriculture.[21]

UNEVEN STATE ENFORCEMENT

As noted earlier, there is little uniformity in state child labor laws, some of which are vague and difficult to enforce. Some states lack resources or commitment to follow up on reports that children are working illegally. Variations in state laws can be dizzying, with some more stringent than federal child labor laws, others more lenient. State enforcement efforts also vary widely.

Oregon law, for example, permits children as young as 9 to pick berries and beans. Hawaii law says 10-year-olds may harvest coffee. California has child-labor-law provisions that are more stringent than those specified in the FLSA for some occupations and industries. California restricts hours of work for minors ages 16 and 17, while the federal law allows unlimited hours of work. Idaho and Maryland have no personnel assigned to enforce child labor laws in contrast to California and New York, which have teams of labor investigators searching for child labor violations. In Minnesota most violations occur in the retail sector, since that is where most teens seek employment. The infractions vary by the type of business. In a restaurant or bakery, the huge mixers or meat slicers are illegally used; at retail warehouses, forklifts are the culprits; at grocery stores, paper balers. The Florida Child Labor Office, which has a $200,000 budget, hears about a possible violation, sends a form letter asking the employer to submit time sheets, personnel files on minors, and a list of power-operated equipment used by minors. The agency is unable to spot-check businesses that typically employ youths ages 14 to 17 and checks most alleged violations via mail because its small size and underfunding preclude on-site investigation of every case. Florida toughened its child labor laws in 1991, but an investigation six years later found the state's enforcement efforts remained almost entirely aimed at teens packing groceries, taking fast-food orders, and working after-school jobs, leaving children working in agriculture vulnerable. A review of records demonstrated that the state had investigated only three cases of children working on farms during the 1993–1997 period. Two involved youngsters killed in citrus groves. The third investigation was begun when a labor investigator encountered a van accident involving migrant workers, including a 15-year-old girl picking tomatoes full time. The enforcement action consisted of one warning to a labor contractor. Limited resources hamper Florida's enforcement efforts. That state has only three inspectors, so that in any given week the Child Labor Office dispatches one inspector into "the field," meaning the entire state.[22]

In Oklahoma a 15-year-old boy was working illegally in an ice plant when his coat caught and trapped his body in an auger. The machine squeezed his lungs until they collapsed. He died a week later. Even though the youth was using prohibited equipment under Oklahoma's child labor law, the employer was fined only $300. The Oklahoma tragedy points out the enforcement problems that may arise when a state relies on the federal government to seek out and punish child-labor violations and why a state should not abdicate its responsibilities to working children. Here, the Department of Labor investigated the 15-year-old's death and quickly concluded that it had no jurisdiction because the small rural ice plant was not engaged in interstate commerce.[23] Texas state law allows farm work at any age and enforcement of federal law is negligible. The result is that even toddlers are out in the fields. The Texas Workforce Commission is the state agency responsible for enforcing state labor laws. In 1997 it had a $780,000 budget, with eight investigators and one supervisor to enforce the law. More than 1,700 cases of child labor were investigated, resulting in fines to about fifty employers. However, not one state fine was levied for children working in agriculture.[24]

In Georgia, which has a $5.3 billion agricultural industry and no reliable estimate of child laborers, state law offers no protection for children who pick and plant crops. We have seen that federal law sets limits but allows children younger than 12 to work in the fields under certain circumstances. To enforce the law, Georgia's Child Labor Division must borrow investigators from another office to check complaints. It has no power to levy fines.[25]

The state Department of Labor, Licensing and Regulation in Maryland has admitted its investigations into child labor complaints have basically ended since the Employment Standards unit was disbanded in 1991 as a response to state budget reductions. During the previous year, the unit found 172 firms employing 488 minors in violation of state child-labor laws. The number dropped to zero with the closing of the unit. The agency was revived in 1994 but with only six employees, compared with thirty, three years earlier. Enforcement now consists of a notice and a copy of Maryland's labor law being sent to the business against which a complaint has been filed. If there is no response, the matter is closed as there is no investigation staff to pursue the offender.

In 1990, in California, the state Department of Industrial Relations issued 833 citations for child labor violations. By 1995, the number had declined to 310 notifications of violations. The department collected only about one-quarter of the $849,000 in penalties assessed that year.[26]

Kentucky has only twenty officials to enforce all labor laws, and none is assigned exclusively to child labor problems. For that matter, only eight states have employees whose sole responsibility is child labor enforcement. In contrast, New Jersey is among the handful of states that enforce child labor laws more vigorously. There, investigators open more than 100 child labor cases in an average month.

New York stands out as a leader in the child labor law enforcement area. The New York law specifies a maximum eight hours a day and forty-eight hours a week for 16- and 17-year-olds when school is not in session, and a twenty-eight-hour work week when school is in session, including a four-hour daily limit Monday through Thursday (See Table 3.4). This compares favorably with the federal law, which sets no limitations on working hours for 16- and 17-year-olds. The twenty-eight-hour-per-week limit makes New York tougher than every major industrial state except California and Pennsylvania, which also have a twenty-eight-hour-per-week limit. By contrast, New Jersey's weekly maximum is forty hours; Connecticut, Massachusetts, and Texas adopted forty-eight hours; and Ohio has no limits.[27] Also, New York is better equipped to pursue child labor law violators. That state has forty inspectors who work exclusively on child labor law cases while there are *no* federal compliance officers whose sole responsibility is enforcement of child labor laws. It should also be remembered that at the federal level fewer than 1,000 compliance officers enforce more than sixty labor laws, and this staffing level remains below that of a decade ago. Of course, as noted above, at the state level, also, the numbers reveal sporadic enforcement. In fact, the total number of state compliance officers in the whole nation working on child labor exclusively is only forty-two officials.[28]

THE KENTUCKY AND NEW YORK SURVEYS

A survey of students, teachers, parents, employers, and labor unions, conducted by the University of Louisville Labor Management Center, revealed that 90 percent of Kentucky teachers believe student employment interferes with education, and most of them believe that state's child labor laws should be

Table 3.4
New York State Teenage Labor Survey

Number of violations or injuries, by type	
Legal rights not explained	277
Asked to work "off the books"	244
Worked after midnight	219
Excessive hours (14–17)	153
No working papers	139
Prohibited machine	126
Job injury	105
Prohibited job	60

Source: New York State Department of Labor, 1988.

more restrictive. One thousand from each group—high school students, teachers, parents and employers—plus somewhat fewer labor union officials were asked questions about the adequacy and effects of Kentucky's child labor laws, which restrict children 17 and under from working in hazardous jobs and set limits on the work students of different ages can do before and after school and on weekends.

Teachers surveyed believed that student employment is detrimental to study and sometimes causes students to fall asleep in class or fail to do homework. Differing with their instructors, seventy percent of the students contended that employment did not affect their schoolwork. Only 20 percent believed outside work interfered with schoolwork, while 11 percent stated that outside work actually improved their educational performance.

A majority of teachers favored a reduction in the hours students are permitted to work. Kentucky students ages 14 and 15 are permitted to work three hours daily during school attendance and eight hours each weekend day. Those 16 and 17 are permitted to work five hours a day when school is in session and eight each weekend day.[29]

Nearly a decade earlier, in 1988, the New York State Department of Labor surveyed 1,106 students or teenage school dropouts, with 621 (56 percent) reporting a violation or occupational injury (see Table 3.4.) The respondents were enrolled in New York City and Buffalo high schools or were school dropouts seeking work or undergoing job training in New York City, Syracuse, and Albany. The following analysis is based on the 621 questionnaires reporting violations or injuries:

Prohibited Occupations:

60 respondents reported working in prohibited occupations, primarily construction.

139 reported that they did not have working papers.

277 reported that their rights under child labor laws were never explained.

Prohibited Machines:

126 respondents reported working with prohibited machines, primarily meat-slicing machines or circular wood saws.

Excessive Hours of Work During School Year:

Sixty 14–15-year-olds worked more than twenty-three hours weekly.

Eighty-four 16-year-olds worked more than twenty-eight hours per week and nine 17-year-olds worked more than forty-eight hours a week.

Most of the children under age 14 worked as newspaper carriers or babysitters. Seventeen of the 13-year-olds reported working from two to seventy hours each week while twelve 12-year-olds reported that they worked from two to thirty-five hours weekly. Two 11-year-olds said they worked (one worked one hour a week; the other worked ten hours each week). An 8-year old reported working one hour a week. Two hundred nineteen, or 35 percent, worked after midnight, and 244 were asked to "work off the books," meaning that their employers asked the adolescents to work over and above the legally mandated hours.

Of the 105 who reported work-related injuries, thirty-five informed the state workers' compensation agency while sixty-five of the youths did not file a report. Five indicated they had sustained injuries but did not mention whether the injury had been reported for worker compensation purposes.

With regard to the permanent nature of the ninety-eight reported injuries, thirty-five were temporary (e.g., sore knee), forty required a short recuperation period (e.g., sprained ankle), twenty-one of the injuries necessitated a long recuperative period (e.g., broken bone), and two individuals suffered a permanent injury (e.g., lost fingertip). The types of accidents included burns, broken bones, falls or something dropped on the worker, cuts, a dog bite, sprains or severe bruises, and an insulin reaction. Only four respondents did not specify the type of injury they had suffered. Thirty respondents indicated that their injuries occurred while they were employed in a legal occupation (primarily cooking occupations, which caused burns). Four had been working on legal machines when they incurred the injuries (primarily, deep fryers causing burns). Ten teens suffered injuries while working in prohibited occupations and six individuals were injured while working on legally prohibited machinery.

DOOR-TO-DOOR CANDY SALES

Much of the discussion thus far has described illegal child labor where employers have broken child-labor laws by employing minors in prohibited occupations using dangerous machinery for longer time periods than permitted by statute. Another type of child-labor abuse has been uncovered in New York, California, Washington, Texas, and other states since the mid-nineties, which involves door-to-door candy selling.

These operations should not be confused with selling Girl Scout cookies. Girl Scouts sell in their own neighborhoods, to people they know, and are driven around by parents. However, in the typical candy-selling scam, vans operated by a host of small, shady operators pick up children, some as young as seven, after school and work late into the night on school days. Children that young are prohibited by the FLSA from working later than 7 P.M.

Small, fly-by-night candy distributors have hired young children to sell boxes of chocolates door-to-door, late at night, and unsupervised, in strange neighborhoods. In Washington state, one 11-year-old girl selling candy alone at 10 P.M. on a school night, 160 miles from her home, was struck and killed by a passing car.

In California, multiple child-labor laws have been violated. Underage children are recruited and are then allowed to work the streets alone, when the state law requires that they work in pairs. Usually, the children are taught to lie about their ages and the nature of the illicit operation. Youngsters selling in New York City's Rockefeller Center claim to be raising money for a charity, when they are not. California minors use the sales pitch that they are selling to help inner-city children escape drugs and crime. For example, one 13-year-old door-to-door seller told a reporter that he was raising money for his school baseball team, when, in fact, he was selling for a local business. As a retired career counselor for the Vallejo school system, who spends much of his time dedicated to exposing the candy sellers, put it: "The lesson the kids learn about work is, the better you lie, the more money you make."[30]

It turns out that most major cities have at least a few for-profit youth sales businesses. Many times, they recruit low-income children, who sell the products after school and on weekends. The businesses often start up and disband in short order, which discourages monitoring by local authorities. The federal government has expressed concern about the potential child-labor violations in candy-sales businesses but is often hamstrung by jurisdictional problems. Often, the business either is not engaged in interstate commerce or does not gross the $500,000 a year required for federal jurisdiction.[31]

STATE TIGHTENING OF CHILD LABOR RESTRICTIONS

Strengthening child labor laws is difficult because there is usually strong opposition from the influential industries that employ children. For instance, child-labor activists have argued that on a national level, restaurant owners have pressured the Labor Department to loosen federal hour restrictions on 14- and 15-year-olds so that they could work through the dinner rush hour, instead of being obliged by law to stop at 7 P.M. Companies that employ teenagers have also called for easing these restrictions on the same age group, claiming the change would reduce unemployment among younger workers without adversely affecting educational performance.

The executive director of the National Safe Workplace Institute, Joseph Kinney, has maintained that "Few people are really interested in protecting children. Who's on the dark side? McDonalds,' grocery stores, retail interests, ranchers, farmers. You've got a huge lobby to make sure there are sufficient children to work the longest hours for the lowest possible pay."[32]

Some states have responded to these concerns and strengthened their child labor laws in recent years, adding provisions that help to protect children in specific situations. For example, Michigan prohibits children from making cash transactions unsupervised after sundown or 8 P.M. This was a response to a situation where children worked a cash register at night and were exposed to robberies. In December 1991, two 17-year-old girls were murdered at a suburban yogurt shop in Austin, Texas. They were working there late without adult supervision.

California has an "agricultural zone of danger" provision in its law that prohibits farmers from allowing minor children of farmworkers in areas where they may be injured by farm equipment or pesticides. That state's work permit system requires parental and teacher permission before a student is allowed to work. The student must also specify the work location and school authorities can evaluate whether it is suitable and legal.[33]

Florida has increased the maximum penalty for a child labor violation to $2,500 per offense. The state also specifically prohibits youths from working in and around explosives, from slaughtering and meatpacking, from wrecking and demolition, and from hoisting machinery. In addition, reflecting a regional idiosyncrasy, 14- and 15-year-olds are prohibited from wrestling alligators. A state official commented, "It's a big thing here."[34]

All of these states have inspectors who check workplaces for child-labor violations, some if there is a complaint and others in conjunction with any inspection.

FEDERAL INACTION

Unfortunately, the positive steps taken by states has not been matched at the federal level. In 1994, for example, Labor Department officials asked for advice about tightening federal child labor laws. The National Institute for Occupational Safety and Health (NIOSH) responded with forty-three pages of recommendations for new child safety rules. The recommendations were supported with statistics documenting death and injury to children in unregulated work. The proposals have been implemented. Some included the following:

1. Drop distinctions between hazardous occupations in agriculture and other industries. Existing rules permit hazardous work in agriculture at age 16, two years younger than in other fields. Thus a forklift, the cause of many disabling and fatal injuries, can be off-limits in the factory but permitted in the barn.
2. Drop the exemption that permits children employed by their parents to perform any farm task, no matter how dangerous.
3. Ban 16- and 17-year-olds from construction sites altogether. Although most young workers injured on construction sites are doing tasks already deemed unlawful, some are struck by falling objects, suffer electrical shock, or are exposed to toxic chemicals while doing work that complies with the law.
4. Bar youths from commercial fishing, from using road-grading machinery and powered conveyors and from extracting petroleum and natural gas. NIOSH counted at least eleven deaths of 16- and 17-year-olds working as roustabouts and the like in oil and gas fields. The NIOSH response was sent to the Labor Department in October 1994, and nothing has happened since.

ENFORCEMENT COORDINATION PROBLEMS IN SWEATSHOPS

The Labor Department's Wage and Hour Division has made some progress in coordinating enforcement activities in garment industry sweatshops, but problems remain. Labor's efforts are impeded because of legal and administrative limitations and the varying regulatory priorities of federal and state labor departments.

For example, WHD has a joint agreement with OSHA, which enforces compliance with standards issued under federal health and safety legislation, to cross-train investigators and refer cases. OSHA and WHD compliance officers receive at least three days of instruction annually on each agency's operations, and WHD and OSHA refer cases on both formal and informal bases. Although experts identify garment-industry sweatshops as dangerous workplaces, OSHA does not target garment shops for programmed health or safety inspections. This is because the Bureau of Labor Statistics (BLS) industry-level injury data used by OSHA for targeting does not identify the garment industry as a high-hazard industry. Thus, OSHA has chosen to rely on an employee complaint or a reported injury, which limits the potential number of referrals it makes to WHD. BLS collects data to calculate lost workday injury rates. The LWDI rate is the average number of injuries that required days away from work or restricted work activity per 100 full-time workers per year. Also, due to the immigrant or undocumented nature of much of the sweatshop labor force, WHD and OSHA report rarely receiving complaints from workers in garment sweatshops. Moreover, compounding the problem, an annual appropriation bill rider prohibits OSHA from conducting safety inspections of most employers with ten or fewer workers in industries with below-average injury rates, unless a worker files a complaint or an accident occurs.

Similarly, in dealing with the Immigration and Naturalization Service (INS), WHD has a joint agreement to cross-train investigators and refer cases. Both agencies' staff personnel periodically participate in joint training sessions. WHD investigators verify the employment eligibility status of workers when inspecting a worksite for FLSA violations and provide information on the results of these inspections to INS. Although WHD officials have received some case referrals from INS, they rarely refer cases to INS. This is because WHD officials believe that greater cooperation with INS would actually impede their own enforcement efforts by undermining worker cooperation in WHD investigations.

In dealing with the Internal Revenue Service (IRS), the federal enforcers have also encountered obstacles in focusing on employers who do not pay federal taxes who may also be violating child and other labor laws. Currently, unlike the OSHA and INS situations, WHD has no agreement with the IRS to cross-train investigators or to refer cases. Although WHD officials say that they do refer some cases to IRS, they also report receiving little information in return for the reason that the IRS Code, in protecting confidentiality, generally limits sharing information with federal agencies for enforcement purposes. Federal agencies receive only very limited information, such as company addresses, when cases involve assessed penalties. However, many child-labor cases do not involve such penalties.[35]

Coordination efforts with state labor departments have also met with varying degrees of success, depending on the emphasis the state placed on combating sweatshops' working conditions. California and New York, for instance, two states that have minimum wage and overtime laws, large garment industries, and state labor departments, have identified garment industry sweatshops as a regulatory priority. These states also have established coordinated enforcement efforts with WHD during the last few years. In California, WHD and the Division of Labor Standards Enforcement conduct joint investigations in the garment and agricultural industries. In New York, WHD and the New York Apparel Industry Task Force conduct separate investigations but share the results with each other.

This cooperation also extends to the cross-referral of cases to take advantage of the different strengths of the state and federal laws to best serve the needs of the workers. For example, in New York, state labor enforcement officials often pursue large back-wage cases because officials have a greater chance of success in state court than WHD has in federal court in cases in which the employer declares bankruptcy. However, New York does not have a "hot-goods" provision, so New York may refer such cases to WHD for action.

In contrast, WHD has coordinated far less with the Florida and Texas state labor agencies, two states with less stringent labor standard legislation than the FLSA. In Florida, WHD officials have an informal agreement to coordinate with the Florida State Workers' Compensation Bureau. But in Texas, WHD officials have no formal agreement with the Bureau of the Texas State Employment Commission, although they do coordinate informally with the state's Last Payday and Child Labor Units. Florida does not have any state minimum wage or overtime laws. Texas does not have any overtime laws, and its hourly minimum wage rate is below the minimum federal rate. In addition, workers' compensation insurance coverage is voluntary in Texas. The Florida Workers' Compensation Bureau collects information on garment industry and other employers who do not pay for mandatory workers' compensation coverage for their workers.

WHD also continues to face a huge and expanding regulatory mandate as its enforcement resources, as measured in compliance officers facing increasing case loads, continues to be inadequate. WHD's regulatory mission was increased several years ago, with the agency given enforcement responsibilities for the Family and Medical Leave Act and the Employee Polygraph Protection Act, in addition to its conventional labor law oversight.

Finally, economic factors have combined to plague compliance efforts. The intense price-competition dynamics of the garment industry have fostered a willingness among manufacturers and contractors to break labor laws. The low domestic start-up costs allow easy contractor entry, ensuring manufacturers a large number of contractors bidding against each other for work. This competition is further heightened by the ability of retailers and manufacturers to import low-priced garments and the typical presence of an immigrant and primarily undocumented workforce, often with limited employment opportunities.[36] Consequently, labor law enforcement alone will not stem abuses in the garment industry. A substantial portion of the exploitation of children and adult workers can be attributed to the lack of federal immigration enforcement, which provides a readily available and cheap labor force of workers who are afraid to report abuses for fear of deportation. This supply of labor provides incentives for abusive employment practices and no impetus for employers to comply with minimum labor standards.

THE TIPP PROGRAM IN CALIFORNIA

As noted earlier, California is one of the states where an effort at federal-state coordination in enforcement has been in operation for several years. Its garment manufacturing and agricultural industries have a history of labor law violations and regularly employ some of the most vulnerable of workers, among them, many children. The need for increased enforcement in the targeted industries was apparent, yet budgetary constraints were hampering such efforts. Consequently, to make the best use of existing resources, in 1992, several agencies joined together to form the Targeted Industries Partnership Program (TIPP), a joint educational enforcement effort by the California Department of Industrial Relations through its Division of Labor Standards Enforcement and Division of Occupational Safety and Health and the U.S. Department of Labor Wage and Hour Division. The partners recognized that no single agency had sole responsibility nor could one agency be expected to shoulder the entire burden of enforcement in the target industries.

The agencies investigate conditions in agriculture and garment manufacturing, two industries in which large numbers of children are employed. What started as two agencies addressing a joint vision of service has evolved into a strong partnership of up to twelve local, state, and federal jurisdictions routinely being brought together to jointly enforce minimum labor and other enforcement standards. Both voluntary compliance and enforcement have increased dramatically. In 1993 (TIPP's first year), penalties assessed against employers totaled $6.5 million, and in 1994, $7 million, more than double the penalties assessed through combined agency efforts in any prior year.

During some TIPP operations, the California Highway Patrol may establish a predawn roadblock in a farming area to search for safety problems on farm worker buses. Labor agents may inspect the housing offered migrant farmworkers and look for code violations and unsanitary conditions. State tax authorities monitor employers who have been found to violate the law and ferret out unpaid taxes, workers' compensation premiums, and mandatory expenses. The main thrust of the operation is to mount a multi-agency effort where information and resources will be shared.

All state and federal enforcement measures are available to the inspection teams, including stop-orders, subpoenas, garment confiscations, hot goods actions, criminal prosecutions, and so on. All state-authorized enforcement measures are executed by the Division of Labor Standards Enforcement (DLSE) investigators. Enforcement and collection of judgments filed by DLSE attorneys is done under TIPP. The state Employment Development Department (EDD) prosecutes any state employment tax actions necessitated by the TIPP investigators and/or audits.

All federally authorized enforcement measures are executed by the Department of Labor investigators. DOL, DLSE, and EDD attorneys work jointly to ensure maximum legal effectiveness. When it is determined that the most appropriate course of action is to file a lawsuit on behalf of employees or against an employer, the prosecution of the lawsuit is carried out by the assigned state or federal attorney. The results of each investigation follow appropriate DOL, DLSE, and EDD procedures. Each agency is required to follow their mandated or administratively required enforcement policies.

The TIPP program operates under the direction of California's labor commissioner. TIPP does not require any new laws to enforce, nor are there any new statutes, regulations, or procedures with which to contend. The difference is that the enforcement and informational databases of the participating agencies are pooled in order to target those employers with a history of various violations who operate within and to the detriment of the garment manufacturing and agricultural industries.

TIPP was launched in 1992 as a two-year pilot program but was extended indefinitely in 1994 when the state Department of Industrial Relations and the U.S. Department of Labor signed a memorandum of understanding to that effect and also agreed to cover other industries and occupations if both parties agreed.

Child labor violations dropped significantly in the garment industry during 1996 to twenty-four, down from 1995's forty-one violations. Violations in the agricultural industry remained relatively level at sixty-five, one additional case over 1995. The two industries demonstrated different violation trends during the 1993–1994 and 1995–1996 periods. In the earlier two-year period, there had been fifteen and twelve violations, respectively, in the garment trades, with a substantial increase in 1995, followed by the sharp decline in 1996. In agriculture there were 153 violations in 1993 and a sharp drop to 74 in 1994, following the relatively level citation numbers in 1995 and 1996. In 1998, California indicated that TIPP might be expanded to construction and restaurants.

When the program began in 1993 with a series of high-profile, well-publicized raids, it sent shock waves through the agriculture and garment industries. In the first summer of TIPP agricultural inspections in Fresno, for example, more citations, including many for child-labor violations, were issued than had been handed out in the previous decade. However, even though the number of citations issued decreased during the 1995–1996 period does not mean that child-labor problems have disappeared, since the number of citations issued do not necessarily reflect the number of children involved in the violations. For example, if fifteen children were found working illegally in a field, one citation would be issued, covering all of them. In addition, for each violation spotted by law enforcement officers, many others are not cited.

For instance, on the first day of the Fresno sweep, a team of state and federal labor officials discovered at least two additional child-labor violations, but were unable to act on them. In one case, the man in charge of harvesting yard-long beans sent home two young children, ages 5 and 9, before investigators could interview them. In another, the employer himself fled before he could be asked why a 14-year-old boy harvesting his crop was receiving no pay at all. Furthermore, there were whole families working in the field. These workers have no child care facilities for their children while they are working, so the children accompany their parents and end up working alongside them.[37]

Furthermore, a number of problems have plagued the joint enforcement effort, notably in the garment industry, with government officials blaming a lack of resources for their inability to keep up with a growing industry where the economics provide minimal incentives for reform. However, only part of the problem can be attributed to staffing inadequacies. Despite the hard work and commitment of inspectors, enforcement has been marred by political infighting, a misplaced focus, and a series of missteps, including a number of controversial raids, and increased friction between state and federal authorities over strategy and publicity. In fact, even officials within the program acknowledge that the state and federal agents no longer cooperate on a continuing basis, nor do they share information.[38]

Despite these problems, the California TIPP program was chosen in 1996 by the National Council of State Governments to receive its Innovations in Government Award, one of eight national winners recognized for establishing programs that open an innovative approach to administration of state government. This is considered to be among the most prestigious public service honors, recognizing governmental initiatives that provide creative solutions to pressing social and economic challenges.[39]

THE ASSOCIATED PRESS-RUTGERS UNIVERSITY STUDY

The most thorough investigation of illegal child labor in the United States was conducted over a five-month period in 1996 when, on behalf of the Associated Press (AP), a Rutgers University labor economist analyzed data from census surveys and other sources and estimated the number of children who worked in violation of child labor laws. This study represents the only comprehensive estimate of illegal child labor in the nation now available. Douglas L. Kruse, the labor economist, concluded, that if nothing else, his research made out a strong case for developing better data on the employment of children, particularly in agriculture where migrant laborers and very young child workers escape the scrutiny of government surveys, with the result that thousands of child workers remain uncounted. Although the number of children traced to any one company was small, there are uncounted thousands of children working illegally because no one, the federal government included, has made an effort to count them all. The result is that there is a virtual absence of any comprehensive estimates about the extent of child labor in the United States.

Kruse relied largely on data compiled from thirty-three months of current population surveys detailing the weekly hours, occupations, and ages of workers. He found 148,000 youths in an average week working illegally and 290,000 youths working illegally at some point during 1996. He calculated the total annual hours worked illegally by minors under age 18 at 113 million and estimated that the illegal employment of young people saved employers $155 million. The cost savings were calculated in part by comparing the employment of minors to those between 18 and 24, without high school diplomas, working in the same hazardous occupations. Members of the latter group also earned an average of $1.38 more an hour. More than 60,000 of the minors were under age 14. Kruse's study was commissioned by the AP in conjunction with a five-part series on child labor and made out the case for more resources being devoted to enforcement of child labor laws.[40]

The study could not account for all children who work illegally because census-takers, like labor enforcement agents, have trouble locating the very children who are among the most easily exploited: children of migrant workers, illegal immigrants, and the very young. Other principal findings included the following:

- Children working illegally averaged $5 an hour.
- The number of children working illegally is close to 4 percent of the 4.1 million children aged 12 to 17 who work in America during any given week.

Some industries were harder to measure than others. Illegal home-based work, like sewing dresses outside the workplace, was not included in the illegal count since there was no accurate way to calculate how many children were involved.

The study did estimate 13,100 children worked illegally in garment industry sweatshops, defined as businesses with a pattern of violating wage, safety, and child-labor regulations.

Agriculture, which relies heavily in some areas of the country on migrant workers, is also hard to examine. To make an estimate, Kruse took the number of child-labor violations the Department of Labor actually found in agriculture, extrapolated a figure for the number of children working illegally, and came up with 4,900, including both crop and livestock work. To put that in context, he figured that 229,600 children, aged 14 to 17, for which data are most complete, were employed in the industry in 1996. This calculation assumes that the Labor Department polices agriculture as thoroughly as other areas of the economy. However, the AP has found that it does not, which makes Kruse's estimates conservative. In fact, AP reporters who visited farms saw scores of children under 14 at work.

To make his overall calculations, Kruse first examined employment data about 15-, 16-, and 17-year-olds in the Current Population Survey, compiled by the Bureau of Labor Statistics and the Census Bureau. He then compared responses with federal and state labor laws to identify violations. He combined thirty-three monthly surveys from January 1995 to September 1997 to obtain a large enough sample. Each survey covered approximately 60,000 households. To calculate how many younger children work illegally, Kruse used other data, including the National Longitudinal Survey of Youth and statistics on adolescent work-related injuries and deaths.

Examining data over time, he estimated that illegal child labor has decreased since the 1970s. However, in recent years, the decline has stopped. He found the number of 15- to 17-year-olds working in violation of federal law during an average school week has varied over the past twenty-six years:

- 156,000 in 1971–1975.
- 169,000 in 1976–1980.
- 100,000 in 1991–1994.

For the 1995–1997 period, the number increased to 114,000. However, the statistical limitations of the study made it difficult to know if the increase was real.

The reluctance of federal inspectors to perform their duties responsibly also created problems. A top Labor Department official stated that she met with resistance when she tried to get investigators into the fields to look for children. "Where would you rather be?" she asked a reporter. "In a nice air-conditioned office and interview some accountant and look at their records, or would you rather go out in a field at five in the morning to see who's working?"[41] She also had to contend with inspectors who simply took the word of farmers who claimed they did not employ children. Moreover, the director of governmental relations at the American Farm Bureau Federation claimed he had never seen anyone working on any farm anywhere under the age of 18.

Another area the study highlighted involved monetary penalties that are supposed to be assessed against employers who hire children illegally. When Congress raised the maximum penalty from $1,000 per violation to $10,000 in 1990, it directed the Department of Labor to use discretion in setting fines by considering the size of the business and the employer's familiarity with the law. The result was that the average fine increased from $212 in 1990 to $887 in 1996, nowhere near the maximum set by law. A "Child Labor Civil Money Penalty Report," which the department tried to withhold but which was obtained by the AP, may explain why. The secret report is used by compliance officers to set fines that are almost always discounted significantly from the recommended maximum set by Congress. Among the reduced fines: $275 for poor record keeping; $400 for a farmer who employs a 14- or 15-year-old during school hours; $500 for the same violation at other businesses.

Fines are reduced 30 percent for businesses with twenty or fewer employees. The maximum fine, $10,000, is imposed only when a child, working illegally, is seriously injured or killed. Other fines are far lower, despite directions from Congress to use the maximum penalty as a deterrent. The fine schedule was formulated by mid-level Labor Department administrators in secrecy, so much so that the Secretary of Labor, Alexis Herman, was unaware of its existence. In addition to civil fines, the law allows repeat offenders to child-labor laws to be charged with criminal misdemeanors, with penalties including up to six months' imprisonment for a second conviction. But no one had gone to jail during the seven years prior to the study, and, generally, incarceration occurred no more than once every decade.

The reason for this inexcusable laxity is that the Labor Department does not seem to know which law breakers are repeat offenders. Investigators are supposed to check department computer files to detect repeat offenders. However, many district offices do not have access to the computer files, and even if they did, the files often would not tell them much, since names of violators are often misspelled or entered in slightly different ways. For example, McDonald's shows up as McDonald's, McDonalds, Mc Donalds, MacDonald's, McDonald's Restaurant, and more. Consequently, a multiple violator can appear to be a string of single violators. In addition, when the AP searched the database using variations in spacing, punctuation, and spelling, it found 129 different recurring violators for 1996 alone, and not one was prosecuted as such.

To compound this outrageous situation, top labor and agriculture officials said they knew that inspectors traditionally resist enforcing child-labor laws and almost never seize interstate shipments of produce or goods tainted by child labor. Enforcement campaigns, moreover, are rare, with only one of limited scope since 1990. Such laxity invites casual evasion of child-labor laws.[42] The outcry against child labor rests on genuine concern about the vulnerability of children and the inhumaneness of much child labor. It too often sacrifices children's health and education, childhood, and personal ambitions. But apparently, public education about existing child labor, and public pressure on Congress and regulators to stop it, are needed to generate proper enforcement of child labor laws.

THE MODEL STATE CHILD LABOR LAW

The Child Labor Coalition, a group of thirty-five national organizations that advocates strengthening child labor laws and enforcement at the state, federal, and international level, recently issued a model state child labor law. Important provisions in the model law provide equal protection for migrant and seasonal farmworker children, as provided for minors employed in nonagricultural industries.

- The model law sets a minimum age of 14 for all employment (whether nonagricultural or agricultural employment);
- The model law sets the same maximum hours of work while school is in and out of session (for nonagricultural and agricultural employment):

When School is in Session:

14- and 15-year-olds—fifteen hours maximum

15- and 17-year-olds—twenty hours maximum

When School is Not in Session:

14- and 15-year-olds—thirty hours maximum

15- and 17-year-olds—forty hours maximum

The model law also would prohibit minors (under age 18) from dangerous agricultural occupations and substances and from operating hazardous tools and machinery, including poultry, fish and seafood processing, door-to-door sales, and pesticide handling. It would also require a certificate of employment for working minors, regardless of occupation. The involvement and information from their parents, educators, and employers would also be required. Other provisions the coalition strongly endorses would include required education for minors and their parents about workplace rights and stiff penalties for violators, including ineligibility for state grants and loans for specified periods and enhanced enforcement provisions such as publicizing names of violators in the media.[43]

FEDERAL LEGISLATIVE INITIATIVE

There also has been legislative action to fight child labor abuses at the federal level. In 1997 Rep. Tom Lantos (D-Calif.), sponsored H.R. 1870 that would, among other things, provide new protections for migrant and seasonal workers under age 14. Commenting on the lack of statistics on children working illegally in agriculture, Lantos suggested that there was no way of gauging whether a reported decline in agricultural child labor violations actually occurred "or whether you are dealing with a more sophisticated pattern of avoidance and escape which can theoretically show a 75 percent decline in child labor violations while in fact child labor violations might have increased."[44]

"It's obvious to me that our government spends tens of millions to produce reliable counts of pigs, chickens, cows, and migratory birds, but it's shocking that when it comes to counting children working illegally in the fields, our statistics are as appalling, unreliable or in fact nonexistent as they are," Lantos maintained.[45]

Lantos's bill is called the Young American Workers' Bill of Rights. It would better protect U.S. children in the workforce by establishing employment limits for all working minors while school is in session; requiring young workers to obtain certificates of employment, which would include approval by parents and schools in order to avoid interference with school requirements; and prohibit additional hazardous work for minors who are under the age of 18 years. Of great significance is the bill's provision to provide the same protections in the areas of minimum age of employment and hours of work for minors who work as migrant and seasonal agricultural workers as for children who work in other occupations. The legislation would also establish criminal sanctions for willful violations of child labor laws that result in the death of a child or serious bodily injury to a child. It would require the Department of Labor to compile and make available to school districts the names and addresses of child-labor-law violators (employers) and the exact nature of the violation.[46]

In late 1997, citing the release of the AP-Rutgers study, Sen. Tom Harkin (D-Iowa) promised to introduce legislation to strengthen penalties for violators of U.S. child-labor laws, double funding for enforcement of child labor provisions, and close loopholes in federal law which allow for the exploitation of children. Harkin's legislation would do the following:

- Increase minimum and maximum penalties for violations. Currently, fines are a maximum of $10,000. In practice, fines in agriculture for violations of wage and hour laws have been about $100 less per violation on average than for retail store violations. The Harkin proposal would assure that there is no differential by type of industry and would require increased penalties for repeat violations.
- Double, from $7.5 million to $15 million, the Department of Labor's budget to enforce federal child labor laws.
- Close the loopholes in federal law which allow employers to hire and exploit children, including prohibiting minors under the age of 15 from working, except for certain exceptions for family-run small businesses and farms. This exemption would permit minors 13 and 14 years of age to work up to two hours a day and no more than 10 hours a week.

Harkin has been a longtime advocate for the eradication of abusive child labor. He was instrumental in the passage of a historic provision in the Treasury-Postal Appropriations bill that authorizes the Customs Service to ban any goods made with indentured child labor from entering the United States. He also is the author of the Child Labor Deterrence Act, a Senate bill first introduced in 1992 to protect children by banning the importation of goods made through child labor. In April 1997 Harkin also reintroduced the Child Labor Free Consumer Information Act of 1997, which calls on manufacturers to voluntarily label their products with a "no child labor" guarantee to give consumers an educated choice when making purchases.[47]

Unfortunately, there has been no action on these bills by the Republican-controlled Congress, and prospects for further action appear dim at this time.

RECOMMENDATIONS

Labor Department sweeps have helped to focus national attention on how significant and widespread the illegal employment of children is today and the undetected nature of the problem. If the Labor Department, using just 500 investigators, could detect more than 16,000 child labor violations during a three-day sweep in March 1990, imagine how many violations could be revealed by a vigorous year-round enforcement program.

Another avenue to pursue would involve a policy of targeting previous federal child labor law violators for investigation, as an effective strategy to deter repeat violations. This would identify industries and businesses that are of special concern for minors who work. Such a policy also would be an efficient use of the limited number of investigators. Presently, the Labor Department has no policy requiring district and regional offices to target investigations to previous violators. The Department guidelines leave the decision about whether to conduct a follow-up investigation of previous violators to the individual investigator. In practice, unfortunately, most offices conduct few, or even no, such repeat investigations, although many officials agree that this would be an important enforcement tool if utilized. In fact, headquarters officials reported great success when they targeted prior violators during Operation Child Watch in 1990, with over 25 percent of the investigations yielding violations.[48] Further inadequacies in this area find the Labor Department lacking any firm policy to publicize the names of child labor law violators; likewise, regional offices have adopted inconsistent policies. At the same time, the Department of Labor's national investigation database has no individual data on repeat violators, penalty collections, or assessments.

Differences between state and federal law in child-labor hour and age limitations can be a problem when employers are unaware of or unable to decipher the dual requirements. Employers often express their concern over such duplication and question whether federal and state requirements can be consistent since the purpose for adopting the statutes was similar. While in some situations, state laws may have to be fashioned differently, most states could adopt requirements that are the same as federal provisions, thereby enhancing compliance and diminishing confusion. Since federal laws are intended as a minimum threshold for child labor regulation, states could eliminate most confusion by adopting at least that threshold standard and only deviating from it if they desire to establish a higher standard. Such a change would increase uniformity and minimize employer confusion.

What can be done to stem the new tide of child labor violations? The last thing most firms want is a new army of investigators harassing law-abiding employers. In any event, in an era of smaller government and limited budgets, such a policy is unlikely. A better alternative is smarter enforcement. Working with the states, Washington could, for instance, create task forces that concentrate on specific areas where abuses are known to be most egregious. One model might be New York state's garment industry task force, whose twenty-four investigators root out violators in New York City sweatshops. California is taking a cross-agency approach, using state tax filings and business licensing and registration records to pinpoint employers with a history of skirting the law. These companies, state officials have found, are the most likely child labor lawbreakers. In agriculture, the most basic change would be eliminating exemptions that allow children to work on farms at younger ages, in more hazardous jobs, and for longer hours than they can in restaurants, stores, and nearly every other business.

Stricter child-labor laws are not always better child-labor laws. If existing child-labor laws were properly enforced, there would be little need for more restriction. But with or without legislation, parents, teachers, and employers must help young people to understand that the key to a successful future is not a paycheck today but a diploma and a degree tomorrow.

Relaxation in the enforcement of federal regulations protecting child workers, along with a decrease in the number of inspectors, and consequently, a decrease in the number of inspections, has contributed to the resurgence of child labor abuses in the United States. Strong enforcement of existing laws and regulations is necessary to protect the health and safety of working children and to support legitimate employers whose businesses are financially endangered by those who hire children under illegal working conditions.

The system can be changed so that children are not put at risk. More education for parents and their working children about child-labor laws and the rights of minors in the workplace is needed in the schools. Loopholes and exemptions need to be closed, so that all employers, regardless of size or industry, are forced to offer the same protections to young workers. Finally, employers with minor workers must realize that they have a special responsibility to our most treasured resource, our youth.

NOTES

1. Michael Doyle, "Conference Focuses on Child Labor, Failure of Laws and Enforcement; Officials from the United States, Mexico and Canada Are Gathering to Swap Ideas," *Fresno Bee*, 24 February 1997, A1.

2. Peter J. McGovern, "Children's Rights and Child Labor: Advocacy on Behalf of the Child Worker," *South Dakota Law Review*, 78 (1983): 293, 297–298.

3. Martha Mendoza, "Untangling the Maze of Child Labor Laws," *Los Angeles Times*, 14 December 1997, A11.

4. Ibid.

5. McGovern, "Children's Rights and Child Labor."

6. "DOL Seeking to Revise Child Labor Regulations," *Daily Labor Report* (May 13, 1994): d2.

7. Farrell Kramer, "Laws Fail Child Farm Laborers, GAO Says," *The Record* (Bergen County, NJ), 22 March 1998, A24.

8. Associated Press, "Laws Short-Changing Kids Hurt in Illegal Work," 10 March 1998.

9. General Accounting Office, *Child Labor: Work Permit and Death and Injury Reporting Systems in Selected States* (Washington, DC: USGPO, March, 1992), 1.

10. Jeff Zimmer, "Survey: 947 Working N.C. Teens Injured on the Job. Work Permit Process Could Lower State's 5th Highest Ranking," *Herald Sun* (Durham, NC), 27 June 1996, C3.

11. "Legal Limits on Young Workers," *New York Times*, 21 January 1988, C6.

12. Skoler, Abbot, & Presser, "Fifteen-Year-Old Employee Gets Double Comp for Coffee Burns," *Massachusetts Employment Law Letter*, 4 (1 July 1993): 4.

13. "U.S. Crackdown Targets Job Hazards Facing Teens," *Commercial Appeal* (Memphis), 17 June 1994, 31A.

14. General Accounting Office, *Child Labor: Information on Federal Enforcement Efforts* (Washington, DC: USGPO, June, 1992), 15.

15. Farrell Kramer, "Labor–Child Farmworkers' Rights Less Protected, Report Says," *Commercial Appeal* (Memphis), 20 March 1998, B4.

16. General Accounting Office, *Child Labor: Increases in Detected Child Labor Violations Throughout the United States* (Washington, DC: USGPO, April 1990), 3, 4.

17. Beth Baker, "Kids At Work," *Common Cause Magazine*, July/August, 1990, 14.

18. Gopal Ratnam, "Child Labor Laws Are Often Violated," *Gannett News Service*, 20 December 1997.

19. *Child Labor Monitor*, Spring, 1998, 5.

20. Ibid.

21. Rae Eileen Glass, "Court Action Results in Texas Grower Agreeing to Check for Child Labor Compliance in Fields," *U.S. Newswire*, 5 May 1998.

22. Lynn Keillor, "Minor infractions: Ignorance of Child Labor Laws Can Land Businesses with Hefty Penalties," *Minneapolis-St. Paul City Business*, 5 July 1996, 15; Gary Kane, "Enforcement Lags on Child Labor Violations," *Palm Beach Post*, 7 February 1994, 1A; Katie Fairbank and Lisa Holewa, "Some States Do Little to Protect Children Who Enter the Workforce," *Las Vegas Review Journal*, 21 December 1997, 36A.

23. Nancy Stancill, "Kids on the Job; Fine Just $300 for Teen Death; States' Efforts to Protect Working Children Are Inadequate," *Houston Chronicle*, 4 January 1993, 1.

24. Fairbank and Holewa, "Some States Do Little."

25. Ibid.

26. Gary Kane, "Enforcement Lags."

27. Sam Howe Verhovek, "New Limits Set on Job Hours for Students," *New York Times*, 29 June 1991, 25; 28.

28. Testimony of Linda F. Golodner, President, National Consumers League, Co-Chair, Child Labor Coalition before the Subcommittee on Workforce Protections, Committee on Economic and Educational Opportunities, U.S. House of Representatives, 11 July 1995.

29. Joe Ward, "Child-labor Abuses Occur Here," *Louisville Courier Journal*, 22 January 1998, 1C.

30. Brian Dumaine, "Illegal Child Labor Comes Back," *Fortune*, 5 April 1993, 86.

31. Nancy Stancill, "Kids On The Job; A Knock So Sweet; Some Scrupulous, Some Break Rules in Door-to-Door Candy Sales Business," *Houston Chronicle*, 13 January 1993, 1.

32. "Employer Groups Say Certain Limits on Child-Labor Hour Statutes Should Be Eased," *Daily Labor Report* (20 October 1994): d10.

33. Ibid.

34. Ibid.

35. General Accounting Office, *Data on the Tax Compliance of Sweatshops* (Washington, DC: USGPO, 23 September 1994).

36. ———. *Garment Industry Efforts to Address the Prevalence and Conditions of Sweatshops* (Washington, DC: USGPO, 10 November 1994).

37. Bill Wallace, "Childhood Lost to Illegal Labor–State Crackdown Deters but Fails to Stop Abuses," *San Francisco Chronicle*, 20 October 1995, A1.

38. Don Lee, "Task Force In Tatters; State-Federal Tensions Hinder Garment Industry Crackdown," *Los Angeles Times*, 4 August 1996, D1.

39. "Honors for TIPP Program," *Cal-OSHA Reporter* (16 December 1996).

40. "Harkin Requests Senate Hearing on Child Labor Abuses in United States," *BNA Employment Policy & Law Daily*, (17 December 1997).

41. Martha Mendoza, "Toughest Laws on Child Labor Not Being Enforced, Fines, Prison, 'Hot Goods' Provision Unsuccessful," *Chicago Tribune*, 18 December 1997.

42. Farrell Kramer, "290,000 Kids Work Illegally, Rutgers Study of U.S. Finds," *Commercial Appeal* (Memphis), 18 December 1997, A13.

43. Nancy Stancill, "Kids On The Job; A Knock So Sweet; Some Scrupulous, Some Break Rules in Door-to-Door Candy Sales Business," *Houston Chronicle*, 13 January 1993, 1.

44. "Herman, Glickman Visit Florida For Talks with Growers, Farm Workers, and Advocates," *BNA Employment Policy & Law Daily*, (15 April 1998).

45. Ibid.

46. "State Action," *Child Labor Monitor*, July 1997, 2.

47. "Harkin to Introduce Domestic Child Labor Legislation," *U.S. Newswire*, 11 December 1997.

48. General Accounting Office, *Information on Federal Enforcement Efforts* (Washington, DC: USGPO, June 1992) 9.

4

Occupational Safety and Health in Nonfarm Employment

> First and foremost, child labor is a safety issue—working children continue to be seriously injured and killed on the job. The National Institute for Occupational Safety and Health (NIOSH). NIOSH, for example, estimates that over 210,000 teens are injured on the job each year in this country, with over 70,000 suffering injuries serious enough to warrant a trip to the emergency room. About seventy teens die each year. This is wholly unacceptable.[1]

RISK FACTORS IN YOUTH EMPLOYMENT

These comments by a high-ranking federal government official highlight an important problem in the United States. Furthermore, many of these occurrences happen where the young worker is employed in full compliance with the law. Work is a common feature in the lives of children and adolescents in this country. Despite its many economic and educational benefits, it also has negative consequences for far too many youth. Occupational injuries to young people happen too often and can have devastating and permanent effects. Over the past decade, deaths and injuries to minors have been recognized as a significant public health problem that deserves attention.

Adolescents typically work at a series of part-time, temporary, low-paying jobs, often going to their jobs after putting in a day of work at school. Many of the industries that employ large numbers of teens, such as grocery and department stores, hospitals and nursing facilities, and recreational services have higher than average injury rates for workers of all ages.[2]

In addition to injuries, hazardous materials and working conditions are also a concern for adolescent workers. Less is known about them than the effects of injuries that have an immediate impact and can be counted and classified as to cause. Exposures of adolescent workers to hazardous materials and working conditions may result in an immediate illness; however, illness might not be detected for months or years after exposure. These workers may be exposed to pesticides in lawn care, benzene at gasoline stations, lead in auto-body repair, asbestos and silica in construction and maintenance work, and high levels of noise in manufacturing, construction, and agriculture. Concerns have also been raised that fatigue from balancing work and school may contribute to injuries among young workers. Moreover, small physical size and inexperience may superimpose additional employment risks for youth.[3]

The National Consumer League says parents should not allow their children to work in what it claims are the five worst teen jobs: delivery and other driving jobs, including operating or riding on forklifts and other motorized equipment; working alone in cash-based businesses; traveling youth crews that sell such things as candy, magazine subscriptions, and consumer items; jobs where employers pay under-the-table wages; and construction.[4]

Understanding the total human and economic impact of occupational injuries and illnesses is crucial to setting priorities and shaping other components of the occupational safety and health agenda. Because the nation lacks a unified and comprehensive system for surveillance of work-related death, disease, and disability, it has been and continues to be difficult to quantify the problem and to measure progress toward the attainment of specific objectives. Nonetheless, we shall attempt to estimate the present status, using available data. Since it is possible in many cases to link occupational deaths, injuries, and illnesses in children and adolescents to human economic activity, they ought, in theory, to be preventable.

PHYSICAL AND PSYCHOLOGICAL LIMITATIONS

Workers of all ages face hazards on the job. However, a number of factors raise special concerns about working youth. Young people entering the labor market may be at greater risk than adults because they lack awareness of risks, the confidence to refuse risky work, and knowledge, training, and experience on how to identify hazards and assess associated risks. They are often greater risk takers, which may result in their ignoring safety instructions and exposing themselves, and possibly others, to a greater risk of injury. The consequences of exposure may be overlooked or not realized due to their lack of experience and knowledge of these outcomes, making them more vulnerable in the workplace. Many of the teens' positive traits—energy, enthusiasm, a need for increased challenge and responsibility, combined with a reluctance to ask questions or make demands on their employers—can result in their taking on tasks for which they are neither prepared nor capable of doing safely.[5]

The physical characteristics of young workers are also important to consider. Teens between ages 14 and 17, especially boys, experience their growth spurts at very different rates. Small teens may not be able to reach parts of machines and may lack the strength required for certain tasks. Job-related back injuries have been shown to be a problem among adolescents, especially among smaller individuals. Large boys may be given adult tasks simply because of their size without regard for their lack of experience and maturity.

Children's physiological and psychological characteristics differ biologically from those of adults, and these differences make them more susceptible to workplace hazards. They are likely to work in excessively hot, damp, dusty, or unsanitary conditions, which favor the transmission of communicable diseases. They may be exposed to toxic chemicals and other hazardous agents, increasing the risk of chemical poisoning and neurological or respiratory disorders. Youths are also exposed to work overload, fatigue, stress, and economic strain, and these in turn can cause injuries, impairing growth and development, plus disability and other adverse health effects. These limitations have contributed to a rash of injuries and illnesses in recent years.

INJURIES AND FATALITIES DURING ILLEGAL EMPLOYMENT

Although work can encourage the development of discipline, teach a child the meaning of money, and provide valuable role models, employment risks are magnified greatly when employment is illegal or exploitative. A recent study revealed that 41 percent of occupational injury deaths of youths investigated by the Occupational Safety and Health Administration (OSHA) occurred while the child was engaged in work prohibited by federal child labor laws. Although it was not possible to determine how many of the deaths resulted from prohibited activities, it is clear than many resulted from violations of laws intended to protect young workers, such as the federal Fair Labor Standards Act (FLSA) of 1938 and state child labor laws.[6] Illegal employment of minors has implications for occupational injuries and illness, because wage and hour violations frequently are accompanied by health and safety infractions.

News reports read like a Dickens' tale. In Millstadt, Illinois, two 13-year-old boys were injured when the blade of a forklift fell off and hit them. Their employment was illegal for several reasons: They were under 14 years of age; employed in manufacturing; and tending a hoisting apparatus or power-driven machinery. The same employer was also cited because a 16-year-old was operating a forklift, another violation of child labor regulations. In another case, a forklift driven by a 14-year-old Florida boy flipped and crushed his right arm and leg, resulting in a two-week hospital stay and several months of physical therapy. In Wisconsin, a 17-year-old was severely injured while using a power-driven circular saw at a construction site. In Snohomish, Washington, a minor was injured operating power-driven equipment at an electrical supply company. The truth is, workers under the age of 18 are being killed and injured at rates much higher than the national averages for adult workers.[7] A study of North Carolina occupational fatalities found that 90 percent were male, and the youngest victim was 11 years old. Homicide was the leading occupational killer of adolescent females, as it is for adult women, mainly occurring in the course of robberies during late night closings at retail firms. More than 50 percent of fatalities involved a motor vehicle. Illegal employment characterized 86 percent of fatalities in workers under age 18.[8]

STORIES FROM INJURED TEENS

17-year old restaurant worker

I'm 5′2.″ The pans I needed to cover the dough were stacked to the ceiling so I stood on a large dough mixer in order to reach them. As I was getting down, I twisted my leg, fell, and fractured my right leg and my knee cap. I had asked for a step stool a number of times.

16-year-old nursing home nurse's aide

A co-worker and I were transferring a patient from the commode to a wheelchair. I thought the patient was going to fall so I turned to get more leverage. I felt a sharp pain in my back. I continued to work 5 more hours to finish my shift. I went to the hospital the next day because my back hurt and I had lost feeling in my left leg.

15-year-old gas station attendant

I was pumping gas the 3–10 shift. It was about zero degrees, and the wind was blowing. Around 5:00, I began to feel some numbness in my fingers and toes. I told my boss about it twice. I worked the rest of the shift and then went home. I woke up in the middle of the night and couldn't feel my fingers or toes. I went to the emergency room the next morning. I had second and third degree frostbite on all my fingers and three of my toes.

16-year-old supermarket clerk

I was in the back room storage area using the safety razor to clean off stickers from the pricing gun. I looked for a second, the razor slipped and I cut my knuckles. I went to the hospital and had to get stitches.[9]

HAZARDOUS OCCUPATIONS ORDERS

The FLSA stipulates that for youth under the age of 18, the Secretary of Labor shall declare certain occupations hazardous or detrimental to their health and well-being. This minimum age applies even when the minor is employed by a parent or person taking the place of a parent. The eighteen hazardous occupations orders now in effect are as follows:

1. Manufacturing and storing explosives.
2. Motor vehicle driving and outside helper.
3. Coal mining.
4. Logging and sawmilling.
5. Power-driven woodworking machines.
6. Exposure to radioactive substances.
7. Power-driven hoisting apparatus.
8. Power-driven metal-forming, punching, and shearing machines.
9. Mining, other coal mining.

10. Slaughtering or meatpacking, processing, or rendering.
11. Power-driven bakery machines.
12. Power-driven paper-products machines.
13. Manufacturing brick, tile, and kindred products.
14. Power-driven circular saws, bandsaws, and guillotine shears.
15. Wrecking, demolition, and shipbreaking operations.
16. Roofing operations.
17. Excavation operations.
18. Messenger service between the hours of 10:00 P.M. and 5:00 A.M.

These hazardous occupations orders also include prohibitions for minors under age 18 against operating certain other machines that may not be readily apparent from a quick reading of this list.[10]

An injury or illness that occurs or surfaces on the employer's premises is presumed to be work-related. In general, all that is needed for an injury or illness to be occupational is for the work environment to contribute, in however minor a manner. The injury or illness is considered to be work-related unless it is known to be caused 100 percent by nonoccupational factors.[11] However, other particularly hazardous work that is not typically prohibited by federal child labor laws includes work in petroleum and gas extraction, commercial fishing, many jobs that require use of respirators, work in sewage-treatment plants or sewers, work on industrial conveyors, many uses of compressed air or pneumatic tools such as nail guns, farm work using all-terrain vehicles, and work around many types of machines with power take-offs or similarly rotating drivelines.[12]

The fact of the matter is that child labor laws, intended to provide extra safeguards for working youth, provide limited protection. The federal child labor laws have not been substantially modified since the 1960s and the Department of Labor is considering new regulations to reflect new knowledge about health and safety risks and changes in youth employment patterns. Many state laws and regulations may likewise need updating. Unfortunately, the agencies responsible for enforcing the child labor laws may lack resources for adequate enforcement.

OCCUPATIONAL DISEASE

Occupational disease encompasses the illnesses and chronic injuries that result from exposure to harmful substances or conditions in the workplace and is not a new phenomenon. The link between certain diseases and substances prevalent in the workplace environment was made more than two centuries ago with the discovery that exposure to creosote, a combustion byproduct that collects on the inside of chimney walls, could cause cancer of the scrotum in chimney sweeps. Other workplace disease relationships, such as coal mining and black lung disease have been established since that time. Occupational disease differs from traumatic injuries in that it takes a long time for the harm caused by exposure to potentially dangerous substances to become apparent. Fractures, sprains, and other similar traumatic injuries are usually caused by a sudden, single, identifiable incident. But in the case of workers who contract debilitating diseases as a result of exposure to hazardous substances, there often is a time lag, known as the latency period, between the first exposure to a substance or activity and the point at which a person becomes ill or disabled. The latency period for illness due to cancer-causing substance exposure can be a decade or more.

Little information is available on the incidence or severity of illness caused in children by toxic occupational exposures. However, we do know that children are particularly sensitive to toxic substances and that they experience a variety of exposures at work, including noise exposure, which may begin the sequence of destructive events in the auditory system that lead to noise-induced hearing loss in adult life.[13]

Numerous factors make difficult the detection and reporting on occupational disease. In addition to the latency period, which may run as long as twenty years, employees may have switched jobs several times or retired during this time, making it difficult to understand the occupational nature of the disease. Sometimes, employees can be exposed to more than one substance. Moreover, different employees may have varying susceptibility to hazardous substances. Finally, employee, employer, and physician unawareness limit the ability to detect full occupational disease. In particular, physicians' training and ability to diagnose occupational disease are notably weak.

Widespread Lack of Awareness

Lack of awareness among health practitioners about the hazards found at work is another cause of underestimation of occupational disease. This lack of information reflects the fact that most physicians are not adequately trained to suspect work as a cause of disease. Very little time is devoted in most American medical schools to teaching physicians to take a proper occupational history, to recognize the symptoms of common industrial poisons, or to recall the known associations between occupational exposures and disease. The average medical student receives only six hours of training in occupational medicine during the four years of medical school. Consequently, most physicians do not routinely obtain histories of occupational exposure from their patients.[14]

Compounding this lack of medical awareness is the limited ability of many workers to provide an accurate report of their toxic exposures. Until recently, they have not been informed of the nature of the hazards of the materials with which they have worked. Employers' reporting requirements are limited under Occupational Health and Safety Administration (OSHA) and state and local right-to-know laws. In many cases, an ill patient will simply not know about his or her past occupational exposure.

Occupational exposures to carcinogens are widespread. NIOSH calculates that over 7 million American workers, including children and adolescents, have the potential for regular occupational exposure to proven human carcinogens. However, the full extent of occupational exposure to carcinogens cannot be known presently, because only about 30 percent of the 70,000 chemical compounds registered with the Environmental Protection Agency (EPA) have ever been tested for potential cancerous ingredients. Consequently, it is entirely likely that millions of American workers are regularly exposed to chemical compounds whose malignant potential has not been defined.[15]

WORK-RELATED INJURIES AND ILLNESSES ASSOCIATED WITH CHILD LABOR

Unfortunately, the most recent data available are from 1993, when an estimated 2.1 million persons aged 16–17 years were employed in the United States. Although many children younger than 16 work, employment data are neither routinely collected nor reported for this age group, and there are no reliable estimates of the number of children in this age group who work. During summer months, when most children are not in school, employment and hours worked by children younger than 18 increases substantially. To characterize workplace-related health and safety hazards for children, NIOSH analyzed 1993 data for workers under 18 from the Survey of Occupational Injuries and Illnesses (SOII), a survey administered by the Bureau of Labor Statistics (BLS) of the Department of Labor, which indicates that substantial numbers of persons younger than 18 sustain work-related injuries and illnesses annually.

The SOII is a collaborative federal/state program administered by BLS and is based on employer reports from approximately 250,000 private industries in the United States. Based on these data, BLS estimates the national incidence of work-related injuries and illnesses. For those injuries and illnesses resulting in lost work days, employers provide demographic information and data about the nature and circumstances of injuries and illnesses. Because employer-provided employment data are not stratified by age, injury and illness rates cannot be calculated for specific age groups.[16]

National Estimates

In 1993, persons aged less than 18 incurred an estimated 21,620 injuries and illnesses involving lost work days (see Table 4.1).

Of these, 24 percent involved lost work days; 43 percent, 2–5 days; 13 percent, 6–10 days; 13 percent, 11–30 days; and 8 percent, 231 days. Most (95 percent) injuries and illnesses (see Table 4.2) occurred among persons aged 16–17 years, and males accounted for 59 percent of the cases.

Table 4.1
Estimated Number of Injuries and Illnesses, and Median Number of Lost Work Days among Persons Aged <18 Years, by State, 1993*

State	No. of injuries & illnesses	Median no. of lost work days
Alabama	330	6
Alaska	86	3
Arizona	592	2
Arkansas	238	6
California	1,418	2
Connecticut	220	4
Delaware	39	5
Florida	1,527	3
Georgia	499	3
Hawaii	141	4
Indiana	706	3
Iowa	340	3
Kansas	225	3
Kentucky	490	3
Louisiana	175	4
Maine	93	4
Maryland	425	2
Massachusetts	519	4
Michigan	544	4
Minnesota	336	4
Mississippi	227	3
Missouri	615	5
Montana	84	4
Nebraska	440	1
Nevada	159	5
New Jersey	248	3
New Mexico	231	2
New York	1,060	6
North Carolina	947	3
Oklahoma	383	4
Oregon	410	2
Pennsylvania	719	3
Rhode Island	158	2
South Carolina	234	2
Tennessee	859	4
Texas	992	3

(continued)

Table 4.1
(Continued)

Utah	303	3
Vermont	24	1
Virginia	686	3
Washington	361	2
Wisconsin	435	4
Wyoming	43	6

* Data not available from Colorado, District of Columbia, Idaho, Illinois, New Hampshire, North Dakota, Ohio, South Dakota, and West Virginia because samples in these states were not designed to generate state-specific estimates.

Source: Survey of Occupational Injuries and Illnesses, Bureau of Labor Statistics, U.S. Department of Labor.

Sprains/strains were the most commonly reported problem (31 percent), followed by cuts/lacerations (17 percent), contusions/abrasions (13 percent), heat burns (8 percent), and fractures/dislocations (5 percent) (see Table 4.2).

Injured and ill persons were employed most frequently by eating and drinking establishments (39 percent), followed by grocery stores (14 percent), nursing and personal care facilities (6 percent), and department stores (5 percent). The most common occupations were food preparation and service workers such as waiters and waitresses, cooks, and food counter and kitchen workers (37 percent), followed by cashier (10 percent), stock handler or bagger (9 percent), health or nursing aide (7 percent), and janitor and cleaner (5 percent).

Common events resulting in injury included falls on the same level (falls to floors and falls onto or against objects, etc.) (21 percent), overexertion (from lifting, pulling, pushing, turning, wielding, holding, carrying, or throwing objects) (17 percent), striking against objects (bumping into, stepping on, kicking, and being pushed or thrown into or against objects) (10 percent), contact with hot objects or substances (9 percent), being struck by falling objects (7 percent), and being struck by a slipping hand-held object (e.g., knife, razor, or tool) (6 percent).

The approximately 22,000 injuries and illnesses involving lost workdays among children less than 18 years of age is probably an underestimate because SOII excludes some categories (e.g., self-employed workers, farms with fewer than eleven employees, private households, and government employees). Employment data suggest that at least 11 percent of working children under 18 are not represented by the SOII. These estimates exclude injuries and illnesses that did not result in lost workdays or in death.[17]

Few studies have been conducted that calculate injury rates across specific age groups. Those that have report that 16- to 17-year-olds have among the highest rates of work injuries treated in emergency departments. In 1996, the rates for male and female adolescents were 6.0 and 3.9 injuries per 100 full-

Table 4.2

Work Injuries and Illnesses Involving Time away from Work among Children <18 Years, by State, 1993[1]

State[2]	Est. no. of incidents	Median days away from work	Most frequent industries (% of total)[3]	Most frequent events & exposures (% of total)[4]
Alabama	330	6	Eating & drinking places (32%) Grocery stores (16%)	Fall on same level (23%) Overexertion in lifting (18%) Struck by object n.e.c. (12%)
Alaska	86	3	Laundry, cleaning & garment services (17%) Grocery stores (16%) Misc. food preparation & kindred products (16%)	Inhalation of caustic, noxious or allergenic substance (17%) Struck against stationary object (16%) Fall on same level (14%)
Arizona	592	2	Eating & drinking places (71%)	Struck by object (37%) Fall on same level (19%)
Arkansas	238	6	Eating & drinking places (40%) Grocery stores (13%)	Fall on same level (26%) Overexertion in lifting (16%) Contact with hot object or substance (11%)
California	1,418	2	Eating & drinking places (30%) Social services (24%)	Contact with hot object or substance (21%) Bodily reaction and exertion, unspecified (13%) Bodily reaction (12%)
Connecticut	220	4	Grocery stores (33%) Eating & drinking places (28%)	Fall on same level (24%) Overexertion in lifting (11%)
Delaware	39	5	Eating & drinking places (46%)	Fall on same level (20%) Overexertion in lifting (14%)
Florida	1,527	3	Eating & drinking places (34%) Grocery stores (23%) Misc. amusement & recreation services (13%)	Fall on same level (27%) Overexertion (18%) Struck against object (12%)

State[2]	Est. no. of incidents	Median days away from work	Most frequent industries (% of total)[3]	Most frequent events & exposures (% of total)[4]
Georgia	499	3	Eating & drinking places (42%) Grocery stores (16%)	Fall on same level (30%) Contact with hot object or substance (16%)
Hawaii	141	4	Construction–special trade contractors (22%)	Contact with hot object or substance (33%) Overexertion (21%) Slip, trip, loss of balance–without fall (10%)
Indiana	706	3	Eating & drinking places (45%) Food stores (15%) Health services (14%)	Fall on same level (25%) Overexertion (18%) Contact with hot object (16%)
Iowa	340	3	Eating & drinking places (47%) Grocery stores (13%) Nursing & personal care facilities (10%)	Struck by falling object (23%) Slip, trip, loss of balance–without fall (13%)
Kansas	225	3	Eating & drinking places (53%)	Overexertion (19%) Struck against stationary object (11%) Fall on same level (10%)
Kentucky	490	3	Eating & drinking places (54%)	Fall on same level (25%) Contact with hot object or substance (15%) Overexertion (10%)
Louisiana	175	4	Grocery stores (37%)	Fall on same level (23%) Overexertion in lifting (23%) Struck by falling object (16%)
Maine	93	4	Grocery stores (37%)	Overexertion in lifting (30%) Struck against stationary object (16%) Caught in running equipment (12%)
Maryland	425	2	Eating & drinking places (50%)	Struck against object (24%) Struck by falling object (20%) Fall on same level (17%)

(continued)

Table 4.2
(Continued)

State[2]	Est. no. of incidents	Median days away from work	Most frequent industries (% of total)[3]	Most frequent events & exposures (% of total)[4]
Massachusetts	519	4	Eating & drinking places (32%) Grocery stores (22%) Department stores (10%)	Overexertion in lifting (20%) Struck by slipping handheld object (10%)
Michigan	544	4	Department stores (14%) Grocery stores (10%)	Struck against stationary object (25%) Overexertion (13%) Fall on same level (11%)
Minnesota	336	4	Grocery stores (19%) Nursing & personal care facilities (11%)	Fall on same level (11%)
Mississippi	227	3	Eating & drinking places (43%) Grocery stores (16%)	Contact with hot object or substance (18%) Fall on same level (15%) Struck by slipping handheld object (14%)
Missouri	615	5	Eating & drinking places (53% Grocery stores (12%)	Fall on same level (21%) Struck against stationary object (17%) Slip, trip, loss of balance–without fall (11%)
Montana	84	4	General merchandise stores (12%)	Skin contact with caustic, noxious, or allergenic substance (22%0 Slip, trip, or loss of balance–without fall (13%) Overexertion in pulling/pushing object (12%)
Nebraska	440	1	Wholesale groceries & related products (10%)	Struck by falling object (65%) Exposure to caustic, noxious, or allergenic substance (11%)
Nevada	159	5	Eating & drinking places (27%) Hotels & motels (31%) Misc. amusement & recreation services (12%)	Inhalation of caustic, noxious, or allergenic substance (23%) Fall on same level (19%) Slip, trip, or loss of balance–without fall (12%)

State[2]	Est. no. of incidents	Median days away from work	Most frequent industries (% of total)[3]	Most frequent events & exposures (% of total)[4]
New Jersey	248	3	Grocery stores (27%)	Fall on same level (28%) Overexertion in lifting (16%) Caught in running equipment (13%)
New Mexico	231	2	Eating & drinking places (58%) Grocery stores (18%)	Skin contact with caustic, noxious, or allergenic substance (20%) Overexertion n.e.c. (18%) Fall on same level (14%)
New York	1,060	6	Eating & drinking places (34%) Grocery stores (32%) Hospitals (10%)	Caught in or compressed by equipment (15%) Contact with hot object or substance (13%) Fall on same level (13%)
North Carolina	947	3	Eating & drinking places (51%) Grocery stores (11%)	Fall on same level (29%) Struck against stationary object (13%) Overexertion in lifting (10%)
Oklahoma	383	4	Eating & drinking places (60%) Grocery stores (13%)	Fall on same level (22%) Contact with hot object or substance (20%) Overexertion in lifting (14%)
Oregon	410	2	Eating & drinking places (57%)	Struck by slipping handheld object (30%) Struck against object (19%) Slip, trip, loss of balance–without fall (10%)
Pennsylvania	719	3	Eating & drinking places (27%) Grocery stores (16%)	Fall on same level (25%) Overexertion in lifting (13%) Struck by slipping handheld object (10%)
Rhode Island	158	2	Eating & drinking places (53%)	Fall on same level (31%) Contact with hot object or substance (24%) Struck by swinging or slipping object (16%)

(continued)

Table 4.2
(Continued)

State[2]	Est. no. of incidents	Median days away from work	Most frequent industries (% of total)[3]	Most frequent events & exposures (% of total)[4]
South Carolina	234	2	Grocery stores (29%) Misc. amusement & recreational services (15%)	Fall on same level (21%) Overexertion in lifting (11%) Struck by swinging or slipping object (10%)
Tennessee	859	4	Eating & drinking places (62%)	Fall on same level (23%) Overexertion (21%) Struck by slipping handheld object (11%)
Texas	992	3	Eating & drinking places (46%) Grocery stores (19%)	Fall on same level (21%) Overexertion (21%) Struck by slipping handheld object (11%)
Utah	303	3	Grocery stores (14%) Hotels & motels (11%)	Fall on same level (29%) Struck against stationary object (12%) Contact with hot object or substance (11%)
Vermont	24	1	Hotels & motels (27%)	Fall on same level (27%) Exposure to sun (22%) Struck by slipping handheld object (21%)
Virginia	686	3	Eating & drinking places (39%)	Overexertion (28%) Struck by falling object (14%) Fall on same level (11%)
Washington	361	2	Eating & drinking places (62%) Grocery stores (17%)	Struck against object (27%) Fall on same level (21%) Overexertion in lifting (17%)
Wisconsin	435	4	Eating & drinking places (37%)	Fall on same level (18%) Overexertion in lifting (14%) Contact with hot object or substance (13%)

State[2]	Est. no. of incidents	Median days away from work	Most frequent industries (% of total)[3]	Most frequent events & exposures (% of total)[4]
Wyoming	43	6	General merchandise stores (17%)	Fall through roof surface (28%) Contact with hot object or substance (14%) Skin contact with caustic, noxious, or allergenic substance (14%)

[1] Data are from the Survey of Occupational Injuries and Illnesses, Bureau of Labor Statistics, U.S. Department of Labor.

[2] Data are not available from Colorado, District of Columbia, Idaho, Illinois, New Hampshire, North Dakota, Ohio, South Dakota, and West Virginia because samples in these states were not designed to generate state-specific estimates.

[3] Classified according to Office of Management and Budget, *Standard Industrial Classification Manual 1987* (Washington, D.C., GPO, 1987). This is a hierarchical coding structure; both specific and collapsed codes are presented in the table, depending on the available data for each state. Top three industries represent 10 percent each of cases reported.

[4] Classified according to Bureau of Labor Statistics, *Occupational Injury and Illness Classification Structures, 1992: Code Descriptions* (Washington, D.C.: U.S. Department of Labor, 1992). This is a hierarchical coding structure; both specific and collapsed codes are presented in the table, depending on the available data for each state.

time workers, respectively—nearly double the rates for employees of all ages. As far as fatalities, data from emergency departments tend to underestimate fatal injuries because many victims of traumatic injury die before ever reaching an emergency room.[18]

Examples of Fatalities and Injuries Involving Motor Vehicles

During a recent congressional hearing, the following revelations of work-related deaths and injuries of young people involving motor vehicle-related incidents were inserted in the record:

> A retail clerk who was just one month past her sixteenth birthday was employed in a gift shop located in a Marriott Hotel in Evansville, Indiana. On 20 July 1996, a customer gave the clerk a hundred dollar bill. The hotel could not make change, so the clerk left the hotel to travel by car to a nearby shopping center to change the bill. Her car skidded on a rain-slicked curve and collided with a pick-up truck. She died at the scene of massive injuries. In the police report, the officer stated that the accident would likely not have happened to a more experienced driver.
>
> A 17-year-old was employed in the service department of a Toyota automobile dealership in Birmingham, Alabama. On 29 December 1995, the youth was sent to the bank in the service manager's car to make a deposit of checks. Upon his return to the vehicle, a robber jumped into [the] vehicle and shot the youth in the leg, seriously injuring him. He was out of work for six days recovering from the wound.
>
> On 29 May 1992, a 17-year-old truck driver participating in a training program was killed when he tried to pass two cars stopped for a funeral procession. He ran head-on into the approaching vehicles.
>
> In September 1994, a 16-year-old male injured his brain and back when he lost control of the pick-up truck he was driving while delivering parts for his employer.
>
> A 17-year-old pizza [delivery] driver was killed on 3 June 1989, when the vehicle he was driving skidded off the road and hit a tree.
>
> On 20 July 1990, a 16-year-old was injured while driving a pick-up to deliver parts in Denver, Colorado. During a rainstorm the driver lost control of his vehicle and was struck by a semitractor trailer. He was treated for injuries to his arms and legs.
>
> On 13 November 1985, a 17-year-old female clerk for an auto parts store was making a delivery of parts when a truck coming the other way turned in front of her. She struck the truck, suffering head injuries, whiplash, a sore back, and cuts to her knees.
>
> A 17-year-old, driving for a furniture store in Waterford, Michigan, fell asleep at the wheel on 20 July 1990. The van he was driving flipped over while he was making deliveries to customers. He was thrown from the vehicle and suffered a fractured spine.
>
> A 17-year-old was picking up a part for Lincoln Auto in the Denver area, and was driving on an interstate when an accident occurred on 23 August 1990. He swerved to avoid a stopped vehicle, ricocheted off another vehicle, and struck a semi-trailer. He struck the windshield and suffered injuries to the head, neck, forearm, and knee.[19]

As Table 4.3 indicates, motor-vehicle-related incidents are the number one killer of young workers, although the data do not tell us how many of these are drivers as opposed to passengers. This is the reason motor vehicle operation is classified as a hazardous occupation for youth under 18 years of age. Nevertheless, legislation has been proposed that would weaken this hazardous order.

Ironically, the advocates of relaxing restrictions on teen driving at work cite higher fatality rates among 18- and 19-year-old workers, perhaps overlooking the point that the restriction on driving at work by 16- and 17-year-olds contributes to the lower fatality rate among youth in the latter age groups. Any legislation in this area must ensure appropriate safeguards to avoid a preventable increase in teen deaths and injuries due to increased occupational driving.[20]

Industry and Types of Teen Work-Related Injuries

The next two tables show how and where teens are injured at work Nearly 75 percent of young people who work do so in the retail and service sectors, so it should not be surprising that most injuries to young workers occur in these sectors. At restaurants, employees burn themselves on hot surfaces. In retail, they hurt themselves lifting heavy boxes or they slip and fall.

The fast-food industry is among the fastest growing and largest sectors employing youth in the United States today. Lacerations and burns are common hazards in fast-food establishments. The delivery of pizzas and other hot food items has proven to be extremely hazardous to working children. The short time span during which pizzas are to be delivered has been shown to encourage reckless driving by young, often inexperienced, motor-vehicle operators. For that matter, commercial driving is illegal under the age of 18. Also, there is some evidence that armed robberies and other violent crimes are being targeted at fast-food restaurants, discount stores, and other places at times when these

Table 4.3
How Teens Are Killed at Work

Number of 16- and 17-year-olds killed by occupational injury in the United States, 1980–1989 (by type)	
Motor vehicle related	24.2%
Machine related	16.9%
Electrocution	11.9%
Homicide	9.6%
Falls	5.7%
Struck by falling object	4.6%
All others	27.2%

Source: D. N. Castillo et al, "Occupational Injury Deaths of 16- and 17-year-olds in the United States," *American Journal of Public Health* 84, no. 4 (1994): 646–649.

Table 4.4
Where Teens Are Injured at Work

Adolescents (14–17 years old) treated in emergency rooms	
Retail	54.0%
Service	20.0%
Agriculture	7.0%
Manufacturing	4.0%
Other	15.0%

Source: D. N. Castillo et al, "Occupational Injury Deaths of 16- and 17-year-olds in the United States," *American Journal of Public Health* 84, no. 4 (1994): 646–649.

Table 4.5
How Teens Are Injured at Work

Estimated no. of adolescent (14–17 years old) occupational injuries in the United States, July-December 1992	
Lacerations	34.5%
Contusion or abrasion	18.2%
Sprain or strain	16.2%
Burn	12.4%
Fracture or dislocation	4.2%
All others	14.6%

Source: D. N. Castillo et al, "Occupational Injury Deaths of 16- and 17-year-olds in the United States," *American Journal of Public Health* 84, no. 4 (1994): 646–649.

stores are primarily staffed by adolescents. These employers are eager to hire teenagers because they are primarily interested in an assured supply of low-wage, unskilled labor, and they prefer to employ individuals or groups who are passive and are unlikely, for example, to unionize in the face of unstable employment. Most adults shun these secondary jobs, characterized by irregular shifts, evening and weekend hours, minimal fringe benefits, and few opportunities to advance into managerial positions. These types of employment opportunities, on the one hand, often fit the needs of teenagers seeking after-school and weekend work. Because the great majority of teens are seeking immediate spending money rather than long-term career objectives, the paucity of advancement makes little difference to them.

"Sacrificing America's Youth," a controversial report from the Chicago-based National Safe Workplace Institute, mentioned that of the estimated 71,600 job-related injuries to minors in 1990, a majority (20,064), occurred in restaurants. Most of the restaurant-related injuries reportedly could have been prevented by the use of protective gloves, slip-resistant shoes, and other simple safety precautions. Some of its harshest criticism is reserved for the fast-food industry:

> The fast food industry typically will hire youngsters off the street and place them in jobs with substantial risk of burns, lacerations, slips and falls. Indeed, many fast food managers know virtually nothing about child labor or injury reporting requirements . . . The hazards in the fast food sector are startling, and the lack of training outrageous.[21]

A more recent report (1999) revealed that teenagers are almost two times more likely to be injured while working in an eating and drinking establishment than in all other industries combined. More than 108,000 work-related injuries among those aged 14 to 17 between July 1992 and June 1994 were analyzed. Fast-food restaurants accounted for 63 percent of the adolescent injuries occurring in eating and drinking establishments, and 26 percent of the total number of occupational injuries to teens. One-fourth of the workforce in eating and drinking firms is aged 16 to 19, according to the Bureau of Labor Statistics. The report also indicated that men were more likely to be injured while cooking than women were. Sixty-five percent of all injuries to males occurred in the kitchen, compared to 52 percent in women. This does not imply that men are clumsy cooks. Rather, previous studies indicated that more men are given cooking and grilling jobs, while more women are put at the counter, dealing with customers.[22]

Occupational Burns among Adolescent Workers

Work-related burns are a leading cause of occupational injury in the United States. A substantial proportion of these burns occurs among restaurant workers, often affecting adolescents. An estimated 400,000 commercial eating and drinking establishments employ approximately 6 million workers. In restaurants, thermal burns accounted for 12 percent of work-related injuries in 1991. The most frequent source of burn injury was hot grease, followed by hot grills and other cooking equipment. Two cases are illustrative: In February 1991, the Minnesota Department of Health (MDH) was notified of a work-related burn sustained by a 17-year-old waitress in a delicatessen, who had slipped on a wet floor. As she fell, she stepped into a bucket of hot grease that had been placed on the floor while the grease in a deep fryer was being replaced. She was hospitalized for three days and required surgery for split-thickness skin grafting. She suffered permanent scarring of her burned ankle. In another case, the MDH was notified of a burn sustained by a 16-year-old crew cook in a fast-food restaurant. He was pushing a container of hot grease from the kitchen to the outside for filtration. When he reached to hold open a door, the container slipped, the lid fell off, and hot grease spilled over much of his body. He sustained second- and third-degree burns to his ankles, arms, chest, and face, and was hospitalized for two weeks. Scarring occurred in all burned areas.

Federal law prohibits cooking and baking by teens 15 years old and younger. Yet, more than 7,000 of the teens aged 14 to 15 who were injured on the job in 1993 were identified as cooks.[23]

Restaurant-related burns, especially those associated with the use of deep fryers, continue to represent a major and preventable source of occupational burn injuries, particularly among adolescents. The risks for burns associated with hot grease emphasize the need for improved surveillance for this problem, as well as improved design of engineering controls and work practices for the prevention of burns in the food service industry.

Working Alone in Cash-based Businesses

Homicide was the leading cause of death among sales workers, retail and personal services, and food preparation occupations in the period of 1992–1995 among workers aged 19 or younger. During that period NIOSH reported that assault and violent acts resulted in 157 fatalities (138 homicides). In 1995, 1,460 young workers 19 years and younger encountered assaults and violent acts in the workplace. Although working with others does not preclude the incidence of crime, a teenager working alone with cash in the register is easy prey. OSHA has proposed recommendations meant to reduce the risk of violence and murder of convenience store clerks. The proposal recommends that two clerks always be on duty. The guidelines initially sought to cover all late-night businesses but were narrowed to convenience stores after hearings were held. If the convenience store guidelines prove effective, similar guidelines for bars and restaurants are also expected to be formulated.[24]

These homicides are not a collection of personal tragedies played out in the workplace—jealous boyfriends barging in or resentful co-workers losing control—but are predominantly robbery-related killings. As employment patterns continue to shift from traditionally heavy industry to retail trade and service sectors, occupational deaths will continue to shift as well, with the result that issues involving workers' compensation and employer liability in homicides will become more common and complex.

Construction Hazards

Construction is one of the most hazardous types of work. More than 7 million Americans work full- or part-time in construction. They build and rebuild highways, bridges, factories, houses, and office towers. They install roofs and wiring, tear out insulation, weld beams, replace industrial pipes and valves, lay brick and carpet, and clean up hazardous waste. It is inherently dangerous work, with hazards both chronic and acute. Dusts constrict the lungs. Vapors attack the central nervous system. Gases kill instantly. Scaffolds collapse and plants explode. The construction industry consistently ranks among the four most dangerous industries, along with transportation, mining, and agriculture, in terms of fatality rates, with an average of six construction workers dying each day.[25]

Because of these dangers, construction employment is prohibited under federal law for those 16 years and younger. From 1992 through 1995, there were 93 fatalities among workers 19 years and younger from electrocutions, falls, motor vehicle accidents, suffocation, and being struck by falling objects. In 1994, there were 7,403 injuries requiring time away from work for construction-site workers under 19 years of age. Although most youngsters injured on construction sites are doing tasks already deemed unlawful, some are struck by falling objects, suffer electrical shock, or are exposed to toxic chemicals while engaged in legal activities. Moreover, construction workers develop disabling and life-shortening diseases more frequently and at younger ages than workers in other fields. In many cases, employers know, or should know, about the insidious hazards that cause these ailments, as well as the more obvious sources of traumatic injury. For instance, a Kansas firm was fined $26,600 for employing two 15-year-olds in construction work, three minors ages 15 and 16 to operate dump trucks, two 16-year-olds to operate power nailers or staplers, and a 16-year-old to operate a bobcat loader. Three minors, ages 16 and 17, operated a circular saw and one minor was seriously injured and required surgery following illegal use of the power saw.[26]

The appropriateness of youth employment in construction should be evaluated. Lack of employee training, the presence of physical and chemical hazards, exposure to the elements, heavy loads, dusts and noise, and misuse of tools contribute to the high rate of injury. Remedies include more and better training for employees and safety and health specialists. Unsafe acts by employees are due to poor training and lack of preparation for the tasks, because safety and health are not integral to the construction process. The nature of construction, multiemployers, worksites, an abundance of small employers, a dynamic workplace and workforce, and acute hazards make safety and health difficult to manage but certainly not impossible.

Critics charge that OSHA compliance officers do not understand the industry, do not inspect the most hazardous companies and job sites, and do not inspect at the right times. In addition, safety and health standards for construction typically lag behind those for general industry. Moreover, the agency has been hampered by the inactivity of its Advisory Committee on Construction Safety and Health, which, for several years, has not had enough members for a quorum. In addition, regulators and researchers cannot make accurate estimates of the incidence of construction industry illnesses and injuries because of spotty data reporting. Some employers flout OSHA record-keeping rules, which require that all but the most minor work-related injuries and illnesses be logged and made available for inspection by workers as well as by the agency. Many observers believe that the BLS annual survey is marred by serious and pervasive underreporting, especially among smaller employers. This underreporting is not all intentional, as smaller firms sometimes lack the time, resources, and understanding to track injuries and illness accurately.[27]

Even large, sophisticated employers with professional staffs have widely divergent reportable rates. The problem of inaccurate reporting is compounded by the fact that injury and illness rates have essentially no predictive value for small employers (and about three-quarters of all construction companies have fewer than twenty employees). A zero rate one year may be followed by an extremely high rate based merely upon one or two incidents in the second year. In sum, OSHA does not currently possess adequate measurement tools for determining the adequacy of an employer's safety and health record, much less the ability to infer valid predictions from past rates.[28]

The Employer's Responsibility for Youth Work Safety

Teenagers need help to work safely. Their inexperience counts against them. In fact, workers with less than one year's experience account for almost one third of the occupational injuries annually. Supervisors and co-workers can help compensate for inexperience by showing teens how to perform their work responsibilities correctly. What may be obvious to an adult or simple common sense to an experienced employee may not be so clear to an adolescent performing a task for the first time. Consequently, the time spent demonstrating to a youthful worker the best way to handle a job will result in the work being done the right way without harm to products or injury to the youth. There are a number of suggestions that management should follow when training minors in the essentials of work safety. First, instructions should be made as clear as possible, and the young workers should be informed regarding safety precautions. Second, the employees should be asked to repeat their supervisor's instructions and given an opportunity to ask questions. Third, they should be shown how to perform the assigned job responsibilities. Fourth, supervisors should monitor the workers and correct any mistakes. Finally, employees should be asked if they have any additional questions. Once young workers have demonstrated their competence, the employer should check again later to ensure that tasks are being correctly accomplished. Employee shortcuts when it comes to safety should never be permitted and supervisors and co-workers should set a good example by following all the appropriate rules as well.

Particularly hazardous jobs are prohibited, but this alone does not eliminate every hazard. Some youthful workers may still need to wear protective equipment such as safety shoes, hard hats, or gloves, depending on the nature of their work. They should know when they need to wear protective gear, where to find it, how to use it, and how to care for it. In other cases, adolescents may simply need to know about safety features of equipment or facilities. For example, they may need to be aware that they must keep exit doors free from clutter, assure that safety guards remain on machinery, or that equipment be turned off or disconnected at the end of each shift.

Every worker needs to be ready to handle an emergency. Employers should prepare their young workers to escape from a fire, handle potentially violent customers, deal with power outages, or face any other risks that affect the firm. They also need to know whom to go to if an injury should occur with the need for first aid or medical care.[29]

Responsibilities of Young Workers

Many young employees are unaware of the potentially life-threatening hazards present in the workplace and many tragedies could easily have been avoided if a few basic safety rules had been followed. Moreover, the employer may have been remiss in not training new, young workers adequately so they would be able to recognize potentially dangerous situations. Unfortunately, young workers are often so intent on impressing a potential employer at a job interview that they often neglect to ask about workplace safety or job training. Some may claim to understand the safety instructions they are given in order to please the trainer when in reality they do not.

The young worker can help ensure his or her own workplace safety by knowing what to look for when entering a new or different work situation, and by knowing what questions to ask a potential or present employer. Young employees should take the initiative and protect themselves by asking their employer the following questions:

1. What are the dangers of my job?
2. Are there any hazards (noise, chemicals, radiation) that I should know about?
3. Will I receive job safety training? When?
4. Is there any safety gear that I'll be expected to wear?
5. Will I be trained in emergency procedures (fire, chemical spill)? When?
6. Where are fire extinguishers, first aid kits, and other emergency equipment located?
7. What are my health and safety responsibilities?
8. Whom do I ask if I have a safety question?

The ability to recognize potential hazards requires not only common sense but also observation, learning, and experience. If the youthful employee has any doubt as to the safety of the materials being handled or employment responsibilities, he or she has the right and responsibility to bring these concerns to his or her supervisor's attention. Ultimately, all employees have the right to refuse to do work that is unsafe, and employers cannot fire anyone for exercising this right.[30]

Parental Responsibilities

Parents should participate in their children's employment decisions and should discuss the types of work, training, and supervision provided by the employer. Workplaces that hire teenagers may not look dangerous, but many of them are. Restaurants have dangerous equipment, as do grocery stores, factories, and construction sites. Keep in mind that a child may have been hired for a relatively safe job, but later might be asked to help with dangerous tasks. One's son or daughter might be closing up the business late at night, which could make robbers think the place would be an easy target. This is an unacceptable risk for adolescents. Parents must ask questions of both their children and the employers and visit the worksites. They should not place much faith in inspectors, because although compliance may be checked in safety sweeps, it rarely occurs. There are so few safety inspectors that some companies have gone decades without a visit.

Responsibilities of Health Care Providers

The best defense against accidental injury or death to young workers is education. It is one of the keys to prevention. The fact of the matter is that when physicians perform preemployment physical examinations on adolescents who apply for work permits, they should inquire about the type of work that is planned. If the work is in clear violation of the law, or involves exposure to toxic or hazardous materials, the physician should advise against such employment. Common-sense advice on using safety equipment (hats, gloves, goggles), as well as being attentive to the general workplace environment, is also recommended.

The injuries for which a child is at risk are influenced by age, cognitive and motor skills, and environment. Childhood injury-prevention counseling by physicians can be effective in changing both the parent's and the child's behavior and in modifying the environment to reduce the risk of injury. Family physicians provide a large portion of the preventive and injury-related health care of children and should make office-based safety education a prominent part of their practices. Pediatricians, particularly, may wish to conduct surveys of medical records of trauma patients in their practice to assess the possible frequency and patterns of work-related injury. They are extraordinarily well positioned to speak out against the abuses of child labor, to urge strengthening of regulations and legislation, and to insist on the need for mandated occupational health and safety training of children and adolescents who propose to enter the workforce. Pediatricians should serve as advocates for working children.[31]

Occupational Disease Prevention

Primary care physicians have an increasingly important role in identifying occupational disease. However, the basic skills in history taking, diagnosis, and management have not been adequately incorporated into traditional American medical education or practice. This is the primary reason why doctors do not recognize work-related conditions.

Missed diagnoses are only part of the problem. Medical education emphasizes diagnosis and treatment of the individual patient, and little attention is traditionally placed on the role of the private physician in public health. The orientation of physicians toward diagnosis and treatment of individual cases and the lack of training in public health may be a more basic obstacle to involvement in preventive activity.

Making occupational disease reporting legally required is one possibility. However, the problems of underreporting, even for legally required reporting of certain infections and venereal diseases, suggests that it cannot solve the problem entirely. Problems with underreporting have plagued the occupational disease reporting systems in California, Michigan, Maryland, New York, Ohio, and Virginia. Other states that require reporting of a limited number of occupational diseases have only recently enacted their reporting requirements. It is premature to determine if only requiring reporting of a few occupational diseases will be more successful. Nevertheless, the requirements, in conjunction with continuing physician education and feedback, could make significant improvements in the number of reports received, as compared with a system dependent on voluntary physician compliance.

Continued efforts by the public health community to work closely with primary care physicians on occupational health could eventually have a positive impact on the recognition of occupational disease and, therefore, its reduction. This process of changing practitioners' attitudes may be lengthy and require both the resources and commitment of the public health and medical care community. Despite these difficulties, the recognition of occupational disease by primary care physicians is crucial for motivating industry to provide healthful working conditions.[32]

Emergency Room Deficiencies

Since many injured children and adolescents receive initial medical treatment in hospital emergency rooms, the quality of the care they receive is an important consideration. Unfortunately, as is the case with primary care physicians, there are significant weaknesses. For instance, only about half of the 25,000 positions in emergency medicine are staffed by physicians certified to provide emergency care. Moreover, less than 20 percent of medical schools require courses in emergency medicine. Hence, part of the problem is a lack of adequately trained individuals. Contrary to the public's expectations, few U.S. medical schools adequately train their students in the fundamentals of emergency care and life support. Additionally, the emergency room practice of hiring medical residents seeking to supplement their modest incomes compounds the problem. Many of these individuals lack training and sufficient experience in any aspect of primary health care. State licensing boards and medical schools should ensure that every medical student receives appropriate emergency room skills. Also, a classification system for employers is necessary to indicate the level of care that would be available to injured youth.[33]

DATA COLLECTION: SCOPE AND PROBLEMS

The magnitude and severity of occupational illnesses in working children are unknown. Children may be especially susceptible to work-related injury and disease because of physiological differences, in size, metabolism, and absorption. Health and safety data on working children and adolescents are fragmented and incomplete. These data are needed to identify minors at high risk of injuries and illnesses, to target prevention programs, and to identify areas for additional legislation.

Erratic reporting is one reason the federal government's occupational health and safety database is inadequate and preventive efforts have had only limited success, especially in industries such as construction. Limited information is available at the national level for characterizing youth employment and calculating rates of injuries and illness. Because data are not routinely collected for youths aged 14 and younger, it is not possible to estimate the number of the youngest workers and, consequently, their rates of injury and illness.

The six data collections system are: the National Traumatic Occupational Fatalities database; the Bureau of Labor Statistics Census of Fatal Occupational Injuries; the Bureau of Labor Statistics (BLS) Annual Survey data; a large workers' compensation database; the National Council on Compensation Insurance data; and the National Electronic Injury Surveillance System. Setting priorities for workplace health and safety depends upon accurate and reliable injury and illness data. All of these occupational health databases have limitations when used to summarize the national scope of workplace hazards. Occupational injuries predominate over illnesses in terms of the number of cases and the overall costs. However, each of these organizations uses different methods for identifying occupational injury deaths and wide numerical disparities are the result. Estimates range from less than 4,000 deaths to more than 11,000 deaths in a given year.[34]

The BLS Annual Survey is the primary data source most frequently cited in the literature. It contains survey results that are extrapolated from a questionnaire sent to a sample of 280,000 private-sector firms, which face an economic incentive to underreport. Moreover, the data undercount injuries and illnesses in working youths and children because the BLS survey does not include self-employed workers, farmers with fewer than 11 employees, private households, and government employees. In addition, the data do not include work-related deaths, or injuries and illnesses that do not result in lost work time. The data also do not reflect the true numbers and rates of workplace illnesses, because many of these are not properly diagnosed, are chronic in nature and often do not develop until workers have left the jobs where exposures occurred. The BLS does not validate injury and illness data that are developed from employer reports.

State Workers' Compensation Data

Data from state workers' compensation systems help to fill a portion of these information gaps, but the state systems have some important statistical limitations. For instance, their varying definitions of industries, workers, and cases covered make cross-state comparisons difficult and a national total of state data even more problematic.

The Massachusetts Experience

Massachusetts is the only state to have mandated that physicians and emergency rooms report teen occupational injuries to the state. It is also the only state funded by NIOSH to analyze that data. The Department of Public Health collects data on work-related injuries to teens under 18. Since 1992, the Massachusetts public health code has required that physicians and hospitals report cases of work-related injuries to teenagers to the Department of Public Health. Workers' compensation records are also used to identify cases of work-related injuries to young workers. These findings are used to guide statewide prevention efforts. Since workers' compensation cases are limited to injured workers with five or more lost work days and only a sample of hospital emergency departments and physicians file regular reports, the data reported are incomplete. Furthermore, only 3 percent of all cases of teen injuries were reported by more than one data source. These findings underscore the need for multiple information sources in order to accurately describe the nature and extent of work-related injuries to adolescents.[35]

State Data Sources

Four data sources are routinely available for identifying state occupational injury fatalities. They are medical examiner or coroner records, death certificates, workers' compensation claim reports, and OSHA fatality reports. The tasks of identifying occupational deaths using these data is complicated by the nature of the data sources. That is, each source has coverage limitations, such as the exclusion of certain industries or types of workers, work-relatedness of the injury may not be identified, or occupational and industry information may either not be collected or may be based on usual, rather than current, occupation and industry, or both. As a result, each data source captures only a certain portion of the total occupational deaths, but when the sources are used in combination, they may capture virtually all occupational fatalities in a given state. Thus, the best injury surveillance systems use data from several sources with each source complementing the others.[36]

The Impact of Data Deficiencies

Death figures cited by OSHA most likely underestimate the total number of fatalities because OSHA does not investigate work-related homicides or deaths that occur in industries regulated by other agencies. The agency also does not have jurisdiction over most transportation incidents. Also, the OSHA fatality figures are drastically lower than those published by NIOSH under its National Traumatic Occupation Fatalities system. The system provides a more accurate count because it draws from death certificates rather than other less complete reporting systems. For instance, the number of 16- and 17-year-old workers killed on the job in 1984 and 1985 as measured by NIOSH was nearly two and one-half times the total identified by OSHA for the same period.[37]

What should be kept in mind, however, is that no single data source contains all the data elements necessary to describe occupational injury deaths. Unfortunately, the systems in place for collecting and coding injury data suffer from a number of limitations that make it difficult, if not impossible, to enumerate correctly the true scope and import of occupational injuries and fatalities. Presently, there are no nationally agreed upon standards for defining, reporting, and recording occupational and nonoccupational injuries.[38]

Accurate injury and illness records have the greatest value when they are used by employers and employees to manage and develop workplace safety and health programs. The records are an effective way to quantify a firm's injury and illness experience. When problems are quantified and presented to employers and employees, they are much more likely to be solved. Hazardous conditions, departments, and jobs also can be identified by reviewing injury and illness records. Once hazards are discovered and corrective actions are taken, the records can be used to monitor the effectiveness of control approaches taken. When information on workplace injuries and illnesses is not available or is incorrect, the ability to identify problems and take corrective action is diminished.[39]

FINAL OBSERVATIONS

While workers of all ages face hazards on the job, a number of factors raise special concerns about young workers. 1) Teens are often employed in industries with higher than average injury rates for workers of all ages. 2) Teens do not receive adequate health and safety training, either on the job or at school. On-the-job supervision is often limited. 3) Often teens go to their jobs after putting in a full day of work at school, which contributes to fatigue, potentially increasing the risk of injury and interfering with school. 4) As new workers, teens are unfamiliar with workplace hazards and often unaware of their legal rights as employees. They may be reluctant to ask questions or speak up about problems. Many teens feel dispensable and believe they will be replaced if they speak up. 5) Adolescent physical development is extremely variable. Smaller individuals may be unable to manipulate machine parts or lack the strength to perform certain tasks. On the other hand, larger adolescents may be assigned tasks simply because of their size without regard to their experiences or capabilities.

Providing safe, healthful, and positive work experiences for today's youth requires a joint effort of many parties, including employers, parents, educators, health care providers, government agencies, and children themselves. Illness and injury do not have to arise at work. Carefully designed information and training, equipment, procedures, and laws that are in place will protect young workers so long as all of these parties recognize and exercise their responsibilities in the workplace.

NOTES

1. Prepared statement of John R. Fraser, Deputy Administrator, Wage and Hour Division, U.S. Department of Labor, before the Senate Labor and Human Resources Committee, Subcommittee on Employment and Training, Washington, DC., 11 June 1998.

2. Bureau of Labor Statistics, *Workplace Injuries and Illnesses in 1993* (Washington, DC: U.S. Department of Labor, 1994), 29–31.

3. S.H. Pollack, P.J. Landrigan, and D.L. Mallino, "Child Labor in 1990: Prevalence and Health Hazards," *Annual Review of Public Health*, 11 (1991): 359, 375.

4. Francine Knowles, "Be Sure Teen's Job Is Safe One," *Chicago Sun-Times*, 1 June, 1999, 47.

5. R.H. Van Zelst, "The Effect of Age and Experience upon Accident Rate," *The Journal of Applied Psychology*, 38(5) (1954): 313, 317.

6. NIOSH Update, "NIOSH Warns: Employment Can Be Dangerous and Deadly for Adolescents," 19 May 1994.

7. Sharon L. Smith, "In Harm's Way: Child Labor in the U.S., *Occupational Hazards*, 57(11) (November 1995): 23.

8. K.A. Dunn and C.W. Runyan, "Deaths at Work Among Children and Adolescents," *American Journal of Disabilities of Children*, 147 (1993): 1044.

9. Work-related Injuries to Teens (Boston: Massachusetts Department of Public Health, 1998).

10. Which Occupations Are Considered Hazardous by State and Federal Lawmakers? (Portland: Oregon Bureau of Labor and Industries, 12 January 2000). Section 2.

11. Occupational Safety and Health Act, 1970 (Chapter V, Sections B.,C.).

12. Comments of the National Institute for Occupational Safety and Health on the Department of Labor/Wage and Hour Division Advance Notice of Proposed Rule Making on Child Labor Regulations, Orders, and Statements of Interpretation (Cincinnati, OH: NIOSH, 1994), 17–25.

13. Philip J. Landrigan and Jane B. McCammon, "Child Labor: Still With Us After All These Years," *Public Health Reports*, 112 (6) (21 November 1997): 466.

14. Jeffrey Brainard, "Universities Fail to Produce Experts in Occupational Safety, Report Says," *The Chronicle of Higher Education* (9 June 2000): A32.

15. Philip J. Landrigan,"The Prevention of Occupational Cancer," *Alliance for Stray Animals and People Journal*, 46(2) (13 March 1996): 67.

16. "Work-related Injuries and Illnesses Associated with Child Labor—United States, 1993," *Morbidity and Mortality Weekly Report,* 45(22) (7 June 1996): 464.

17. Landrigan and McCammon, "Child Labor."

18. D.N. Castillo, D.D. Landen, and L.A. Layne, "Occupational Injury Deaths of 16- and 17-Year-Olds in the United States," *American Journal of Public Health,* 84(4): 646–649.

19. Prepared Testimony of Linda F. Golodner, President, National Consumers League, Co-Chair, Child Labor Coalition, before the House Committee on Economic and Educational Opportunities, Subcommittee on Workforce Protections, Washington, DC, 12 September 1996.

20. Ibid.

21. "Sacrificing America's Youth: The Problem of Child Labor and the Response of Government" (Chicago: National Safe Workplace Institute, 7 September 1992) (4), 35.

22. Kitty J. Hendricks, "Adolescent Occupational Injuries in Fast Food Restaurants: An Examination of the Problem From a National Perspective," *Journal of Occupational and Environmental Medicine,* 41(12) (December 1999): 1146–1153.

23. "Occupational burns among restaurant workers—Colorado and Minnesota," *Morbidity and Mortality Weekly Report,* 42 (37) (24 September 1993): 713.

24. D.N. Castillo and B.D. Malit, "Occupational Injury Deaths of 16- and 17-year-olds in the U.S.: Trends and Comparisons with Older Workers," *Injury Prevention,* (December 1997): 277–281.

25. Katherine G. Abraham, William L. Weber, and Martin E. Personick, "Improvements in the BLS Safety and Health Statistical System," *Monthly Labor Review,* 119(4) (April 1996): 3.

26. "Five Worst Jobs for Teens," *Child Labor Monitor* (July 1997): 5.

27. "NIOSH Had Stiffer Child Worker Safety Rules, But Was Ignored," *The Commercial Appeal* (Memphis), 17 December, 1997, B7.

28. Prepared Testimony of Robert A. Georgine, President, Building and Construction Trades Department, AFL-CIO, before the Senate Labor and Human Resources Committee and Small Business Committee on S. 1423, the Occupational Safety and Health Reform and Reinvention Act, *Federal News Service,* 6 December, 1995.

29. Preparing Teens to Work Safely (Washington, DC: U.S. Department of Labor) n.d.

30. "Tips for Young Workers," Workers' Compensation Board of B.C., in *Prevention at Work* (July/August 1995).

31. D. Glotzer and M. Weitzman, "Childhood Injuries: Issues for the Family Physician,"*American Family Physician* 44(5) (November 1991): 1705–1716.

32. Noah S. Seixas and Kennth D. Rosenman, "Voluntary Reporting System for Occupational Disease: Pilot Project, Evaluation," *Public Health Reports,* 101 (May/June 1986): 297–282.

33. Paul Raeburn, "Emergency Room Staffs Called Undertrained," *Chicago Sun-Times,* 5 September 1994, A7.

35. "Menial Jobs Hard on Teenage Backs," *The Back Letter,* 9(5) (May 1994): 56.

36. M.A.J. McKenna, "Are After-School Jobs Killing Our Kids? Solutions Needed to Stop Work-Related Injuries to Teens," *The Boston Herald,* 24 January 1994, D29.

37. Patricia J. Schnitzer and Thomas R. Bender, "Surveillance of Traumatic Occupational Fatalities in Alaska—Implications for Prevention," *Public Health Reports,* 107(1) (January–February 1992): 71–74.

38. "Improved Enforcement, Data Gathering Needed to Reduce Work-Related Deaths Among Children," *Occupational Safety & Health Reporter*, 23(16) (15 September 1993): 414.

39. A.J. Rubens, W.A. Oleckno, and L. Papaeliou, "Establishing Guidelines for the Identification of Occupational Injuries: A Systematic Appraisal," *Journal of Occupational and Environmental Medicine*, 37(2) (February 1995): 151–159.

5
Risks for Child Labor in Agriculture

> Many people look at farming as the idyllic dream of rural America. They don't see all of the hazards that range from animals to pesticides, from machinery to allergies, from play areas to old barns and all the places in between.[1]

THE NATURE OF THE PROBLEM

The above quotation demonstrates that farming is one of the most dangerous industries in the United States. Yet injury, illness, and death on the farm are not restricted to adults. Each year, approximately 100,000 children under 20 years of age are injured on farms and more than 100 are killed. Approximately 1.5 million children under 20 live, work, or have a regular presence on farms in the United States. Included in this total are children of farm families, farmworkers, and migrant and seasonal workers. Children who work in agriculture are exposed to myriad hazards. These hazards include: working around heavy equipment, driving tractors, forklifts, and combines, working with livestock, falling from ladders, and drowning in irrigation ditches and ponds. Children are working with knives, machetes, and other sharp cutting instruments; risking exposure to pesticides through direct spray and drift; and carrying and lifting heavy buckets filled with produce. In addition, children are working in a stooped position for hours on end and being exposed to high levels of heat and sun, sometimes without access to fresh drinking water or without being allowed appropriate rest periods. The agricultural workplace is a hostile environment, filled with high risks of injury and possible death. It is not an environment for children and youth who are not even aware of the dangers they face and the possible long-term impact that an accident can have on their future.

Agriculture, although generally agreed to be one of the most dangerous industries, employs a proportionately larger number of these children than other industries. When agriculture depended upon small and family farmers for most agricultural products, children working for their parents or local farmers was common. Today, a different kind of child labor exists on U.S. farms, fewer of which are owned by families or local farmers. These children work as hired labor on a migrant or seasonal basis (that is, moving to find employment or working intermittently) or have parents who work as migrant and seasonal workers.

More American children are killed while working on farms each year than in any other industry. But laws that date to the 1930s and an overwhelmed enforcement system fail to protect young people working in the fields. To illustrate, a 13-year-old may not, under federal law, be employed to perform clerical work in an air-conditioned office, but may be employed to pick strawberries in a field in the heat of the summer; a 16-year-old may not operate a power saw in a shop or a forklift in a warehouse, but may operate either on a farm; and a 14- or 15-year-old working in a retail establishment may work only between the hours of 7 A.M. and 7 P.M. (9 P.M. during the summer) and may not work more than eighteen hours in a school week or three hours in a school day, but the same child may work an unlimited number of hours picking grapes, as long as he or she is not working during school hours. Moreover, parents who employ their children on a farm may have their children work on the farm at any age and in any occupation, regardless of how hazardous a task they perform. Parents who employ their children in other industries, however, have restrictions on what occupations their children work in.

Fatality rates among young farmworkers dwarf those in other fields. In 1999, 38 percent of all work-related adolescent deaths occurred on U.S. farms. More than half those fatalities involved tractors, most often while teens were driving.[2] Family farms are excluded from reporting requirements, and many accidents are not identified as work-related. Since these data exclude children under the age of 16, the real impact is much greater than depicted with data pertaining to adolescents and adults.

DATA-GATHERING LIMITATIONS

While many minors are injured while working on farms, little specific information on farm work-related injuries is available, probably because data on employment of youths less than 16 years of age are not routinely collected or reported. In 1996, an estimated 261,000 youths 16–19 years of age were employed in agriculture, accounting for 4 percent of working youths in this age group. Eighty-one percent of these workers were wage and salary employees, 11 percent were self-employed, and 7 percent were unpaid family workers. The Bureau of Labor Statistics reported 114 agricultural work-related deaths of youths 16–19 years of age for the 1992–1996 period, accounting for a disproportionate 15 percent of work-related deaths among this age group during this period. Further, Bureau of Labor Statistics (BLS) reported 87 agricultural work-related deaths of youth less than 16 years of age during this period, a group for which employment data are not available. The best available nationally representative estimates indicate that, on average, 155,000 15-to-17-year-old children may work in agriculture at some point in the year.[3]

Death rates of children, in all likelihood, are inaccurate. For example, only three work-related deaths to children younger than 18 were reported to the Occupational Safety and Health Administration (OSHA) by employers in fiscal year 1997. Although employers are required by law to report work-related deaths to OSHA, the small number of deaths may mean that employers are not notifying OSHA of work-related deaths as they are required to do. Or, because farms with fewer than 11 employees are not required to track this information for OSHA, they may be less likely to report deaths to OSHA. In this regard, smaller farms may be more hazardous than larger ones; as a result, these data may not reflect the number of injuries and fatalities occurring on farms not covered by safety and health regulations.

Data-Source Deficiencies

Concerns about the quality of injury and illness data relate to the data source and the link between the injury or illness and the workplace. Much of the data on occupational injuries are self-reported by employers, and it is unknown whether employers report events accurately, especially if an injury or fatality involves transient or undocumented workers or if the employer or child is not covered by applicable child labor or safety and health laws. Also, health practitioners may have difficulty determining whether an injury to a young child is occupationally related. This is especially the case for chronic injuries or illnesses from sustained exposure to pesticides. One may question whether health officials are always adequately trained to recognize the effects of pesticide exposure on children. In addition, whether children are appropriately classified in order for the injury or fatality to be recorded in these systems is questionable. For example, two children in Florida died after having been run over by farm machinery. While these children were not legally classified as working, their deaths still resulted from their being on a farm and with their parents, who were working at the time of the deaths. Farmworker advocates and others claim that it is a common practice for children to help out their parents on a farm on an informal basis, but these kinds of deaths may not be included in estimates of work-related deaths. Nonetheless, available data indicate that although the relative number of injuries experienced by child farmworkers is not as high as in other industries, the severity may be greater, and these children may suffer a disproportionate number of fatalities. For example, BLS data show that, between 1992 and 1996, about 140 children younger than 18 were killed while doing agriculture work, which was about 40 percent of all fatalities suffered by children working in all industries.[4]

Recent estimates from the National Institute of Occupational Safety and Health (NIOSH) revealed that the estimated injury rate for 14-to-17-year-olds in farming was 4.3 per 100 full-time-equivalent workers—less than the rate for 14-to-17-year-old workers in all industries. However, fractures and dislocations were more common in agriculture (14 percent) than in other industries (3 percent), which may indicate that agricultural injuries may be more severe.[5]

Consequences of Less Legal Protection

Even though farm children may perform tasks that are prohibited in other industries, be exposed to workplace hazards at an early age, and perform tasks that are inappropriate for their age, safety requirements of the Occupational Safety and Health Act of 1970 are not enforceable on 95 percent of U.S. farms. As a result, most farm owners lack the direction provided by mandatory safety standards to address the complex problem of controlling risk for both adult and youth workers. Children working on small family farms may perform hazardous agricultural tasks, such as operating machinery, working from ladders greater than 20 feet high, and working in confined spaces. Although youths aged 14 and 15 who have received safety training on specific topics through specialized programs may perform work activities otherwise prohibited for minors less than 16 years, compared with adults, these youths may lack work experience, physical size, and cognitive abilities that are less well developed than in adults.[6] Despite the fact that several federal agencies engage in selected activities promoting child safety and health in agriculture, until now, there has been no national coordinated effort to protect young people. Unfortunately, estimates are based on inadequate surveillance systems and provide little information about the causes and consequences of injury and may underestimate the problem. Agriculture may be much more hazardous than numbers indicate. Many farm states, like Iowa, do not distinguish farm-related deaths from other accidental fatalities and are therefore not included in the statistics.[7] Then, too, children commonly work with their hired farmworker parents on evenings or weekends but are not considered to be official employees. As a result, their injuries, illnesses, or fatalities are probably not reflected in available data.[8] For example, a study in New York state of migrant children who worked on farms indicated that fully one-third of these children were injured while working.[9] Surveillance systems and other descriptive efforts can provide useful information on the scope and spectrum of agricultural injuries but can seldom identify specific factors, such as faulty machinery, risky behaviors, or particularly hazardous environments, which can be the focus of preventive efforts. The conventional statistics on farm accidents provide an outsider's view, the view that makes sense to occupational safety and other public health experts, insurers, legislators, and others not directly involved in farming. The insider's view, the view of farm operators, may be different. Farm operators may take into account their own close calls (something happened that was almost a serious accident but was not) in farming and the accidents of people they know.

Their close calls and their knowledge of the accidents of others may be factors affecting their farm safety practices, but economic pressures and the human tendency toward procrastination may delay their utilization of safer operational procedures.

Home Treatment

Farm accident statistics often come from hospital, clinic, and doctor's office records. Such studies are useful and important, but they provide no information about injuries treated only at home. It may be that a great deal of treatment is done at home—for financial reasons or because of the press of work that has to be done immediately, the cultural acceptance of pain and the cultural norms that treat bodies as expendable, the practice in farm families of doing as much as possibly can be done without outside assistance, and the distance that must be traveled to reach medical care.

Home treatment may reflect the extent to which health care is affordable and available, the valuing of home-based solutions to problems, the sense that pain and injury are part of life, the press of work, and the availability of substitute workers. It is possible that on all these counts, people in farming may be pushed to home remedy. For them, health care may be less often affordable and less available. They may value home-based solutions to problems more than other people and may more often feel the press of work and the lack of substitute workers.

Whatever the factors underlying the high level of home treatment, the data suggest that it would be important to evaluate the adequacy of home treatment of farm accidents. To put all planning energy devoted to health care for farm families into safety education, public health concerns, physicians, hospitals, paraprofessionals, emergency response, and health insurance might be to miss the importance of home treatment in a farm family. Of course, youth treated in this manner may not appear in accident statistics.[10]

Characteristics of Occupational Injuries of Farm Youth Aged Less Than 20

Approximately 14,400 occupational injuries occurred to children or adolescents under the age of 20 who lived on, worked on, or visited a farm operation in 1998, according to a random telephone survey of 50,000 farm operations conducted in 1998. An injury was defined as any condition occurring on the farm operation resulting in at least four hours of restricted activity. Most injuries happened to youth who were part of the farm household. Approximately 43 percent of the injuries (10,143) to household youth were work-related and happened at a rate of 1.4 injuries per 100 youth. Of youth visiting the farm, approximately 2,200 injuries were work-related, for a rate of 0.3 injuries per 100 youth.[11]

Characteristics of Occupational Deaths of Farm Youth Aged Less Than 19

During the 1992–2000 period, a total of 337 children and adolescents died from injuries resulting from their work in agricultural production, which included agricultural crop and livestock production and agricultural services labor. Two hundred and eighty of them were engaged in nonmanagerial farm occupations. Twenty-seven percent of the fatalities (92) occurred while the youths were operating tractors, while 19 percent (73) of the deaths involved the operation of motor vehicles. Most farm children work for their parents, so the majority of fatalities occurred on their family's farm. Farm children are twice as likely to die from an accident as their urban counterparts because farm children are often expected to help with chores and handle responsibilities at a young age. Due to this fact, and the nature of farming, they are exposed to potentially dangerous situations much more frequently than are children in towns or cities.

Ranchers and farmers in rural America learn to drive at a very early age and often let their children use farm vehicles to do chores. A farm family pastor commented on the accidental death of a 10-year-old farm boy: "From the time I could reach the pedals I was driving a tractor and a truck. . . . The Lohrs are a farm family, and Riley was feeding horses and out doing chores when the accident happened."[12]

The Impact of Farm Culture and Traditions

A question asked by many mothers and fathers, grandparents, and others with a stake in children's safety is, "How young is too young?" Or, asked another way, "At what age is it okay to let my son or daughter drive a tractor?" A farm safety expert who was raised on a farm answered these questions in this fashion:

> Like many people who grew up on a farm, my first real experience operating a tractor was as a little boy at the age of ten. I vividly remember a blustery November day on my dad's old Farmall 460 tractor. First I sat on my dad's lap where I learned to steer, use the clutch, and shift gears. Then, I rode on the back of the tractor to learn how the disc behind me would respond to various conditions and hydraulic controls. I'd carefully balance myself, one foot on the draw bar, the other on the cast-iron rear-axle housing. One hand would be on the back of the tractor's seat, and the other on the old steel fender. Little did I know of the dangers I faced as a young operator or extra rider, especially as we bounced through that field together disking cornstalks. I remember making that first round by myself, with dad watching, heart racing, and palms sweating. My father, on the other hand, remembers being seven when he was asked to drive an old Allis Chalmers WC attached to a bale lifter.[13]

Advocates for increased safety measures appreciate the traditions of farm life, but insist the country must better protect these children as it does those in all other industries.

Parental Involvement

Child deaths and injuries in agriculture involve a situation different from that in other industries. They often involve the parents of the child or other relatives, who, by their own actions, contribute to the horrendous incidents that occur each year. In other cases, although the parents have not intentionally put their child in danger, they witness the incident leading to the death or injury, and suffer from the thought that they might have been able to prevent it. In some cases, they have tried but failed to prevent the incident—perhaps seeing a loose gate or wheel start to fall off but being unable to reach it in time.

All this has made farming, a virtually unregulated industry made up of proudly independent families, more deadly than traditionally dangerous occupations, particularly for children who routinely work on farms but are never seen on construction sites or in quarries. The economic pressure on modern-day family farms, combined with an ethic of independence and a fierce resistance to regulation, has led many farmers to accept high risks as a way of life and injuries as isolated accidents. Some are just that, despite parental supervision.

The toll of child injuries and deaths has led to parents taking part-time jobs off the farm to help them hold on to the land. This has meant later nights in the fields, more hurried work and more dependence on machinery. It has also meant a greater need for children to pitch in for longer hours and sometimes with less supervision.

Parents are often not aware of the significant consequences associated with farming hazards. Parents may believe that "our kid is a good kid and wouldn't be involved in such an accident." Consequently, children are allowed to work with or play on and around dangerous farm machinery (not viewed as dangerous). To change this perception, parents must take a more active role in the decisions that children make with regard to farming tasks. This includes discussing the pros and cons of a chosen job and its associated tasks. It is the parents' responsibility to cultivate good safety attitudes and teach children to respect the dangers associated with the farm environment

Many autumn accidents occur when farmers don't take the time to turn off machinery before removing stalks from combine heads and chutes. With the speed that objects are drawn into the combine head, even with the fastest human speed, it is very difficult to withdraw a hand once it is caught.

Most (if not all) accidents that occur on a farm are preventable. Recognizing this requires a change in attitude and behavior—a change that must begin with the children's parents.[14]

Accidents—Do They Go with the Territory?

Whether it is a difficult harvest or simply the fact that accidents are going to happen, there are too many accidents within agriculture. Loss of life, loss of limb, and injury to fingers cannot be experienced without asking why. Why did it happen? How could it have been prevented? Apparently farmers only recognize farm safety when there is a death (pretty obvious) or there are missing limbs. It seems that farmers have to see or feel it to admit an accident can occur. For instance, a farmer for thirty years mentioned that he was pretty lucky in that he never had to deal with a safety issue on his farm. He was asked by a neighbor about the time he fell from a silo, was unconscious for a period of time, hospitalized for three days, and badly bruised. His neighbor did not consider the incident a farm accident because there was no death or loss of limb.[15] Another farmer criticized this mind-set, maintaining: "Farmers need to recognize that the 'she'll be all right' attitude is not good enough when it comes to safety. Accidents can't be fixed with a piece of four-by-two and a slap on the back. We need to educate our youngsters and their parents as to the risks of farming."[16]

One farm parent described her experience: "It's just something that touches me. . . . I was raised on a farm in western Oklahoma. I think back on some of the things I did as a kid, and I wonder how I lived through it."[17] Anyone who has grown up on a farm knows that it is not the bucolic life that is pictured in television commercials. Children in farm families are about the only children at significant risk for occupationally related illness and injury.[18]

Sadly, all the bone-chilling analysis doesn't begin to tell the story of the continuing tragedy unfolding every day on U.S. farms. Numbers alone don't reveal that 20 percent of the victims of all farm accidents are children and teenagers. Other industries have no such agonizing figures to report because children don't live and work in factories or mines, but they do live and work on farms.

The equation for danger on the farm is so basic we stumble over its simplicity. On a farm, the workplace and the home place are the same place, and it is considered a wonderful privilege for children to grow up helping out on the farm. Nevertheless, it is still real work, and it still presents very real dangers. The farm is a great place to raise a family, with this exception: farming, of necessity, brings all its workers into direct contact with powerful machines, large animals, and toxic materials. In most industries, other than agriculture, people work together in centralized facilities where safety practices can be easily organized and enforced. Each worker may have responsibility to perform only one basic skill. But the farmer works alone, is usually self-taught, and must be proficient in dozens of skills, many of them life-threatening if not performed properly.

Researchers now know more about why farm accidents occur. Despite that fact, little can be done to combat human nature. An Iowa farmer put it this way: "The problem is, people take it for granted that they're going to get hurt, and there's nothing they can do about it. They feel like eventually everybody gets hurt or loses a hand." Bearing this out, while the fatality rate for farm children may have declined 39 percent, nonfatal injuries are 10 percent higher.

Farm Safety 4 Just Kids, a farm-safety advocacy group, has found that children ages 10–14 are at the greatest risk for farm-related injuries, often due to low levels of experience with farm equipment.[19]

The Anti-Regulation Environment

Farmers in America have a tradition of being fiercely independent and self-reliant, a quality often necessary to survive the demands that farming places on the individual. Such character is reflected in the fact that agricultural groups have successfully lobbied to exempt most family farms from OSHA and child labor regulations. Thus, children of all ages are exempt from any regulatory requirement and may operate any machine or perform any task their parents deem appropriate. The long tradition of having children work on the family farm is exemplified in summer vacation from school. This practice originated in our culture so that children could help with planting and harvest.

In April 2001, the Nebraska legislature unanimously approved an amendment to the existing law which would allow 12- and 13-year-olds to detassel corn. The previous minimum age had been 14. Governor Mike Johanns was confident that detasseling companies would not take advantage of young workers and claimed summer work was good for many children.[20]

Several years earlier, eleven northern Illinois children became ill after spending just thirty minutes detasseling corn in a field that had been sprayed with pesticide a weekend earlier. The youths, aged 12–16, suffered from nausea and dizziness, symptoms of chemical exposure. A state official contended that tests showed no overuse of pesticides, but admitted the possibility that pesticides had caused the detasselers' ill health.[21]

At the federal level, OSHA has had little contact with agriculture. Farmers have lobbied to be exempt from regulation, creating a situation where the agency with the mandate to protect the safety of workers has no jurisdiction over one of the most dangerous occupations. Congress prohibited the Occupational Safety and Health Administration from spending money to inspect farms with ten or fewer employees. The majority of farms in the United States fall into this category.[22]

Tough economic times force some farmers to hang on to older, more dangerous equipment or to trim the payroll by employing their children for longer hours or more dangerous duties. Farmers' devotion to a way of life and a chance to pass that on to their children can endanger youths, whether they're working on the farm or not. Despite the risks of death and disfigurement, many farmers reject efforts to regulate farming as impractical and intrusive. Farmers apparently don't see the need for all the precautions. Perhaps they have been desensitized by years of exposure to too many brochures, booklets, videos, and strategically placed decals all telling them how to do their jobs without getting hurt.[23]

For that matter, many farmers are cautious about cooperating with researchers because they fear their findings may lead directly to more legislation and regulations of farm operations. In a seeming contradiction, the American Farm Bureau Federation (AFBF), the largest, most influential, and very conservative farm organization, while acknowledging that " . . . current federal law governing the employment of minors does not meet the needs of agriculture and needs to be updated," nevertheless adds its voice to the anti-regulation chorus by maintaining that it . . . will oppose any efforts to unnecessarily restrict the employment of workers under age 18 in agriculture." In particular, the AFBF "will work to ensure that farmers will be able to continue to employ their own children and those of their friends and neighbors as has been traditionally done in agriculture."[24]

Safety Misperceptions and Economic Pressures

The agrarian philosophy has greatly influenced the public's image of agriculture. This philosophy holds that farm life produces better people and that farmers are more democratic, honest, independent, virtuous, self-reliant, and politically more stable than city dwellers. It also recognizes that farm life is filled with hardships, which further undergirds the family-farm image as a cherished one in American culture. Despite the alarming statistics, with scores of children seriously injured or killed each year due to tractor-related accidents, this myth has caused the public to overlook hazards inherent in farming. Consequently, the public does not perceive farm safety to be a priority. As a result of these rather idealistic beliefs, children continue to suffer.

Although farmers recognize the hazards they face, the "nothing can happen to me" attitude prevails as the primary motivation for neglecting the need for safety. Most farmers strive to produce and supply in order to make a reasonable profit. To achieve that objective, many operate in the most economical way. Unfortunately, such an approach may mean that safety is relegated to the back burner as safe practices are often overshadowed by issues of cost and customer demand. It is this fierce sense of independence, driven by economic necessity, that all too often pushes farm children into harm's way.[25]

Unsafe Work Practices—Fact and Fiction

Overall, while farmers generally believe in safety and believe they are safe, they do not consistently practice safety. For whatever reason, most farmers utilize unsafe practices in the course of their farming activities. They may be in a hurry or so tired that they make mistakes. Some are unwilling or unable to purchase and use appropriate safety equipment, or maybe they are planning to repair or replace safety devices later. Some may be unaware of the proper way to perform certain tasks or unaware of the potential risks involved. Of course, there are also some who knowingly take chances, perhaps having done things that way many times before without incident.[26] Many agricultural workers are killed when their tractor or attached equipment runs over them after being jolted off the vehicle. Seat belt usage would prevent these deaths, yet three-quarters of all farmers never use one. Thus, it is clear that a persuasive message cannot target safety in general, because farmers already believe themselves to be safe. But persuasive messages must target specific safety behaviors, such as the use of seat belts, or having a "One rider at a time" rule for their tractor.[27]

An Iowa study revealed that children begin operating equipment at an average age of 12 years. Coupling this with the finding that the parents believe their children are not capable of operating equipment until age 15 exemplifies the most important issue, the disparity between parents' levels of safety knowledge and safety behavior.[28]

Children have a reasonable awareness of farm hazards, but their knowledge is not manifested in safe farm practices. They invariably perceive farm activities to be conditionally hazardous. A Colorado survey of three dozen farm adolescents, ages 14 to 18, indicated that the subjects have been and are at risk of injury on the farm while working, playing, and playing in the context of work. They recognize the importance of safety rules, but bend or break those rules on a personal assessment of risk. They take more risks while playing than while working, but playing often occurs in the context of work and involves some of the same equipment or machinery. In fact, many of the youths reported modeling the unsafe practices of parents, grandparents, and other authority figures as opposed to performing chores the way those individuals taught them.[29]

The Cost-Benefit Mind-Set

Farmers view injury entirely different than those who have employer health coverage. It is not a benefit to farmers; it's an expense. Since they don't believe anything is going to happen to them, why should they go to the expense to make it safer? Farmers do not view herbicides, augers, and tractors as dangerous. They see these things as good and helpful and necessary. They seem to be saying, "How can anything so good for my crops and my cattle be a bad thing?"

Farmers put their energy, their thinking, and their money into those things that promise a financial return. There is no readily apparent financial incentive in farm safety, so it receives very little of their attention. Consequently, in response to calls for stricter legislation or policies, farmers stress that safety is adequately addressed, that they know safety is in their best interests, and that the government need not remind them of that fact. In other words, farmers believe that new legislation would merely hinder their business, not increase their concern for safety.

Safety Education—Obstacles and Limitations

There have been genuine efforts to try to address farm-safety issues in the last fifteen years, but the nature of the farm workplace does not lend itself to the application of strategies that have worked in other workplaces. Despite technological advances, "One still has to climb on top a granary to close the lid, and falls are a leading cause of injuries."[30] Information from the National Safety Council cites hurrying as the cause of many farm accidents—not taking the time to shut down the power take-off while oiling the chains, for example, or not taking the time to shut off the auger while unclogging it from a grain bin.

Safer equipment and better education have trimmed farm fatalities, but other industries have made greater strides. The manufacturing sector had four deaths per 100,000 workers in 1994. According to federal figures, 70,000 farm residents were injured on the job in 1993. Another 600 people died. That rate of 35 deaths per 100,000 workers made farming more hazardous than any other industry in 1993.[31]

Farmers and farm workers receive little formal safety training; most training is learned on the job, largely by trial and error and through word of mouth. Educating farmers about safety is expensive and time-consuming, and farmers seem reluctant to participate in educational forums. Only a small number attend Co-op, Farm Bureau, or National Farmer's Organization meetings. Individual training sessions offered at the time equipment or supplies are purchased seem unlikely.[32]

Although almost all county extension agents conduct some occupational safety and health programs annually, the time spent on such activities is minimal. For instance, a Wisconsin study of the efforts of eighty-nine county-level agriculture and agribusiness agents showed that:

> These activities occupied an average of 4.8 days per year. Most of the reported activities were group programs for the agricultural labor force that involved other extension agents and included the use of videotapes. The greatest barrier to more programming was lack of time on the part of both the agricultural work force and the agents. Most extension agents placed greater emphasis on training in how to work safely around hazards than on how to recognize and permanently correct hazards. Agents could be more effective with more time, better materials, and with more emphasis on hazard correction in workplace safety programs.[33]

Other federal agencies haven't been able to do much, either. The U.S. Department of Agriculture and its Extension Services, which help sponsor Farm Safety Week, have been subject to farm safety budget cuts in recent years. And the Consumer Product Safety Commission has no jurisdiction over farm equipment, although it monitors the use of all-terrain vehicles, which sometimes are used on farms. Critics decry inadequate safety regulation and say industry standards are only voluntary.[34]

It is unfortunate that the lack of adequate safety standards to protect people on the farm still exists. Moreover, there is a major discrepancy in resources allocated to farm safety compared with those in other dangerous occupations such as mining. Total federal spending for farm safety is less than 0.3 percent of annual federal occupational expenditures.[35]

Assignment of Age-Appropriate Tasks

Farm youth spend most of their waking hours in one of the nation's most dangerous workplaces. They routinely encounter hazards in farm chores. They must know what to do during busy seasons when adult family members may be preoccupied with other tasks. By understanding the stages of a child's growth and development, adults can help protect farm youth from needless harm. Farm accidents that involve children may seem unpredictable, stealing young lives at random, in situations that could not have been avoided. However, most farm accidents can be prevented. In these cases, the child acted in a way that was consistent with his or her developmental ability, and was injured or killed because of it.

Children who are physically and mentally ready for farm work should be allowed to perform only age-appropriate tasks. They should receive training in the proper way for the task, have their training continually reinforced, and be supervised by an adult as they work.[36] A pediatric emergency physician summed it up best, stating:

> Understanding the stages of a child's growth and development is important in assigning appropriate tasks and work. Parents need to make decisions regarding developmentally appropriate farm tasks. Sometimes this means a child cannot tackle the whole job, but may be able to handle smaller parts of it.[37]

Remember that, while children can be mature most of the time, they can quickly revert to childlike behavior. Parents should discuss farming risks with their children, citing personal experiences whenever possible. Children mimic their parents. That's why parents need to be good role models.[38]

Risks Associated with Development Stages

Farm parents expose their children to the greatest danger when they overestimate their children's ability to perform adult tasks on a farm. Children pass through several developmental stages, each carrying its own risks. Children aged 5 and under, in the preschool stage, are curious and without fear of the consequences of their actions. They have short memories and attention spans, especially when it involves obeying rules. They are impulsive and strong-willed. Children in this category are physically and mentally unprepared to evaluate the potential hazards on a farm. Common sense tells us that preschoolers have no place in work areas or livestock enclosures except in the arms of a responsible adult.

Grade-school children, ages 6 to 11, are slow to react and their reaction time is one-third that of a 17-year-old. They are less coordinated physically, with poor eye-to-hand coordination. They become easily bored with tasks, even after being initially enthusiastic about their job assignments. Assigning simple chores to early-grade-schoolers is a good way to teach them responsibility and provide experiences that give them a feeling of satisfaction and accomplishment. Working with farm equipment can often become repetitive, but it requires constant concentration. Grade-school children lack the maturity and coordination to work with large farm equipment. Instead, this age group is more suited to working with simple hand tools, feeding animals that require little contact, or cleaning out empty pens. This age group likes to explore and be creative. Parental attention and praise are very important. School-age children generally try to complete any assigned task to please their parents, even though the task may not be appropriate for them. They do not feel they can tell their parents "No" even if they themselves know the task is beyond their capability. This attitude results in many accidents. For example, a tired or weak child is more likely to become entangled in farm machinery.

Most rural adolescents participate in farm labor. Therefore, their injuries are commonly work-related. This age group is greatly influenced by peer pressure. Adolescents do not like to look like failures; they want to impress others and tend to believe they are immortal. Many risky behaviors, intended to impress, result in accidents.

Age should not be used as the sole measure of maturity. Some other variables that distinguish individuals are judgment and body size. Experience and observation help to improve judgment. A parent who takes proper safety precautions is the best teacher. Improper behaviors that parents perform automatically—for example, stepping over a moving power take-off device—will likely be copied by a child. There is a tremendous difference in the size of adolescents. Growth occurs in spurts and varies between siblings. A task that was appropriate for one son or daughter at age 12 may not be appropriate for his or her brother or sister at the same age.

Early teens in the 12-to-14 age group are a bit clumsy due to rapid physical growth. They often challenge authority and want to do things their own way, desiring to emulate older siblings. The greatest threat facing this age group is that they are unable to handle equipment and unable to recognize their limitations. At this age, children's tasks should be monitored and limited. This is also the time to reinforce the importance of farm safety devices.

High-school-aged teens from 15 to 18 are competitive, always in a hurry, with fluctuating emotions. They often cut corners and should therefore be continually reminded of safety precautions. They can handle adult tasks, but only after hours of supervision and only on well-maintained, safe equipment. A child's development, rather than age, is most important.

One study of young farmworkers found the majority of their injuries occurred during the first day on the job or the first time they performed the task after a long period of time. Parents need to take the time to repeat teaching of tasks and safety rules, especially after long lapses in performing jobs, such as seasonal tasks during planting or harvest. Teaching a few rules at a time and testing children before they actually perform the tasks also helps prevent injuries.[39]

Other Factors to Be Evaluated

Before allowing children to perform farm work, especially tasks involving operation of equipment, parents and farm managers should evaluate additional factors that may expose youth to increased risk for injury. The National Institute for Occupational Safety and Health (NIOSH) recommends that parents and farm managers carefully consider the following questions before assigning work tasks to youth:

- Does the youth possess the physical capacity to perform the task safely?
- Does the youth have sufficient and appropriate training and experience?
- Can the youth recognize and control potential hazards?
- Can the youth read and understand safety instructions in operating manuals and on signs?
- Is the youth mature enough to exercise good judgment?
- Has the youth been trained to cope with emergencies?
- Do work procedures accommodate physical characteristics of the youth?
- Is adult supervision available?[40]

Parents and grandparents should be sensitive to the development and needs of children. When assigning tasks to children, they need to consider a child's age, maturity level, attention span, and physical size. If children are not physically ready for a task (for example, if they are too short), they should not be asked to perform the task. They also need to assess the alertness level of children. If children have been in school all day, they may be fired. Fatigue will increase the likelihood of an accident. A little time spent evaluating children before assigning tasks may end up saving lives.[41]

The North American Guidelines for Children's Agricultural Tasks

In June 1999, a long-awaited publication was released to the public by the Marshfield Clinic. The North American Guidelines for Children's Agricultural Tasks (NAGCAT) was developed for use by farm parents and anyone else involved with children 16 years of age and under working in farm situations. Parents normally know best what tasks their children can handle, but sometimes they need help in assessing age-appropriate farm tasks. The guidelines contain practical recommendations that match a child's physical and mental development, regardless of age, to the requirements and dangers of 62 specific farm jobs. The guidelines are a checklist that helps adults match a child's physical and mental abilities with the requirements of these jobs. The guidelines were created by a task force of 150 persons from the United States, Canada, and Mexico, including farm parents, teen farmworkers, agricultural safety specialists, and child development professionals. For each job they provide a process parents can go through to evaluate the specific job their child is able to safely perform at his or her current developmental age.[42]

Following are some of the questions that parents are supposed to answer in determining whether a child, approximately 14 to 16 years old, should operate a hay cutter. Answering "No" to any of these questions means the child shouldn't perform the tasks:

1. Does the child have the ability to drive a tractor?
2. Does the child have the ability to hitch and unhitch the hay mower?
3. Does the child have the ability to connect and disconnect hydraulics?
4. Does the child have the ability to connect and disconnect a power takeoff device used to drive the mower?
5. Does the child have good peripheral vision? For example, looking straight ahead, can the child see your finger entering his or her field of vision at shoulder level?
6. Is the child able to stay focused on a task for 50 minutes?
7. Does the child have a quick reaction time?
8. Can the child recognize a hazard, solve the problem, and respond without getting upset?
9. Do you trust your child to do what is expected without being supervised?
10. Has an adult demonstrated cutting hay on-site, and has the child done the job about five times under close supervision?
11. Can an adult supervise as recommended?

The guidelines are not meant to be a foolproof formula, but they are a big step toward objectivity when assigning farm chores. Farm equipment is more powerful and complex than it was forty years ago. When something goes wrong, it often happens quickly, with deadly consequences.[43]

DANGERS POSED BY TRACTOR OPERATION

Rollover Mishaps

Tractor accidents are the most common cause of fatal farm injuries to children, followed by injuries from farm wagons and combines. Accidents involving farm animals account for only 2 percent of the deaths. Augers, tractors, and power take-offs are the most common causes of nonfatal injuries. Four to five times more boys than girls are involved in farm accidents.[44]

There are over 4 million tractors on American farms. Farming, as we know it, cannot exist without them. But at least 3 million tractors in the United States are more than ten years old and most were not equipped with ROPS (roll-over protection structure) and seat belts at the time of sale.

Older tractors often are used in situations typically associated with tractor rollover accidents, such as mowing the road ditch area, using a front-end loader, and hauling fallen trees.

Perhaps the most frequent cause of fatal accidents for all age groups is tractor rollovers. Once a multiton tractor hits a hole and starts to tip over, nothing will stop it, and it is difficult for the operator to jump free. Tractor manufacturers agreed as early as 1985 to begin selling only machines with rollover protection, but hundreds of thousands remain in use without the structures. Many also lack seat belts. In fact, a recent survey by the Centers for Disease Control and Prevention found that although almost 40 percent of tractors in use in Iowa feature rollover protection structures, an estimated 156,000 tractors do not. Two-thirds of them are used more than 100 hours annually.

A modern tractor usually weighs more than ten tons. When it rolls over onto a person, the result is usually a fatality. Even an older-model tractor weighs several thousand pounds, more than enough weight to cause massive internal damage to a person's body. These same older models are also the ones most likely to have a higher center of gravity, a narrow tricycle style front-end, and most dangerously, no rollover protective structure.[45]

Use Seat Belts and Retrofit Older Tractors

ROPS affords some safety during tractor overturns, but operators need more protection. All operators of tractors equipped with ROPS must wear seat belts. Without a seat belt, the operator will not be confined to the protective zone. During an overturn, the operator could be thrown from the protected area and crushed by the tractor, or even the rollover protective structure itself, if the operator is not wearing a seat belt.

However, one should never use seat belts on a tractor without ROPS. In this case, the operator has no chance of survival because the seat belt will keep the operator in the cab as the tractor rolls over and crushes the individual. It is not certain whether the operator would be thrown clear from the tractor if seat belts were not worn, but that remains the operator's only chance of survival.[46]

Retrofit Older Tractors

Protective structures such as rollover cages and bars have been standard equipment on most tractors since the mid-1970s and can be easily fitted on older models. But many veteran farmers, especially those who have never rolled over, resist the $300 to $500 cost for ROPS. Retrofitting can pose a difficult decision because its cost for an older tractor can exceed the machine's actual value. However, the true cost is in the lives that could be saved, not the least of whom are children and adolescents.[47]

When a farmer told David Baker, University of Missouri Extension safety specialist, that a rollover bar for his tractor would cost too much, Baker replied, "We're not trying to save the tractor. What's the value of the person operating it?" The best way to prevent tractor rollovers involving young persons is to prohibit them from operating older models, high risk tractors.

Tractors also should be equipped with master shields. Sometimes, farmers remove master shields to work on their tractors and don't replace them. This can put both mature and youthful operators at even greater risk for injury from a power take-off (PTO).[48]

Roadway Mishaps

Because a tractor may be operated on public roadways, it is subject to all highway regulations, except that a driver's license is not required. This, in the writer's opinion, is a misguided abdication of public safety responsibility resulting from the ingrained farm culture on the part of farmers and farm lobbyists. Consequently, as a result of their misguided thinking, lives of children and adolescents are placed in jeopardy. No other vehicles can be operated by minors without licensing requirements attesting to the operator's driving competence. The exclusion of tractor operation from licensing requirements has turned out to be a Pyrrhic victory for antiregulation advocates, as the toll of children and adolescents injured or killed on the roadways continues to mount.

Some tractor accidents can be attributed to elderly operators who do not possess quick enough reaction times. Others can be traced to children driving large tractors on which they can't quite reach the pedals. Compounding the situation is the fact that tractor accidents are almost never witnessed or investigated, and no legal requirements exist for their operation by family members of any age.

Tractor Operation by Children—Misguided Perceptions

As discussed earlier, farm parents' safety perceptions often conflict with their behavior, which turns out to jeopardize the safety of their children. This is clearly the case when grade-school-age children and young teenagers are permitted to drive tractors despite not being developmentally mature enough to handle physical and cognitive demands inherent in this farm task. Clearly, many rural youth are assigned chores involving tractors at an inappropriately early age. Numerous empirical studies and surveys unanimously support this conclusion.

According to the results of a survey conducted by *Successful Farming* magazine, by the time farm boys reach 10 to 12 years of age, 65 percent are operating tractors by themselves, and nearly 30 percent are operators as early as 7 to 9 years of age, since licensure is not required.[49]

A questionnaire was developed to investigate the behavioral determinants of tractor safety for youth and administered to 235 Future Farmers of America (FFA) students from ten schools in Illinois. Nearly one-third of the respondents (31.3 percent) began operating a tractor at age 8 years or younger; more than one-half (60.7 percent) at or before 10 years of age, and nearly three-fourths (72 percent) of the respondents began driving a tractor at or before age 11. The average mean age at onset of tractor operation was 9.8 years.

Over two-thirds (67.4 percent) of the respondents indicated that they frequently operate tractors. More than two-thirds (67.3 percent) operate tractors without supervision; only 5.1 percent operate these huge vehicles only under direct adult supervision. The range of tractors operated was between one and thirty tractors, with a mean of five tractors being operated (5.2); the mode was two tractors. More than 85 percent of the respondents operate more than one tractor. Nearly three-fourths of the students operate six or fewer machines.

When asked about the number of tractors operated that were equipped with ROPS, over one-third (38.6 percent) indicated that none of the tractors that they drove had seat belts. An additional 15.5 percent indicated that they operated only tractors equipped with seat belts. Regarding their behavioral intentions, nearly 52 percent indicated the intention to keep extra riders off tractors they operate; however, only 34 percent stated that they do not plan to be an extra rider on tractors. Less than one-third (29 percent) intend to use seat belts on tractors equipped with ROPS.

These responses are particularly disappointing considering, the lifesaving potential of the ROPS/seat belt combination. There have been no documented cases of tractor rollover fatalities when seat belts have been used in conjunction with ROPS.[50]

Farm Parents' Perceptions of Children's Exposure to Hazards

One significant study explored behavioral intentions and factors influencing those intentions of Wisconsin dairy farmers to allow their children younger than 14 years to: (a) drive a tractor with more than 20 horsepower; (b) be a second rider on a tractor without a cab that is driven by the father; and (c) be within five feet of the hind legs of a dairy cow. There were a total of 3,448 children (not limited to younger than 14 years) reported by the 1,151 study participants. When asked to indicate their intentions regarding their children who were younger than 14 years on a scale of very likely (+1) very unlikely (+7), farmers reported they were quite likely to allow children 10 to 14 years old to drive a tractor and less likely to allow a child near a dairy cow or be an extra rider on a tractor without a cab. None of these hazardous activities would be "unlikely" to occur. The primary influence on farm fathers' attitudes for two of the three behaviors was a desire for children to gain work experience in farming. There is ample evidence in the lay farm press that supports the influence family farmers exert over their children's roles on the farm, along with the tendency to gradually pass farm ownership and operating styles to the younger generation. Desire for children to develop a strong work ethic and build self-confidence also are important beliefs of farm fathers. Attributes of hard work and personal integrity are also highly valued.[51]

Another survey involved the participation of 5,870 farms where children were allowed to operate tractors. Parents were asked the age at which children were first allowed to do so. Responses ranged from 4 years to 16 years, with an average age of 11 years. Approximately three-quarters (78 percent) reported children operating tractors by age 12, and over 90 percent by age 14. Respondents also indicated that most of the training prior to operation was provided by the children's parents.

The fact that young children are still operating tractors on Indiana farms suggests that traditional tractor safety programs designed for high school agricultural education programs may occur too late to be effective intervention strategies. Many Indiana farm children begin operating tractors before they are eligible (by age) to participate in these traditional tractor safety programs. This is corroborated by the number of respondents who reported that most of the tractor safety education children received prior to operating a tractor, if any, was provided by the parents. These results also suggest that while more emphasis should be placed on educating parents about the risks associated with young operators, programs must also focus on improving parents' ability to provide adequate safety training. Considering that tractors and machinery consistently rank as the leading cause of childhood farm work-related fatalities, the high number of young children riding on and operating tractors presents a serious challenge to injury prevention efforts.[52]

The Gap between Words and Deeds

The following two studies illustrate the ambivalence felt by parents regarding the age at which their children should be allowed to drive tractors and operate dangerous farm machinery. In one survey, researchers revealed the discrepancy in what parents believe about children using farm machinery and what they actually practice on the farm. Seventy-nine percent of parents believed it was acceptable to let children drive a tractor, but 90 percent were actually allowing their 7-to-9-year-old children to ride. Thirteen percent believed 7-to-9-year-olds should operate tractors, yet 29 percent of 7-to-9-year-olds operated tractors. Sixteen percent thought children 7 to 9 shouldn't be within ten feet of rotating machinery, but 27 percent were allowing the behavior.[53]

In the second study, more than a quarter of the adult farmers participating in a national survey allowed their 7-to-8-year-old children to drive tractors even though only 10 percent of the 342 respondents felt children in that age group should be allowed to operate a tractor. But 27 percent of the parents actually let their 7- or 8-year-olds drive tractors. Also, 65 percent of the parents said it was all right to let children younger than seven ride on tractors and other farm equipment with their parents. But in practice, 83 percent of the parents admitted letting children younger than seven ride tractors. The majority of the respondents said their children were safe riding a tractor because the parents are in control of the situation. But it is that false sense of security that leads to unnecessary accidents involving farm children.[54] Moreover, there is an undercount of tractor-rollover-related fatalities because persons less than 16 years of age are not included in the database used to derive work-related fatalities in agriculture.[55]

Much new farm machinery is quite easy to operate when everything is going as planned, so it is tempting to believe that a youngster can handle this equipment. The problems occur when something unexpected happens; children do not have the experience to adjust and make good decisions in unforeseen circumstances. While it is likely that driving a tractor influences physical and psychological development of children in a positive manner, the reality that a child may be placed into an adult, hazardous work situation cannot be ignored.

Hazards Posed by Augers and Power Take-Offs

While tractors are responsible for a major portion of deaths among farm children, augers and power take-offs appear to be responsible for the most severe, nonfatal accidents. These injuries tend to be extremely disfiguring and incapacitating. An auger is a screw device in a cylinder designed to move corn and grain against gravity. Material within an auger moves at a rate of 210 cm/second; thus, an arm or leg caught in an auger will move 150 centimeters before the injured person can react. Due to the rotational motion of augers and power take-off shafts, body parts can be rapidly entangled, resulting in amputation and massive crushing injuries. The limb literally becomes screwed into the machine. Because these injuries tend to result in major amputations, prosthetic fitting is often made quite difficult.

Toddlers are often intrigued by the moving material in the auger and may reach into the auger without knowing the probable consequences. Older children often try to unclog the machine without first turning it off and are thus injured. Many of these injuries, apparently, are the result of the common practice of removing protective covers from these devices, and often more than 50 percent of augers have their safety devices removed prior to being operated. Like tractor-related injuries, auger injuries occur equally in all age groups. The severe amputations that often result require an average length of hospital stay of 16.3 days and multiple reconstructive surgical procedures.[56]

A Mayo Clinic study investigated injuries to eighty-seven farm children during the November 1974–July 1985 period. Thirty-seven injuries were caused by corn augers, which move corn up into a storage bin. The highest incidence of permanently disabling injuries came from the augers and power take-offs, devices that allow implements to be attached and driven by a tractor engine.[57]

Another study demonstrated the most common times for auger-related injuries are right before lunch, in the middle of the afternoon, and right before dinner. These are times when the operator is tired, anxious to take a break, and possibly loses his or her concentration.[58]

Power take-offs are used to transmit power from tractors to implements such as grinders and mowers. Their shafts operate at speeds of 9 to 17 revolutions per second. An unguarded shaft can wrap clothing, shoelaces, or even part of a body around it at a rate of nearly 7 feet per second. Because an average human takes at least half a second to react, it is often too late by the time the operator realizes what's happening. Power take-off injuries can be prevented by shields that are standard parts of the equipment. The shields on older take-off units offered only partial protection, but newer models are fully shielded. Prices vary, but farmers could replace outdated shields for as little as $25. Instead, many farmers remove the shields. Without the guards in place, a worker's limb, hair, or clothing are more likely to be caught, causing serious injury or death. Most power take-off (PTO) accidents can be prevented by keeping machine guards in place and taking care to keep a safe distance from the machinery.

During harvest, power take-offs are often used to spin augers, which lift grain into storage bins the same way that drill bits expel wood shavings from a hole. The awesome power of power take-offs was illustrated in the highly publicized case of John Thompson, an 18-year-old North Dakotan, whose arms were torn from his body and reattached at a Minneapolis hospital in January, 1992.

His chore one early January afternoon was to unload barley from a dump truck, using an auger that carried grain to a bin as a conveyor belt would. A tractor engine supplied the power. Connecting the engine to the auger was a flat, one and one-half inch power take-off bar. As the bar spun, the auger turned. While playing with one of the family dogs, he stumbled and, in a split second, fell into the power take-off. Although his arms were reattached by seven hours of microsurgery, the prognosis was one of permanent disability. Thompson has the use of his arms, but only time and more operations will determine if his hands will be fully functional. John's father had removed and failed to replace the protective shield on the auger.[59]

Musculoskeletal Disorders

Another area of concern involving farm children and adolescents is work-related musculoskeletal disorders (WMSD) that occur when there is a mismatch between the physical requirements of the job and the physical capacity of the human body. More than 100 different injuries can result from repetitive motions that produce wear and tear on the body. Back pain, wrist tendonitis and carpal tunnel syndrome may all stem from work-related overuse. Specific risk factors associated with WMSDs include repetitive motion, heavy lifting, forceful exertion, contact stress, vibration, awkward posture, and rapid hand and wrist movement.

Despite the ongoing changes in the scale of farming operations and the types of machinery in use, very little has changed about the way work is performed by most farm workers or in tasks—harvesting, weeding, irrigating, and so forth—that can generate back injuries and/or musculoskeletal disorders. These tasks are still common in all agricultural field work. Agricultural field work continues to be demanding, to be performed in stooped postures, to require lifting, carrying, and handling of significant weights in awkward positions, and often to involve repetitive, damaging hand work. This work summarizes the kinds of risk factors consistently linked to musculoskeletal disorders, and which can be successfully addressed through ergonomic interventions.[60]

The Ergonomic Solution

Ergonomics is the science of designing jobs, selecting tools, and modifying work methods to better fit workers' capabilities and prevent injury. Ergonomic principles are based on a combination of science and engineering and a thorough understanding of human capabilities and limitations. When these principles are applied to the design of a job, task, process, or procedure, the incidence and severity of musculoskeletal injuries decrease.

Many characteristics of farm work are typical for ergonomic factors associated with an increased risk for musculoskeletal trauma and degenerative disorders. Poor ergonomic design is linked with increased traumatic injury, which is common in agriculture. Conditions in farming are similar to those in work settings that have already successfully applied ergonomic principles to hazard reduction. Ergonomically reengineering work procedures to eliminate hazards produce permanent and meaningful reductions in musculoskeletal symptoms and injuries. These innovations can reduce the large number of sprain/strain injuries and overexertion injuries which may develop into long-term work-related musculoskeletal disorders by reducing risk factors with low-cost, non-labor-displacing measures.[61] Unfortunately, any comprehensive involvement by the federal government, which would be essential in producing a meaningful approach vis-à-vis ergonomic programs has been indefinitely shelved when the Congress succumbed to political pressures and defeated proposed funding legislation.[62]

Noise-Induced Hearing Loss

Noise is the leading cause of hearing damage in 28 million Americans in all walks of life. While anyone can be at risk for noise-induced hearing loss in the workplace, agricultural workers have higher exposure to dangerous levels of noise. Mechanization, combined with long hours, brings about extensive noise exposure for people who work on farms. Large and powerful machinery is a principal source of noise exposure at levels likely to damage human hearing. Noise may reach these levels in fields where tractors and other types of machinery are used and in barns where feed mills, ventilating fans, pumps, and animals are the major sources of it. Unless some type of noise-control measures are utilized, permanent hearing loss may result. Continued exposure to noise above 85 decibels over time will cause hearing loss.

The hearing damage depends mainly on how loud the noise is and the duration of exposure to it. The frequency, or pitch, may also be a factor, with high-pitched sounds being more likely to cause hearing impairment than low-pitched ones. Farmers and farmworkers need to understand what constitutes dangerous noise conditions. Permanent hearing damage will, in turn, cause other health and safety problems such as an inability to recognize warning signals, which may create a serious situation in the farm workplace.[63]

Noise-induced hearing loss seldom involves total hearing loss or deafness. However, the damage cannot be repaired, and hearing aids can do little good. Constant exposure to noise affects the inner ear. The first sign of hearing damage is an inability to hear higher-pitched sounds. With continued exposure to noise, the ability to tell musical tones apart becomes impossible. Eventually, with continual exposure to excess noise, the ability to hear normal conversation is impaired.

The greatest risk to farmers is spending prolonged periods being exposed to normal farm noise that often is slight to moderately higher than the acceptable levels. Tractors, grinders, augers, chain saws, lawn mowers, and even squealing pigs have decibel levels that exceed 90. It is this prolonged exposure to farm noises that often causes hearing loss for farmers. Noise created by animals is not easily controlled by engineering measures, and, in confinement barns or other facilities where animal noise levels are unacceptable, hearing protection devices must be used, thus effectively reducing noise levels by 10 to 15 decibels.[64]

Teenagers who work on farms are much more likely than others to develop hearing loss, apparently as a result of spending time around noisy machinery such as tractors and combines. Researchers interviewed and tested 872 vocational agriculture students at twelve high schools in the farm country of central Wisconsin. Some of the students worked more than forty hours a week on a farm; others lived in town and had no direct exposure to farm labor. The rate of hearing loss was about twice as high in the students who spent a lot of time working on a farm, as compared with those who didn't. The results were adjusted to account for the possible effects of age, sex, family history of hearing loss, and use of amplified music, snowmobiles or motorcycles.

The proportion of students with evidence of hearing loss in at least one ear at either high or low frequencies was 71 percent for those living and working on a farm; 74 percent for those working on a farm but living elsewhere; 36

percent for those living on a farm but not working there, and 46 percent for those reporting little or no exposure to farm work. The results, combined with reports of increased hearing loss in adult farmers, suggest that adult hearing loss may begin in childhood. As in previous studies, hearing loss was much more common in the left ear than in the right. That is because the left ear is more likely to be exposed to engine noise, since drivers habitually look over their right shoulder, partially shielding the right ear. Many males, who operated tractors, harvesters, and other equipment, had the hearing of 50-year-olds. Females, who had less exposure to the machinery noise, were found to have better hearing. Economic pressures could increase the exposure of children to noisy and hazardous farm machinery, the study concluded, since teen-age children of farmers are increasingly called upon to do jobs previously handled by hired workers.[65]

Even more alarming is the early age at which such hearing losses can begin. There is evidence of early, noise-induced hearing losses among high-school, vocational-agriculture students, and, in one instance, 15 percent to 20 percent of freshmen entering a predominantly rural university had impaired hearing. Another study estimated that one-fourth of the male farming population incurs a significant hearing handicap by age 30, and half by age 50. Currently, intervention programs to educate agricultural workers about the risks of noise exposure have been few and far between. Farmers, therefore, lack information on noise hazards, warning signs of hearing impairment, and appropriate preventive measures. Studies indicate that only 10 percent to 42 percent of farmers report using hearing protectors around farm noise; of those who do, the majority use them only 20 percent or less of the time. Pilot hearing conservation programs in farm communities have resulted in significant increases in farmers' use of protective devices, indicating that farmers are willing to implement preventive measures when educated and motivated to do so.[66]

Noise-induced hearing loss knows no age discrimination; older workers, as well as teenagers, have suffered hearing loss from farm-related activities. What can be done to prevent the development of noise-induced hearing loss among farmworkers? Blocking noise can lower the potential for hearing losses. This includes simple machinery maintenance techniques such as keeping all equipment well-lubricated, properly adjusted, and maintained. Maintenance can increase the life span of equipment, reduce down time, create safer working conditions, and reduce noise. Limiting exposure in a noisy area reduces the risk of hearing damage. In addition, fully insulated tractor cabs are now available for most popular makes of tractors. The use of acoustic materials has allowed many manufacturers to produce a cab that meets recommended noise levels.

Ear Protection

If other means of noise reduction cannot reduce noise to acceptable levels, ear protection should be worn. The two basic types of protection devices are earmuffs and earplugs. There are excellent choices in design of these designs on the market, depending on the workers' preference and the working conditions. Both earmuffs and earplugs will effectively reduce the level of noise entering the ear, but will still allow a worker to hear equipment running. Even workers who have suffered some hearing loss can save whatever they have left with consistent use of earplugs or muffs when working around noisy equipment.[67]

As we have seen, farmworkers as a group are more geographically spread than workers in other industries and are often fiercely independent. To make matters worse, a large portion of the farm labor force is excluded from the hearing conservation programs mandated by the Occupational Safety and Health Administration for the rest of American industry. It has been pointed out that information can best be disseminated to farmworkers through agencies and associations with which they commonly deal. Migrant farmworkers are most difficult to reach. Because of the presence of noise in farm operations, information on prevention of noise-induced hearing loss should be given a prominent place in materials that farmers read. Use of hearing protectors should be actively promoted, and these devices should be made readily available. It may be necessary for local health departments to take the lead in this area. Special efforts need to be directed toward protecting children who are involved in farm work, since many have experienced hearing losses by age 17. The list of farm machinery capable of producing noise-induced hearing loss is endless. Many manufacturers of farm equipment are now designing their equipment to reduce noise. However, the nature of farm equipment and the manner in which it is used, will continue to make noise a problem area for quite some time.[68]

Dangers Posed by Farm Animals

Youngsters are often fascinated with animals and enjoy the adventure of exploration. Unfortunately, this can be a disastrous combination on farms and ranches. Large animals account for many injuries, particularly to children. The numbers vary, depending on the region and emphasis on livestock production. Data from Iowa indicates animals were the number one cause of injuries to children 19 years and younger in five out of seven years (1990–1996). Likewise, in North Dakota, animals have been the leading cause of farm-related injuries to children under the age of 18. Most children are injured doing tasks beyond their developmental capabilities. The child must be told why he or she shouldn't go into the bull's pen without someone around or why Dad is working on the other side of the livestock chute. Early teenagers face a great risk. Starting at age 12 to 14, youth start acting as if they know everything, and they feel invincible. It may also be a time when adult supervision of farm chores is decreased. When something goes wrong—when an animal becomes cross—the early adolescent may not be able to react. It is all based on the child's ability to handle a situation. Parents should not take for granted that the child is ready for the activity just because he or she grew up on a farm.[69]

Large animals tend to cooperate better when they're handled with knowledge and skill. It is important to know how animals perceive and react to the world around them. Understanding cattle behavior is critical for anyone who moves, handles or loads cattle. Animal scientists point to two very important concepts: the flight zone and point of balance.

The flight zone is the space surrounding an animal or group of animals. If an animal's flight zone is entered, it will move away until it feels safe. If a person stops or retreats from the flight zone, the animal usually stops moving away. The size of an animal's flight zone varies with the type of animal, the angle and speed of the handler's approach, the animal's familiarity with the handler, whether the animal sees or hears the person approaching, whether the animal is wild or tame, and the animal's recent experience. An animal's point of balance is related to its flight zone. The shoulder is the point of balance for most cattle. If approached in front of the point of balance, the animal moves backward. Approaching from behind the point makes the animal move forward. Dennis Murphy, Penn State farm safety specialist, relays this guide to handling animals:

- Cattle generally are color-blind and have poor depth perception, making them extremely sensitive to contrasts. A shadow across a walkway may look like a deep hole to the animal, making it balk. This is often why cattle often hesitate when passing through unfamiliar gates, barn doors, or chutes.
- Cattle have good hearing and will try to move away from the source of unfamiliar or unpleasant noise. They are calmest when surrounded by familiar sounds.
- Animals draw on experience when reacting to a situation. An animal that has been chased, slapped, kicked, hit, or otherwise mistreated will fear humans.
- Plan the process of moving animals before trying it.
- To reduce risk in handling and treating livestock, use a well-built restraining chute.[70]

Many people fail to realize the dangers of working with farm animals. One out of every five injuries on the farm involves animals. Injuries caused by animals are the second leading cause of farm accidents. The only good news is that injuries caused by livestock are less likely to be fatal. Injuries caused by animals include bites, kicks, or getting pinned between the animal and a fixed object. Horse-related injuries are most commonly caused outside of pens, in lanes, and along public roads.

The best way to avoid livestock injuries is to understand animal behavior. Livestock patterns should be recognized, and youth should be taught these patterns. Domesticated animals living under fairly uniform conditions will form habits. Habits are also caused by regular changes in environmental conditions, such as when daylight turns to darkness. Animals are most active at the time of greatest change, such as at dawn or dusk. They will be least active either in the middle of the day or the middle of the night.

Domesticated animals have strong maternal instincts. Most animals are docile during pregnancy, but change abruptly after giving birth. For example, a sow at the end of gestation may begin nesting, and after birth, will exhibit maternal tendencies and may become aggressive if crowded in a small area. Experienced farmers may recognize aggressive behaviors as maternal tendencies, even before nest building begins. However, persons new to a livestock operation, such as children, may not be able to identify and anticipate the animal's aggressive behavior. When working around animals, children should be encouraged to:

- Be calm, move slowly, and avoid loud noises.
- Wear steel-toed shoes.
- Approach large animals at the shoulder, not at the hind legs.
- Children should avoid animals with newborns.
- Children should avoid stallions, bulls, rams, and boars.
- Always have an escape route when working with animals in close quarters.
- Wear helmets when riding horses.[71]

NOTES

1. Megan Finnerly, "Education, Common Sense Can Be Protection," *Intelligencer Journal* 6 July 2000: A-6.

2. Andrew Conte, "Teens in the Workforce: Teen Farm Workers' Jobs Riskiest," *Cincinnati Post,* 15 March 2000, l.

3. "Lack of Knowledge Makes It Difficult to Track Children, Injuries in Agriculture," *BNA Employment Policy & Law Daily,* 26 March, 1998.

4. These data, from the Survey of Occupational Injuries and Illnesses, are collected from a sample of records employers with eleven or more workers must complete to report any work-related injury or illness requiring more than first aid.

5. These data are collected through the National Electric Surveillance System, which collects information on emergency room visits from a nationally representative sample of hospitals.

6. "Childhood Work-Related Agricultural Fatalities—Minnesota, 1994–1997," *Morbidity and Mortality Weekly Report,* 48(16) (30 April 30 1999): 332–335.

7. Isabel Wilkerson, "Farms, Deadliest Workplace, Taking the Lives of Children," *The New York Times,* 26 September 1988, A1.

8. *Child Labor in Agriculture: Changes Needed to Better Protect Health and Educational Opportunities,* (Washington, DC: U.S. General Accounting Office, August, 1998) 28.

9. "Youth Agricultural Work-Related Injuries Treated in Emergency Departments—United States, October 1995–September 1997, *Morbidity and Mortality Weekly Report,* 47(35) (11 September 1998): 734–736.

10. Paul C. Rosenblatt and Paul Lasley, "Perspective on Farm Accident Statistics," *The Journal of Public Health*, 7(1) (Winter 1999): 52–59.

11. National Agricultural Statistics Service, *1998 Childhood Agricultural Injuries*, 6 October 1999.

12. Kit Miniclier, "Eaton Boy, 10, Driving Car to Farm Chores, Dies in Crash." *Denver Post*, 20 July 1999, B-01; Table. *Workers Age 19 Years and Younger: Fatal Occupational Injuries to Workers Age 19 Years and Younger by Selected Characteristics, 1992–2000* (Washington, DC: U.S. Department of Labor, Census of Fatal Occupational Injuries; in Cooperation with State and Federal Agencies, 2000), 10.

13. John Shutske, "How Old Should Kids Be to Drive a Tractor?" *Farm Safety & Health Digest* (October, 1999): 1.

14. P. Wagner Jay, "Dangerous Harvest: Farm Safety a Top Concern in Fall '93," *Des Moines Register*, 31 October 1993, 1.

15. Marilyn Affleck, "Young Farmers' Viewpoint on Farm Safety," *Farm Safety News*, n.d.

16. "Work Deaths Include Some Under-Fives." *The Dominion* (Wellington) 28 August 1988, 16.

17. Rebecca Pilcher, "Children Learn about Farm Safety at Washington County Day Camp," *Arkansas Democrat-Gazette*, 20 June 1999, B1.

18. Grant Madsen, "Class Demonstrates Dangers of Working With Farm Equipment," *Salt Lake Tribune*, 19 March 1999, B8.

19. Ann Franzenburg and Cheryl Tevis, "A New Day Dawns for Farm Safety: Ten Years of Triumph and Tragedy," *Successful Farming*, February 1997, 31.

20. Jake Bleed, "Bill Would Allow Younger Detasselers," *Omaha World Herald*, 20 April 2001, 7.

21. "Detasselers' Illness Not Result of Pesticide Misuse," *The State Journal Register* (Bloomington, IL), 10 August 1996, 7.

22. Wilkerson, "Farms, Deadliest Workplace."

23. "Ohio Farm Bureau Wages Education on Safety Issues." *PR Newswire*, 24 August 1994.

24. "Regulation of Employment of Young People in Agriculture, *American Farm Bureau 107th Congress Backgrounder*, 14 May 2001.

25. T.W. Kelsey, "The Agrarian Myth and Policy Responses to Farm Safety," *American Journal of Public Health* (July 1994): 1171–1177.

26. C.L. Connon, E. Freund, and J.K. Ehlers, "The Occupational Health Nurses in Agricultural Communities." *AAOHN Journal*, 41(9) 1993: 422–428.

27. Kim Witte , et al., "Preventing Tractor-Related Injuries and Deaths in Rural Populations: Using a Persuasive Health Message Framework in Formative Evaluation Research." *International Quarterly of Community Health Education*, 13 (3) (1992–1993): 219–251.

28. C. Hawk, J. Gay, and K.J. Donham, "Rural Youth Disability Prevention Project Survey: Results from 169 Iowa Farm Fatalities," *Journal of Rural Health*, 7(2) (1991): 170–179.

29. A. Rowntree Darragh, L. Stallones, P. L Sample, and K. Sweitzer, "Perceptions of Farm Hazards and Personal Safety Behavior among Adolescent Farmworkers," *Journal of Agricultural Safety and Health*, Special Issue (1) (1998): 159–169.

30. John Everly, "Teens Teach Farm Safety to Youngsters; Dangerous Chores: Cascade Students Help Raise Awareness of Key Precautions," *Telegraph Herald*, (Dubuque, IA), 23 September 2000, 1.

31. Brian Williams, "Harvest Times the Perfect Time for Farm Safety, Health Week," *Columbus Dispatch,* 12 September 1995, 2D.

32. Jack L. Runyon, " A Review of Farm Accident Data Sources and Research: Background," *National Safety Database,* October 1993.

33. Larry J. Chapman, Ronald T. Schuler, Cheryl A. Sjkolass, and Terry L. Wilkinson, "Agricultural Work Safety Efforts by Wisconsin Extension Agricultural Agents," *The Journal of Rural Health,* 11(4) (Fall 1995): 295–304.

34. D.J. Murphy, N.E. Kiernan, and L.J. Chapman, "An Occupational Health and Safety Intervention Research Agenda for Production Agriculture: Does Safety Education Work?" *American Journal of Industrial Medicine* (4) (29 April 1996): 392–396.

35. Andrew Blum, "The Bitter Harvest; Lawyers Struggle to Make Farming the Country's Most Dangerous Work, Safer," *The National Law Journal,* 31 October 1988: 1.

36. Nancy Templeman, "Keeping Kids Safe on the Farm," *Roanoke Times & World News,* 18 September 1997, 2.

37. Charles A. Jennisen, "The *Register*'s Readers Say Dole Out Farm Duties Carefully," *Des Moines Register,* 2 June 1999, 12.

38. Robert E. Leiby and David L. Dunbar, "Make Farms Safe; Watch for Children; Adults Must Be Good Role Models, Firm Against Riding Along on Tractors," *The Morning Call* (Allentown, PA), 9 September 1996, B8.

39. "Knowing How Old Is Old Enough Can Save Kids' Lives, Says Progressive Farmer," *PR Newswire* 4 June 1996.

40. "Childhood Work-Related Agricultural Fatalities—Minnesota, 1994–1997," *Morbidity and Mortality Weekly Report,* 48(16) (30 April 1999): 332–335.

41. Thomas L. Bean and Jennifer Wojtowicz, "Farm Safety for Children: What Job Is Right for My Child?" *Fact Sheet: Ohio State University Extension, AEX-99.1,* 1992.

42. "Guidelines for Children's Tasks Culled from Study," *The Pantagraph* (Bloomington, Il) 19 November 1999, C1.

43. Rick Barrett, "Quiz to See If a Child Can Handle a Job," *Wisconsin State Journal,* 27 September 1999, 3A.

44. J.A. Swanson, M.I. Sachs, K.A. Dahlgren, et al, "Accidental Farm Injuries in Children," *American Journal of Disabilities of Children,* 141(12) (1987): 1276–1279.

45. F.P. Rivara, "Fatal and Nonfatal Farm Injuries to Children and Adolescents in the United States," *Pediatrics* 76 (1985): 567–573.

46. R.B. Smith, "Perils in the Fields," *Occupational Health & Safety* 62(5) (1993): 780.

47. Victor Volland, "Durbin Seeks Answers on Farm Danger," *St. Louis Post-Dispatch* 28 July 1992, 8A.

48. "Use of Rollover Protective Structures—Iowa, Kentucky, New York, and Ohio, 1992–1997, *Morbidity and Mortality Weekly Report,* 46(36) (12 September 1997): 842.

49. C. Tevis and C. Finck, "We Kill Too Many Farm Kids." *Successful Farming* 87(3) (1989): 18A–18P.

50. B. Campbell, "Of primary concern, it's getting safer, but farming is still the most dangerous industry," *American Agriculturist* 187(9): 22–23.

51. Barbara C. Lee, Louise S. Jenkins, and James D. Westaby," Factors Influencing Exposure of Children to Major Hazards on Family Farms," *The Journal of Rural Health,* 13(3) (Summer 1997): 206–215.

52. S.A. Freeman, S.D. Whitman, and R.L. Tormoehlen, "Baseline Childhood Farm Safety Data for Indiana." *Journal of Agricultural Safety and Health*, 4(2) (1998): 119–130.

53. David A. Bird, "Averting the Tragedy: Children's Farm Accidents," *Journal of Extension*, 31(4) (Winter 1993): n.p.

54. "Heartland Horizons Study Probes Risk to Farm Children," *BC Cycle* (23 March 1989).

55. "Public Health Focus: Effectiveness of Rollover Protective Structures for Preventing Injuries Associated with Agricultural Tractors," *Morbidity and Mortality Weekly Report*, 42(3) (29 January 1993): 57.

56. Raymond C. Bredfeldt, Ann E. Heath, Jessie A. Junker, and Georgia L. Cuddeback, "Childhood Farm Injuries: A Neglected Aspect of Patient and Resident Education," *Family Medicine* 21(3) (1989): 218.

57. Associated Press, "Children Working on Farms Are Found at Risk for Injury," *New York Times*, 8 December 1987, A18.

58. "ISU Study Shows Need for Grain Auger Safety," *Extension News* (Iowa State University), 28 August 1998, n.p.

59. Sharon Schmickle, "Bucolic Image Belies Farm Accident Rate; Each Year, 1 in 7 Farms Is Scene of Serious Injury," *Minneapolis Star-Tribune*, 18 January 1992, 1A.

60. OSHA, "Preventing Work-Related Musculoskeletal Disorders," February, 1999.

61. T.J. Stobbe, "Occupational Ergonomics and Injury Prevention," *Journal of Occupational Medicine* 11(3) (July–September 1996): 531–543.

62. Ibid.

63. Joe Turco, "Deafening Sound—Listen Up While You Can," *Statewide Perspective* 17 November 2000.

64. "Farm Safety—Taking Care of Your Health-Hearing," Adapted from the *New Brunswick Farm Safety Committee Brochure*, n.d.

65. Don Colburn, "Teenaged Farm Workers Suffer Hearing Losses," *Washington Post*, 6 January 1989, Z5.

66. J.K. Ehlers. C. Connon, C.L. Themann, J.R. Myers and T. Ballard, "Health and Safety Hazards Associated With Farming," *AAOHN Journal* 41(9) (1993): 414–421.

67. Joyce Price, "2 Groups Shout a Warning about Noise Pollution" *Washington Times*, 8 January, 1990, A3.

68. Clifton D. Crutchfield and Steven T. Sparks," Effects of Noise and Vibrations on Farm Workers," *Journal of Occupational Medicine: State of the Art Reviews* 6(3) (July–September 1991): 362.

69. Lori Gilmore, "Caution: Children at Work, Home and Play," *The Angus Journal*, September 1998.

70. Robert E. Leiby and David L. Dunbar, "Wise Farmers Don't Shrink from Animal Psychology," *The Morning Call* (Allentown, PA), 23 August 1995, B7.

71. Farm Safety Association, "Safety with Farm Animals," September 1985.

6
Sweatshops and Corporate Codes of Conduct

> Indeed, the building's hallways are strewn with orange peels, rotten bananas, and garbage. Vagrants were seen sleeping on the steps. Bathrooms are cramped and dirty, with no toilet paper, sinks, or windows. Metal gates cover door windows, and side windows are draped in sheets. The ventilation is so bad, and the odors and steam so overpowering, that many workers cover their noses and mouths with cloth all day.[1]

SWEATSHOPS

Background and History

Newspaper articles, containing information about garment industry sweatshops similar to that in the above quotation, in the last few years have reported that the number of sweatshops is on the rise. They state that working conditions in hundreds of establishments in the garment industry have become similar to those tolerated by workers almost a century ago. They describe a growing number of businesses that regularly violate federal and/or state wage, safety, health standards and child labor requirements.

"Sweatshops" have been commonly described as establishments employing workers at low wages, for long hours, under poor conditions. The sweatshops of the 1880s and 1890s were typically located in small factories or crowded and dilapidated tenements where immigrant families lived and worked. In the men's clothing industry in New York, overcrowding and sanitary conditions were probably at their worst in the 1880s. The workers, all immigrants, lived and worked together in large numbers in a few small, foul, ill-smelling rooms, without ventilation, water, or nearby toilets. Many immigrants slept on unswept floors that were littered with work, and meals were eaten on the work tables. Factory inspectors reported similar findings in Chicago. Garment sweatshops were typically located in the worst tenement buildings, often in basements or attics, over saloons or stables, and were frequently noxious with refuse.

Subcontracting of tasks to different groups of workers was the typical approach used in the tenement shops of the 1880s and the 1890s. The term "sweating" originally described a subcontract system in which middlemen earned their profit from the margin between the amount they received for a contract and the amount they paid workers with whom they subcontracted. The margin was said to be "sweated" from the workers because they received minimal wages for excessive hours worked under unsanitary conditions.

The immigrants worked in establishments where production was labor intensive. The "sweating" of workers was reported in various labor-intensive industries, such as cigarmaking, shoemaking, and the making of artificial flowers and other decorations. However, according to the House Committee on Manufacturers' 1893 report on the sweating system, sweatshops were most widespread in the apparel industry. The large number of sweatshops corresponded to the industry's high labor intensity, on which the immigrants had a significant impact. The immigrant tailors changed the method of production in the apparel industry by introducing the "task system." This system subdivided the manufacture of garments into separate tasks suitable for unskilled workers, whom the tailors employed in small shops, usually operated in tenement houses.[2]

Working hours were unlimited; people worked until they fell asleep from exhaustion. Quite common was a working day of fifteen or sixteen hours, from five in the morning until nine at night, with a break of three to fifteen minutes for lunch. During the busy season, they worked all night. A fair average wage for a New York cloak maker was nine dollars a week, for six working days of fourteen or fifteen hours each. Pants makers were paid even less. Their weekly wages were reported to average five to seven dollars. Many children also worked in these conditions.

Tenement shops, by far, posed the most serious sweatshop problems, and production in tenement houses was extremely widespread. In 1901 there were a minimum of 20,406 apparel shops in tenements, with at least 50,381 employees in New York City.[3] Diseases, such as smallpox and tuberculosis, and the danger of fire were among the hazards that plagued the tenements. Unsafe working conditions were highlighted by industrial accidents, such as the Triangle Shirtwaist Factory Fire of 1911 in New York City, which claimed the lives of 146 women.[4]

With the surge of unionism and a socially conscious government by the end of the 1930s, sweatshops had been wiped out in the United States. A Smithsonian exhibit includes the August 1, 1938, cover of *Life* magazine, which declared America's victory over sweatshops.[5] But the story doesn't have a happy ending. With the evolution of global entrepreneurs, always in search of cheaper labor, along with the weakening of the American labor movement, sweatshops began blossoming again in the 1960s in the United States. Sweatshops were thought to have declined in recent decades. Unfortunately, not only do sweatshops still exist, but child labor is rampant in them, both in the United States and worldwide—where American corporations have shifted jobs in search of ever lower labor costs—and not only in the garment industry. People think it's fine when they see the label "Made in USA." But maybe the dress or shirt was made in a sweatshop by children. According to one estimate, of 290,000 illegally employed children in 1996, 59,600 were under 14 years of age, and of those 14 and younger, 13,100 worked in garment industry sweatshops.[6]

Task Force Investigation

In New York state, members of a task force appointed by the governor, investigate garment sweatshops, where they inspect working conditions, review employee records and examine registration certificates. To meet registration requirements, contractors must provide workers' compensation insurance as well as comply with other state laws that govern the production of apparel and accessories to apparel. The task force issues violation notices to businesses that break state laws covering registration, child labor, wages and benefits, working hours, and industrial homework. Task force investigators also may seize materials distributed to "homeworkers." In addition, when task force investigators find sweatshop conditions that seem to violate state or federal safety and health laws, or local building and fire codes, the task force will alert the appropriate regulatory agency.[7]

In 1,500 surprise inspections, the task force found 101 minors working in eighty firms. The youngest was age 7. The greatest obstacle to investigators is getting workers who view officials as corrupt, hostile, and ready to deport them, to report abuses.

The Immigration Control Act of 1986, which imposes criminal penalties on employers who knowingly hire illegal immigrants, briefly stemmed the tide of illegals. But its deterrent effect quickly wore off, as the law became a means of segregating the labor market. Legal immigrant workers got hired by fairer employers; undocumented workers, by the unscrupulous, ready to extort labor for silence about immigration status. "If you have the dual problem of continued illegal immigration and increased exploitation . . . you have a recipe for the resurgence of sweatshops," said Muzaffar Chisti of the International Ladies Garment Workers Union.[8]

Developments in the 1990s

The problem of noncompliance in the garment industry remains widespread, with conditions in shops of the 1990s having been described as similar to those of turn-of-the-century sweatshops. A legal definition of a sweatshop is an employer that violates more than one federal or state labor law governing minimum wage, overtime, child labor, industrial homework, occupational safety and health, workers' compensation, or industry registration.[9] Due to extreme price competition in the industry, there is a willingness on the part of contractors and manufacturers to break the law. One of the largest manufacturing industries in the United States, the garment sector is dominated by fewer than 1,000 manufacturers who parcel out production to about 20,000 contractors and subcontractors, all of whom enter and exit the industry easily due to low domestic start-up costs. Retailers' and manufacturers' access to low-priced imports and the presence of an undocumented workforce with limited job opportunities heighten this competition. By threatening sanctions against employers who hire illegal immigrants, the government has actually given employers a powerful tool with which to silence immigrant workers who lack proper documentation. As such, they have faced worsening labor conditions and a new boom in sweatshops. According to the government's General Accounting Office (GAO), some 2,000 of New York's 6,000 garment shops in 1994 were sweatshops. For the same year, the GAO estimated that 4,500 of the 5,000 garment shops in Los Angeles were also categorized as sweatshops.[10]

A Queens, New York, site had scary-looking electrical wiring, cluttered aisles, and plastic bags of fabric piled ceiling-high, just waiting for a lighted cigarette to send them up in flames. Its emergency exit door was barred by a padlocked steel gate, another fire department violation. Scattered among the eighteen or so sewing machine operators were teen-age workers who probably were undocumented. Workers had tampered with the freight elevator, so the door didn't close automatically when the elevator cab wasn't there, paving the way for a serious accident. These were some of the sights that greeted members of the New York State Apparel Industry Task Force as they did their investigative work. With twenty investigators and a $1.5 million annual budget, the force tries to police over 6,000 garment factories, both legal and illegal, throughout the New York metropolitan area as well as locations upstate. Thomas Glubiak, chief investigator, said that one of his investigators found a 14-year-old girl helping her father with his work in a garment shop.[11]

Transactions are often in cash, and sweatshops actively work to avoid detection, so it is difficult to count them. Each contracting shop typically employs twenty-five to fifty workers, but can have as many as 100 workers. There has been a three-fold increase in the number of tiny subcontractors, under twenty workers, from 1977 to 1992 at the same time that larger shops with better conditions have closed down. The GAO has reported estimates of sweatshops in major garment producing centers:

- New York City: In 1994, the GAO reported an estimate that 4,500 of 5,000 garment shops were sweatshops.
- Miami: 400 of the total 500 garment shops are sweatshops.
- El Paso: 50 of 180 are sweatshops.
- New Orleans: 25 of 100 apparel firms are sweatshops.
- The GAO also reported that there are apparel sweatshops in parts of New Jersey, Chicago, Philadelphia, San Antonio, and Portland, Oregon.[12]

Sweatshops operate illegally as part of the underground economy. They typically are fly-by-night operations that can pack and move quickly from one place to another, sometimes across state lines. Sweatshops flourish because of the huge competitive advantage they hold over legitimate businesses that pay fair wages, provide safe working conditions, pay taxes, and contribute to the economic and social health of the nation. Although sweatshops routinely can produce garments at lower cost than honest shops, a company that enters into a contract with a sweatshop faces the possibility of civil penalties, criminal fines, and the loss of goods that are illegally produced. Doing business with a sweatshop also means a company encounters the risk of having its public reputation damaged.

The U.S. garment industry is structured like a pyramid, with the manufacturers at the top of the pyramid; contractors, who are generally legal immigrants, in the middle, and the garment workers at the bottom. This industry structure has created a situation that engenders abuse of labor laws because contracting out the production part of their business has enabled manufacturers to minimize their investment and insulate themselves from instability and risk. By characterizing their relationship with contractors as independent, they have avoided legal responsibility for workers' compensation, unemployment insurance, and fringe benefits. In short, garment manufacturers have preferred contracting for two reasons: they can control how much or how little contractors are paid, and they can take advantage of the prevailing assumption that they are not liable for wage violations in their contractors' sweatshops.

The presumption that contractors are independent contractors was rejected in September 1999 when California Governor Gray Davis signed into law a bill to crack down on sweatshop abuses in that state's $30 billion garment industry. Workers and advocates called the new law a solid first step toward cleaning up the state's sweatshops. In the preceding ten years, three other attempts were made to pass similar legislation, only to be vetoed by Republican governors. This is the toughest garment manufacturer's law in the United States. For the many garment workers who are being paid starvation wages, this law gives them a process to recover their unpaid wages relatively quickly because the manufacturer, not just the contractor, is held responsible, creating joint liability, and because the law provides for a strict timetable for resolving wage claims. Joint liability is one of the most important and misunderstood provisions, creating joint liability for manufacturers with private labels and is the only reliable method for cleaning up sweatshops in the garment industry.[13]

A variety of measures have been taken in order to combat rampant labor law and human rights abuses in sweatshops. In addition to the New York state task force, the U.S. Department of Labor (DOL), at the federal level, has pursued several courses of action to eradicate sweatshops. One measure the DOL has pursued is the compilation of a list of garment manufacturers and retailers that can ensure their clothing is not being made in sweatshops where wage and safety laws are disregarded. In 1995, at the behest of Secretary of Labor Robert Reich, the National Retail Federation promulgated a code of conduct that retailers would abide by in order to comply with labor laws. Another approach was having garment manufacturers sign voluntary compliance agreements in which they would monitor their contractors for legal compliance.

The El Monte Sweatshop

A much publicized sweatshop was discovered in El Monte, California, in August 1995 in a fenced seven-unit apartment complex, surrounded by barbed wire and spike fences, reminiscent of a POW camp from World War II. It was raided by state labor inspectors, who found Thai immigrant sewers being held against their will. One of these workers reported that she worked seventeen hours a day for as little as sixty cents an hour in order to pay off her $5,000 debt to the smugglers who had brought her into the United States. Another worker suffered headaches and vision impairment because of the long hours of nonstop sewing. In addition, one worker showed investigators the twenty-eight square-foot workroom area where he slept on a blanket on the floor under a stairwell located near sewing equipment. In order to turn a profit the contractor made workers work "eighteen hours a day straight . . . locking them in for several years."[14] The operators were convicted of civil rights violations and received prison terms of up to seven years. Most of the workers received $5,000 to $80,000 in a settlement with three Los Angeles garment makers, and most apparently remained in the United States.[15]

Sweatshop Characteristics

No single characteristic marks a garment factory as a sweatshop. However, there are many characteristics common to sweatshops. Examples follow:

- Fire hazards: Perhaps there may be only one exit . Fire exits might be blocked or locked. Fire extinguishers are not mounted on the walls or are missing from the mounting. There are no fire exit signs. Electrical exit signs are not lighted.
- Electrical hazards: Wires are exposed. Protective covers are missing. Many extension cords are in use. Wires are frayed, unconnected or dangling.
- Safety hazards: Machines and fans lack safety guards. Belts and pulleys are exposed. Steam pipes are not insulated. Aisles are less than 36 inches wide. Trash, clothing, or other obstacles block aisles and doors. Stairs do not have handrails.
- Health hazards: Ventilation is poor (heavy dust deposits may mean inadequate ventilation). If employees have hand rashes, the shop might be using toxic dyes. Restrooms are dirty. Lighting is poor.
- Structural dangers: Elevators work with doors open. There are holes in the factory's floors or ceilings. There is excessive play in floors. A basement shop does not have a certificate of occupancy posted.
- Wage violations: Employees are not paid on time. Workers do not receive wage statements with their pay. There are no overtime rates for piecework. Paydays are missed or there is no regular payday. There are more employees than time cards. The time

clock is broken or not used. Payments for weekend or overtime work are made separately in cash. Hours on the job are not recorded for pieceworkers.

- Child labor: Hours are not posted for children under 18. Children under 16 are working in the shop. A young employee responds with contradictory dates of birth when questioned about age. Children are seen outside the factory. A large increase in piecework production indicates that children may be helping their parents.
- Industrial homework: The shop's production seems to be greater than its capacity. Employees are seen carrying large packages or bags into and out of the factory. Daily production rates vary. Parts of clothing (examples: cuffs, collars) might be missing. Inventory is missing.
- Registration violations: A State Labor Department registration certificate is not displayed. The wrong employer's name is on the certificate.
- Tax irregularities: A company's identity changes frequently without a change in officers. The shop does not use a journal or daybook. The company has no bank account. The shop uses an individual who cashes checks instead of a bank. Deliveries to the shop have different names in the address.[16]

In recent years Department of Labor inspections of garment contractors found violations of wage-and-hour laws at 61 percent of factories in Los Angeles and at 63 percent of factories in New York City. In the San Francisco Bay area, where local garment firms cooperated with federal regulators, the rate of violations was only 13 percent. Some analysts say the apparel industry may be too complicated and politically powerful to be fully reformed. John Dunlop, a Harvard professor and former secretary of labor in the Ford Administration believes that "[t]here are powerful, intractable economic forces at work in the sweatshop issue. If we can't eradicate sweatshops and child labor at home, how do you think we're going to do it for Indonesia and Bangladesh."[17]

Industrial Homework

The sweatshop issue has been revisited since January 1989, when the Reagan Administration lifted the ban on industrial homework, which had been in effect since 1940 on all industries. The prohibition remained in effect only on women's apparel and "unsafe" jewelry production. Industrial homework is usually piecework unfinished at the factory and completed at home by an employee working in a totally unsupervised and illegal setting. One observer caustically noted that industrial homework " . . . is like an assembly line that comes crashing through your living room window, dispensing stuff at you that you have to run like hell to keep up with."[18]

More than sixty years ago, when the ban was imposed, industrial homework was prohibited in seven industries; women's apparel, jewelry manufacturing, knitted outerwear, gloves, button and buckle manufacturing, handkerchief manufacturing, and embroideries. The only exceptions were for workers who were disabled or too old to get to a place of business and workers who had to care for the disabled. In these exceptional cases, special certificates had to be obtained from the Department of Labor. The bans had been imposed to counter widespread exploitation of immigrant and child laborers There was evidence that employers were routinely violating both minimum wage and child labor laws with respect to home-based workers. Recently, there have been reports of an expansion of illegal home sewing of women's apparel by immigrant labor. This means that this area will continue to be a public policy issue. Furthermore, the growth of clerical homework, especially using home computers, has caused the Service Employees International Union and the Communication Workers of America to call for its prohibition.

The Pros and Cons

Better knowledge of the characteristics of home-based workers will help evaluate the various arguments put forward in the long-standing and continuing controversy about the desirability of this form of work organization. The conflicting views about the desirability of this type of labor arise from the two contradictory theories on which they are based. The first depicts homeworkers as a relatively advantaged group of individuals who have chosen to work at home to gain flexibility and to better control their time. In this view, homework allows family members to care for their children or elderly or disabled relatives while at the same time participating in the labor market. Homework also facilitates the employment of the disabled, according to this theory. That these homeworkers must forgo fringe benefits is not considered important, because they typically receive such benefits from their spouses' employers. The other theory portrays home workers as an exploited group, forced to work for low wages, with few if any benefits, in substandard working conditions, and often relying on the supplementary labor of young children. For that matter, female home-based workers are more likely than are all female workers to have children under the age of 18. One or the other of these two views underlies most of the arguments that have been advanced for or against home-based work.[19]

The Recent Evidence

Research throughout the country has uncovered illegal homework arrangements in industries ranging from textiles to microelectronics. There have also been abuses in the jewelry industry. Manufacturers cut agreed-upon piece rates, ask their factory workers to prolong their workdays by taking work home, and employ vulnerable workers, new immigrants, the elderly, and children to keep wages down. Indeed, child labor restrictions are virtually impossible to enforce in the privacy of people's homes, although to meet minimum income requirements, piece workers are under extreme pressure to employ their children. The issue is not over whether homes in rustic settings resemble traditional sweatshops, but rather the practice of "sweating," previously discussed, which produces payment by low piece rates and imposes long hours to reach a living wage.[20]

A trend, ignored amid the furor over apparel industry sweatshops abroad, is proving almost possible to extinguish here: illegal home sewing. Apparel contractors are hiring tens of thousands of workers in big cities to sew clothes in their homes. Most are Asian immigrants. Many are under the legal age of 16 who often work for less than the minimum wage.

The Texas Labor Department finds enforcement is nearly impossible because home sewers are scattered, difficult to find, and uncooperative with inspectors. Home sewers work for contractors who supply pre-cut fabric, keep no time records, and pay cash by the item: $1.25 for a simple blouse and up to $8 for a dress. Statistics on the number of home sewers are imprecise. Estimates range from 20,000 to 80,000 in the Dallas-Fort Worth area, and there are thriving home-sewing industries in Miami and in Orange County, California, as well.

Enforcement verges on the hopeless. Manufacturing is scattered in neighborhoods where workers rarely answer their doors. Few complain. Some are afraid of being deported. Others are satisfied with the pay: A family of eight working in a one-bedroom apartment can clear $600 a week in cash, often free of taxes. They avoid child-care expenses, also. Children as young as five work with their parents. Teachers complain that students sleep during classes because of late night hours sewing.

Home sewers take more than twice as long per garment as employees in efficient factories. But contractors avoid rent, electricity, and workers' compensation expenses, and home sewers pay for their own industrial sewing machines that cost $2,000 to $3,000 each. Home sewing may have made U.S. apparel making competitive with Third World countries. However, it has come at the expense of those who obey labor laws. Joe Allen had nearly 3,000 workers in his Texas factories before home sewing began to proliferate. Retailers demanded price cuts, and Allen's firm ended up losing $1 million before going bankrupt. "This decimated a legitimate industry for everybody playing by the rules," he says.[21]

Under California law, garment fabrication must be done in a shop that is legally registered with the state labor commissioner. In August 1996, five garment contractors under investigation had been registered, indicating that the manufacturers had followed that state's registration requirements. However, contractors involved in illegal industrial homework typically attempt to hide this activity from not only government enforcement officials, but also from manufacturers for whom they work.[22]

In New Jersey, inspectors for a state task force reported finding a boy working at home with gloves on because it was only 10 degrees and a woman doing piecework in her apartment with material piled perilously close to a furnace. "Workers are afraid to complain or inform on their employer because they fear being sent away deported, fired, or not finding work elsewhere," stated state

Assemblyman Louis J. Gill, co-sponsor of an Assembly bill to ban industrial homework.[23]

In Silicon Valley, a largely poor, immigrant workforce is engaged in high-tech industrial homework, assembling circuit boards at home on a piece-rate basis. Their hours are long; the work, which involves soldering of metal and exposure to solvents, is dangerous; and pay often falls below minimum wage requirements.[24] A former electronic pieceworker, who said he was paid as little as $1 an hour to assemble electronic products at home, settled his lawsuit with a Silicon Valley high-tech company. Mao, a Cambodian immigrant living in San Jose, was one of dozens of pieceworkers, predominantly Asian immigrants, who assembled printed circuit boards and cables at home for as little as a penny per component for some of high tech's major companies. At least fourteen local electronics manufacturers that contract to build products for companies such as Hewlett-Packard and Sun Microsystems engaged in piecework, some as recently as 1998. The work, which took place in workers' kitchens, living rooms, and garages, often involved whole families, including children. Workers routinely used toxic chemicals without supervision or protection. Nearly all home assemblers were paid no overtime, and many did not earn the minimum wage in violation of state and federal labor laws.[25] John Fox, a union international vice president, said working at home gave companies opportunities to exploit workers. "There is no control," he said. "Their children help them. Before you know it, children under 12 have become helpers."[26]

Weaknesses and Remedies

In practice, industrial homework regulation has been ineffective. As far back as the 1930s, New York state's extensive regulation system, requiring records from both employers and home workers, was administratively unworkable and unenforceable. Similarly, the British system in which wage councils review employers' biannual submission of lists of their home workers, has been ineffective in preventing wage exploitation and hazardous working conditions. In practice, employer registration systems impose the burden of enforcement on individual workers whose dire need for employment inhibits them from complaining. The ban policy has not worked, not only because it is difficult to enforce in scattered industries, but also because it is not much of a deterrent to operators who are already violating numerous federal and state work-standard, tax, and health laws.

Realistically, the need for regulation exists. Far better than a series of ad hoc state laws would be a consistent and well-enforced federal policy that provided necessary protection against exploitation in all types of homework, not just garment making, without shutting off legitimate and much-needed opportunities for work. A better approach would be to legalize homework, but set licensing requirements that ensure that home workers receive decent pay and benefits and that piece rates do not unfairly undercut factory work.

Properly regulated, homework can offer many people a convenient way to mix work and home responsibilities. Operating illegally, as it does now in many areas, it can become a means by which unscrupulous contractors exploit workers. An outright prohibition in areas such as garment making, where exploitation has historically been common, has the appeal of simplicity. In addition, joint liability, which finds the manufacturer sharing responsibility with the contractor, needs to be judicially expanded beyond its recent narrow application.

In present circumstances, many immigrant children, still being exposed to Dickensian working conditions, may be unable to leave hazardous environments long enough to complete an education, vital to their economic futures. These young people are being denied an education because they may not know they have a choice.

AGRICULTURAL "SWEATSHOPS"

They are children, yes. But is this childhood? She sweats into the soil of a vast Ohio field. A baseball cap keeps the sun and her unruly dark hair from her almond eyes. Adult rubber gloves engulf the small hands that snap cucumbers from their vines. Her name is Alejandra Renteria. She is 6.[27]

Working Conditions

Due to circumstances similar to those described above, the conditions on many American farms can only be referred to as "sweatshops in the fields." Hand labor is especially vital to the production of blemish-free fruits and vegetables that American consumers have learned to demand. Laboring in the fields often means stooping over rows of produce for hours under the hot sun with no breaks. According to the U.S. Department of Agriculture's own data, agriculture is one of the most accident-prone industries in the United States.

The New York Times reported on August 5, 2000, that there were 150,000 children ages 16 and younger employed in U.S. agriculture and that they often work ten to twelve hours a day, six days a week, facing dangers from pesticides and risking exhaustion and dehydration. Farmers claim to prefer older workers, but many underage workers present documents showing they are 18. The Department of Labor says that agriculture provides 6 to 7 percent of the jobs held by young people, but accounted for 43 percent of youth workplace fatalities in the 1990s. Child farmworkers are divided into three groups: unaccompanied migrants, usually teenage illegal immigrants from Mexico or Guatemala; children of migrant farm laborers, who often force their teenagers to work and sometimes take children as young as 7 into the fields to pick alongside them; and last, about 40,000 minors who are the children of farm owners and who start milking cows and harvesting at an early age to learn how to operate the farms that they may someday inherit.[28]

Approximately 25 percent of farm labor in this country is performed by children. Studies show that at least one-third of migrant children, as young as 10, work on farms to help earn family incomes; others may not be hired laborers but are in the fields to help their parents or simply due to a lack of child care services. Growers often do not provide them with toilets and drinking water, and some child pickers say growers occasionally order them to resume picking even when the twenty-four hours required by law have not passed after pesticide are sprayed. In July 2000, the Department of Labor fined an El Paso, Texas, farmer when children as young as 7 were found working in onion fields. The farmer paid $3,000 in fines and entered into a compliance partnership agreement with the Wage and Hour Division that required daily monitoring of field operations for compliance with child labor laws.[29]

Even when children do not work, they may be at risk. Due to the scarcity of child-care facilities, many farmworker children are present in the fields and thus are exposed to pesticides on plants and in the dirt. Children have a smaller body mass than adults, and their metabolisms differ from those of adults. As a result, it is thought that the consequences of pesticide exposure may be more severe for children.

Despite the publication of a variety of statistics, it may be impossible for the Department of Labor to accurately report the exact number of children working on farms. A provision in the annual appropriations bill forbids the federal government from inspecting farms with fewer than eleven workers. This provision is intended to keep small farms free of the same regulations that giant agribusinesses must comply with. This exemption has seen some growers allow an independent contractor to hire workers, allowing the grower to be free and clear of worker-safety or child labor laws. Another tactic employed by growers to circumvent the laws is to register an entire family as working under the social security number of the head of a household. This creates the illusion that there are only a few workers being employed, when, in reality, there could be hundreds. There is little regulatory agencies can do to help. In addition to being barred from inspecting farms that claim fewer than eleven workers, labor officials have to ask a grower's permission to inspect a farm. This makes it more difficult to measure the problem of child labor in agriculture.[30]

Due to budget cuts, the Consumer Product Safety Commission, charged with collecting data on young, injured farm workers, decided to stop collecting data on injuries caused by farming equipment like tractors and pesticides in its reports on consumer products. "We can't spend our limited resources on things that we aren't sure are considered consumer products," stated Art McDonald of the Commission.[31]

As a practical matter, farm-working juveniles have second-class status: they enjoy fewer rights than their non-farm-working peers, and they are exploited while the government looks the other way. They are vulnerable to occupational injury and illness because their jobs are dangerous; they are worked too hard because employers don't have to limit their hours; and they are underpaid because the farm labor contractors can get away with it.

Nobody seems to care. It is a national disgrace.

THE PESTICIDE DILEMMA

The Enormity of the Problem

No discussion of agricultural sweatshops would be complete without discussing pesticide dangers. Children living on or near farms are exposed to disproportionately high amounts of dangerous pesticides, putting them at serious risk for adverse health effects. These children are likely to have the highest exposure to pesticides of any group of people in the country. Many of the children with the greatest pesticide exposure are from migrant farmworker families who are poor and usually people of color or recent immigrants.

There are approximately 25,000 pesticides on the U.S. market, with about 600 in wide use. Pesticide use in this country alone amounts to 2.2 billion pounds annually, or roughly 8.8 pounds per person. Virtually all of these pesticides in use have undergone inadequate testing for safety. Most of what testing has been done has concentrated on acute toxicity and cancer-causing potential, ignoring the possible endocrine-disrupting effects or damage to human immune systems.

Of the twenty-five most heavily used agricultural pesticides, five are toxic to the nervous system; eighteen are skin, eye, or lung irritants; eleven have been classified by the U.S. Environmental Protection Agency (EPA) as carcinogenic; seventeen cause genetic damage, and ten cause reproductive problems (in tests of laboratory animals). Annual use of pesticides causing each of these types of health problems totals between one and four hundred million pounds.[32]

Illnesses Caused by Pesticides

Pesticides are toxic by design. Their purpose is to kill or harm living things such as insects, weeds, and organisms that cause plant diseases. They can also harm human beings. The health hazards of pesticides fall into three main categories:

1. There are short-term or acute effects, including skin rashes, systemic poisoning, and even death. The number of poisonings is not precisely known. There is no national reporting system, and even in states that keep track of pesticide-related illnesses and incidents, there is widespread underreporting. Many illnesses are not recognized as pesticide poisoning because of similarity to influenza and other common ailments. Farmworkers often do not report suspected pesticide-related illness for fear of losing their jobs, or other employer retaliation. Furthermore, most doctors do not recognize the signs and symptoms of pesticide poisoning and are unaware of the hazards posed by

different pesticides used in agriculture. There are even some physicians in rural areas who are better informed about pesticides, but trivialize their hazards and risks because they fear loss of business from farmers or ostracism from the business community.

2. The long-term or chronic effects include cancer, damage to the brain and nervous system, birth defects, and infertility. The cancers in children most frequently associated with pesticides are leukemia and brain cancer.

3. There are also effects on preexisting conditions such as asthma, allergies, and chemical sensitivities. Pesticide can exacerbate these conditions, causing harm at significantly lower levels of exposure than in those without these conditions. Consequently, pesticides are rarely recognized or considered as potential precipitating factors in the resulting illness.[33]

The Worker Protection Standard

EPA's Worker Protection Standard (WPS) is a regulation aimed at reducing the risk of pesticide poisonings and injuries among agricultural workers and pesticide handlers. The WPS contains requirements for labeling, pesticide safety training, notification of pesticide applications, use of personal protective equipment, restricted entry intervals following application, posting and signs, decontamination supplies, and emergency medical assistance. Initially, the WPS was a very simple statement; workers were not allowed to enter the field until the sprays had dried or the dust had settled. WPS was amended several times before it was finalized in 1995. This resulted in a very complex rule that is difficult for the agricultural community, both the farmer and the workers, to understand. It is very weak and poorly enforced. Most farmworkers have no idea what pesticide residues are on the crops they cultivate or harvest, or of their potential health effects.[34]

The WPS still leaves a significant number of workers unprotected. For example, the problem of drift of airborne pesticides onto adjacent fields where people may be working, or onto adjacent work camps where people may be living, is not adequately addressed by the WPS. Although warning signs are required to be posted, they may be posted immediately before a pesticide application, and the required location of the signs is intended to target the workers on the farm being sprayed. However, there is no mechanism by which workers in the field are ensured they will be warned prior to the spraying of an adjacent field. If even a slight breeze is blowing in their direction, those workers will be subjected to a potentially injurious exposure, despite the fact that all relevant laws have been followed. A survey of children working on farms in New York revealed that nearly half had worked in fields still wet with pesticides and over one-third had been sprayed directly or indirectly. Unfortunately, the current WPS has not considered pesticide exposures to children. No separate pesticide reentry intervals specifically for children have been established as yet even though recommendations have been submitted to the Department of Labor regarding minimum reentry times for 10- and 11-year-olds working in potatoes and strawberries.

These intervals ranged from 2 to 120 days. They were adopted into regulations but ruled illegal by the U.S. Court of Appeals for the D.C. Circuit in 1980 in *National Association of Farmworkers Organizations v. Marshall,* 628 F.2d 604. Although children as young as 10 can legally work in the fields, reentry intervals are calculated based on a theoretical 150-pound male.[35]

Poor Enforcement

Reentry intervals are intended to prevent farmers and farm labor contractors from sending harvest workers into fields for a specified number of hours after particular pesticides have been applied, in order to permit the chemicals to degrade into less toxic substances. The field sanitation regulation requires farmers and contractors to provide drinking water and sanitation facilities, which can be used in cases of acute pesticide exposure. These safe work practices are woefully underenforced. For instance, less than half of the seventy high-profile California pesticides have reentry intervals of more than one day, and many have no reentry interval at all. The protective equipment and sanitation requirements are widely ignored; a recent targeted enforcement effort documented the manner in which even the most elementary hygienic practices are disregarded. In California, less than 3 percent of all farms are inspected each year by the state, and in many other states, the inspections are even rarer. Without strong enforcement of existing standards, violations are likely to be common. The Environmental Protection Agency (EPA) should expeditiously reevaluate the WPS in order to determine whether it adequately protects children's health. Children are not mini-adults and are more vulnerable to toxic exposures. With exposure to the same amount of chemicals as an adult, children will absorb more. This is because they have much more skin surface for their size, they take in more breaths per minute, and their immune and detoxifying systems are not fully developed. Pesticides can also interfere with a child's developing brain and nervous system. In its reevaluation, EPA should, for example, consider using standardized data on size and age-specific weight and height for modeling children's exposure when more specific data on children's exposures to individual pesticides may be lacking.[36]

Another Legal Deficiency

The Food Quality and Protection Act (FQPA) of 1996, which was an effort to reduce or eliminate the use of those pesticides which pose the greatest hazard to human health, is also deficient in not requiring biological or environmental monitoring of drift and other exposures to farmworkers, children and rural residents. The failure to collect information on these ongoing exposures leads the EPA to ignore them. Nor are there any provisions for mandatory reporting of all pesticide uses, and of pesticide-related illnesses. The resulting lack of information undermines the ability of regulators and researchers to determine if unacceptable exposures or health consequences are occurring.[37]

The Fresno County Incident

In California, suspected pesticide-related illnesses and suspected work-related illnesses and injuries are reportable conditions. On July 31, 1998, the Occupational Health Branch of the California Department of Health Services (CDHS) received a report from the California Department of Pesticide Regulation (CDPR) of a pesticide exposure incident in Fresno County involving thirty-four farmworkers, both adults and minors. CDHS investigated this incident by reviewing medical records of the thirty-four workers and interviewing twenty-nine. The workers ages ranged from 13 to 64 years, with a median age of 31 years. The findings indicated that the workers became ill after early reentry into a cotton field that had been sprayed with three pesticides. The primary pesticide used was carbofuran, which, when used on cotton, has a restricted entry interval (REI) of forty-eight hours and requires both posting of treated fields and oral notification of workers. Neither warning was provided. After weeding for approximately four hours, the workers were transported to a second field two and one-half miles away that had been sprayed two days earlier with three pesticides, whose REI was twelve hours. Within approximately one-half hour of entering the second field, the workers began feeling ill and stopped working. The symptoms most commonly reported by the thirty-four farm workers were: nausea (97 percent), headache (94 percent), eye irritation (85 percent), muscle weakness (82 percent) tearing (68 percent), vomiting (79 percent), and salivation (56 percent).

Thirty workers were transported immediately to a medical clinic; the other four went home, showered, and sought medical care three to seventeen days later. All workers received hospital treatment for symptoms, and twenty-eight lost at least one day of work. The CDHS continued to monitor these workers to assess the acute and chronic effects associated with these pesticide overexposures. In this incident, workers entered a field at 6 A.M. to complete weeding begun the previous day, This was well before the required forty-eight-hour reentry interval and without labeling and oral notification. The results were moderately severe illness. The incident demonstrates that 1) posted and oral warnings based on the REI are necessary to prevent illness among workers performing hand labor in fields recently treated with pesticides, and 2) failure to adhere to an REI can result in serious health consequences for the exposed workers. No worker without prescribed protective clothing should enter a treated area to perform a hand-labor task until the REI expires. The length of the REI depends on the specific pesticide but generally can be no less than 12 hours. Additionally, this incident demonstrates that sole reliance on these control measures may be inadequate, creating a case for the substitution of safer, less toxic, alternative pesticides when feasible, or integrated pest management techniques, where pesticide usage is prohibited.[38]

Non-Reporting of Inert Ingredients

The EPA requires that pesticide labels disclose only the product's active ingredients, that is, those toxic materials that kill the insect or weed or other target organism. However, pesticides also contain many other ingredients, called "inert," which deliver the active ingredient to the target. Many of these may also be toxic, but the government does not require them to be identified on pesticide product labels. States are preempted by the federal government from requiring such labeling for pesticides. In 1998, New York, Connecticut, Alaska, Massachusetts, and other states submitted a federal petition to the EPA to require full-product labeling of inert ingredients. Rather than responding to the petition, the EPA referred the matter to two advisory committees, neither of which has a definite timetable for resolving this pressing issue. After four years, no recommendations have been made to the EPA, and none are expected in the foreseeable future. This is an example of effective lobbying and political pressure by the agricultural chemical industry.[39]

The So-Called Right to Know

The Worker Protection Standard, which has been noted, requires safety training for all workers who enter crop fields where pesticides have been applied, as well as explicitly granting certain rights to workers, including a basic "right to know." Also, under state law, growers and farm labor contractors are required to inform workers of the risks they face and to train them in safe handling techniques. Written illness prevention plans are formally required. These "right to know" provisions are supported, in principle, by the "right to act" provisions of federal and state labor law, which guarantee to workers the right to join labor unions and bargain collectively with employers. The fact of the matter is that the "right to know" movement among industrial workers and urban communities exposed to toxic chemicals has exerted a modest beneficial impact on public policy toward pesticide-exposed farmworkers. Yet, these worker-oriented regulations have not been observed in practice.[40]

The California Study

A study in California was conducted to determine whether farmworkers are aware of new regulations mandating safeguards designed to protect them from illness or injury caused by occupational pesticide exposure. It also sought to determine whether and how they had received the required safety training, and whether they believed they were at risk of pesticide illness in their workplace. Nearly 500 interviews were conducted in Spanish in two California counties in the summer of 1997. Fewer than one in five workers had ever heard of the Worker Protection Standard containing a basic "right to know," or the Environmental Protection Agency. Most of those who claimed to know something about either could not provide anything substantive upon closer questioning. Residents of two farm labor camps in Yolo County were the most likely to have received some training (66 percent), but in most cases it was provided by nonprofit agencies, not their employer. Only a relatively few farmworkers living at private camps had received training. Overall, only about 16 percent of farmworkers said that they had received on-the-job pesticide safety training. Clearly, these results suggest that the news about WPS and "right to know" has not yet reached most farm workers in California.[41]

Legal Compliance in Michigan

Unfortunately, noncompliance with the law is rampant. To illustrate this fact, consider that the state of Michigan, the nation's fourth largest user of migrant farmworkers, has never had one single report of a pesticide-related health problem in a farmworker. Dr. Kenneth Rosenman, a professor of medicine at Michigan State University, who carries out a contract with the Michigan Department of Public Health to compile statistical summaries of the occupational illness reports, states in a recent article, "Although the large employers comply with the mandatory reporting law and submit occupational disease reports, less than 1 percent of all employers report and less than 1 percent of all physicians report. For example, no occupational disease report has ever been received from a migrant health clinic."[42]

Primary Care Providers and Pesticide Issues

What is the knowledge and awareness of pesticide issues in the educational and practice settings of primary care providers? A primary care provider is defined as physician, nurse, nurse practitioner, physician assistant, nurse midwife, or community health worker specializing in one of the following areas: family medicine, internal medicine, pediatrics, obstetrics/gynecology, emergency medicine, or public health. Americans look to their primary care providers for guidance on health concerns. Increasingly, such concerns include the effects of environmental and occupational hazards, including pesticides, on their health. While some progress has been made in introducing environmental health issues into the curriculum of medical and nursing schools, most health professionals still do not have adequate knowledge and tools to address patient and community concerns.

Primary care providers are not sufficiently trained at any stage of their education about pesticide exposure. The main concerns in provider knowledge about pesticide exposure are:

- Pesticide exposures are often underreported.
- Providers often do not know how and where to report pesticide exposures; sometimes the reporting is considered burdensome given their demanding work environments.
- Health conditions associated with pesticide exposures are often misdiagnosed because of many confusing symptoms.
- Providers do not often see acute pesticide poisoning, and they do not possess enough knowledge to recognize chronic cases.
- Providers have not received training on pesticide exposures during their years of formal education.
- Pesticide exposures and associated health conditions are difficult topics to teach because they require additional knowledge on toxicology and other topics that are often not included in the curriculum of health professional education.

One of the most difficult obstacles is simply gaining the attention of students, faculty, and primary care providers to the issue of pesticides. Curricula are crowded, providers are busy, and time is at a premium.

Importance of Environmental Histories

Few primary care providers ask patients the questions that would be likely to alert them to the possibility of a pesticide-related illness. Although it is important for primary care providers to take environmental histories, a full environmental history can sometimes take up the entire patient visit. However, getting primary care providers to ask just a few simple questions, such as, "Where do you work?" and "Do you think your problems are related to something that happened at work?" could go a long way toward uncovering pesticide-related health concerns: low-dose chronic effects as well as acute, high-dose poisonings; and effects on children.[43]

Data Limitations

As was the case with the reporting of occupational injuries and fatalities in nonfarming activities, there are serious data-gathering deficiencies in the reporting of pesticide-related illnesses and deaths. In the absence of comprehensive nationwide information, EPA uses four databases to provide some indication of the extent of acute pesticide incidents and illnesses. These databases are: (1) the American Association of Poison Control Centers' Toxic Exposure Surveillance system, (2) the data reported to EPA under the Federal Insecticide Fungicide Rodenticide Act (FIFRA) of 1947, (3) the National Pesticide Telecommunications Network, and (4) the California Pesticide Illness Surveillance Program. However, each of these databases has limitations:

- The American Association of Poison Control Centers maintains information on poison exposures. However, its database does not isolate pesticide exposures that occurred in agricultural work (or from any other occupation). In addition, some poison control centers do not report to the national database, and reports that poison control centers receive by telephone may lack medical confirmation.

• Under section 6(a)(2) of FIFRA, registrants are required to submit information they obtain about unreasonable adverse effects of their pesticide products. The 6(a)(2) database was designed to gather information on the effects of pesticides rather than on the extent of pesticide incidents. Therefore, the database contains detailed reports on serious and rare incidents, but little information on less serious incidents.

• The National Pesticide Telecommunications Network (a cooperative effort between EPA and Oregon State University) is a toll-free telephone service that provides the general public and health professionals with information on pesticide health and safety and pesticide incidents. While the network categorizes pesticide by the age, sex and occupation of the affected person, the network's data rely on self-reporting, and most of the information has not been verified or substantiated by independent investigation, laboratory analysis, or any other means. Moreover, many farmworkers, particularly migrant or seasonal workers, may not have ready access to a telephone to report pesticide incidents.

• The California Pesticide Illness Surveillance Program, often cited as the most comprehensive state reporting system, obtains most of its case reports through the Workers' Compensation system. Therefore, illnesses that occur in farm children who are not officially workers are unlikely to be reported in this system. Also, according to EPA and farmworker advocacy groups, farmworkers may be reluctant to report pesticide exposures because of the potential for retaliatory actions such as loss of jobs or pay cuts.

Notwithstanding the limitations of California's program, EPA used this information in 1999 to make a nationwide estimate that there were 10,000 to 20,000 incidents of physician-diagnosed illnesses and injuries per year in farm work. However, EPA recognized that its estimate represents serious underreporting (other estimates are as high as 300,000). Moreover, according to officials from the California Department of Pesticide Regulation, because California's crops and pesticide regulations are different from those of other states, it is inappropriate to extrapolate California's data to the rest of the nation. In addition, there are other reasons why acute pesticide incidents are underreported, including farmworkers' hesitancy to seek medical care for financial reasons and physicians' misdiagnoses or failure to report incidents.[44]

Complications Stemming from Misdiagnoses

Farmers and farmworkers suffer from pesticide exposure and other ailments that often are misdiagnosed or improperly treated because doctors never have faced the malady or the patients don't think to pass information along. Physicians, for instance, commonly misdiagnose lung irritations or infections from pesticides or other toxic substances as pneumonia. Or they see the farmworker before symptoms begin and send him or her home before fluid buildup and breathing difficulties start.

There definitely needs to be some specialized training for doctors who work in rural medicine. South Carolina may have the best system in the nation. A network of experts helps physicians by teaching them to spot peculiar agricultural illnesses or by providing information for treatment. Under that network, physicians are linked with various extension agents, poison specialists and other experts who have more experience in treating specific problems. To make a real difference, farmers and farmworkers must also become aware of what they need to tell doctors. When a farmworker goes to a doctor for treatment, it is up to that individual to say, "I work on a farm." Then it's up to the doctor to ask the questions. A farmworker who thinks he or she has problems because of exposure to some sort of toxic substance also needs to learn to urge his physician to contact poison control centers because those institutions often have suggestions for treatments that are immediately available.[45]

Financial Problems

The EPA has concluded that making use of existing surveys, particularly the Consumer Product Safety Commission's (CPSC) National Electronic Injury Surveillance System (NEISS) and the National Center for Health Statistics' National Hospital Discharge Survey (NHDS), and supplementing them with additional data collection specific to pesticides, as well as increasing coverage of hospitals in rural areas, would be more cost effective than initiating a new data collection system. However, funding was never allocated by the EPA to expand data collection and coverage of hospitals in rural areas, and the agency has not collected hospital emergency room data since 1987.[46]

CODES OF CONDUCT

The egregious sweatshop conditions in the garment industry described earlier have led many garment manufacturers and retailers to examine their production processes, and upon discovering oppressive labor conditions, many of which involve child labor, voluntarily to adopt codes of conduct to meet certain legal and ethical standards. Provisions prohibiting child labor are one of the most common elements of these codes.

The Apparel Industry

In reviewing the development of codes of conduct in the garment industry, it is important to recognize the enormous changes that have occurred in the industry in recent decades. Once concentrated in the United States and other industrialized countries, the garment industry has gradually spread in successive waves to countries with lower production costs to become a worldwide industry whose geographical distribution is constantly changing. A number of factors have contributed to this globalization. Many developing countries have based or are basing their industrialization on labor-intensive export sectors, particularly the apparel sector. Developing countries have almost doubled their share of world clothing exports since the early 1970s to account for more than 60 percent of exports at the present time. At the same time, companies in the United States and other industrialized nations have adopted strategies to relocate certain labor-intensive activities, such as clothing assembly, to low-wage countries through direct investment or outsourcing.[47]

The Apparel Industry Partnership

Reacting to criticism from human rights advocates, Levi-Strauss, Nike, and other corporations developed voluntary codes of conduct in the early 1990s. In the United States, the Clinton Administration in 1997 formed the Apparel Industry Partnership (AIP), composed of corporations, unions, nongovernmental organizations (NGOs), and multinational organizations, to seek agreement on a set of standards and a compliance process.[48]

However, the AIP soon encountered criticism of its provisions. A religious coalition known as the People of Faith Network called the agreement "deeply flawed" and recommended that the coalition draft a more credible code of conduct for participating companies. The group alleged that the code of conduct proposed by the AIP "does not hold companies to even the most limited improvements in workers' lives," fails to require that companies pay their workers "a living wage," and did not adequately protect workers against being "legally denied their rights."[49]

The Fair Labor Association

The AIP led to the creation of the Fair Labor Association (FLA) in 1998, a group that is to develop an independent, external monitoring system to ensure that companies agreeing to the partnership's proposed code of conduct for the apparel industry live up to its standards. The code of conduct sets out protections in nine areas: child labor, forced labor, discrimination, harassment, freedom of association, wages, health and safety, hours of work, and overtime compensation.[50]

The FLA's job is to accredit independent monitors, determine whether companies are in compliance with its standards, and assure consumers that the apparel and footwear they purchase has not been made under exploitative conditions. Companies seeking to participate in the new process must provide comprehensive information to the association, monitor their factories themselves, and submit to independent monitoring of factories that manufacture clothing and footwear. On June 12, 2001, the FLA announced that 982 companies had registered to apply for membership in the FLA. The announcement was made at the third annual meeting of the University Advisory Council, the organization of 155 colleges and universities affiliated with the FLA.[51]

Criticism of the FLA

Over the course of the AIP negotiations, several organizations refused to join the FLA because of what was termed a bias in favor of the companies. Two unions, the garment workers' UNITE and the Retail, Wholesale and Department Store Union (RDWU), and the Interfaith Center for Corporate Responsibility (ICCR) pulled out of the partnership in late 1998. Not only these groups, but others in the U.S. sweatshop activist community criticized the agreement reached in the charter document. Primary criticisms focused on the level of monitoring, on the fact that companies may select their preferred monitors from a roster of groups accredited by the FLA, and on what was considered to be inadequate language on wages.

The FLA does not demand that its members pay their workers a living wage, only the higher or prevailing or minimum wage. By setting such a standard, any impact the FLA might have on a country's garment industry would be eliminated by that country reducing its minimum wage to the prevailing wage, assuming the legal minimum were higher to begin with. Thus, the market, which has reduced real wages for garment industry workers over the past two decades, would continue to disadvantage the people who make clothes. Additionally, if it had any effect, the FLA's provision would most harm the countries in which workers might be able to voice some resistance to a reduction in the minimum wage, as companies would flee to more authoritarian states like Burma, where the military dictatorship can do whatever it wants to both wages and the workers.

The FLA does not implement an effective enforcement procedure. After having as few as 30 percent of its factories monitored by an external organization accredited by the FLA, a licensee would be given a seal of approval. After that, even the worst offenders would have only 15 percent of their factories monitored by an external firm.

Despite inadequate standards and monitoring, companies will be able to use their participation in the FLA as a marketing tool. Once certified, they will be able to sew a label into their products saying they were made under fair conditions—a label that could fool consumers and which would amount to false advertising. Additionally, numerous legalisms would allow a licensee to manipulate the process; for instance, clothes could be made by 14-year-olds in El Salvador for eighty hours a week "under extraordinary business circumstances" and technically be in accord with FLA standards. Also, neither the FLA nor the licensee would provide for full public disclosure.[52]

The FLA initiative still suffers from other weaknesses, as well as some important open questions. After three years, program participants had not yet reached agreement on the benchmarks for determining compliance on issues not fully defined by the code of conduct, or by international standards, such as definitions of sexual harassment, or the extent of benchmarks on occupational safety and health matters. Also, the channel for third party complaints had not yet been established. The decisions reached on these matters, as well as the initial implementation of independent monitoring under the program, will be the real tests of its success.

United Students Against Sweatshops (USAS)

College students across the nation typically are outfitted in sweatshirts, T-shirts, shorts, and baseball caps emblazoned with the logos and mascots representing their campuses. Students and other fans spend an estimated $2.5 billion a year on the products, according to the U.S. Department of Labor. But when some students realized that much of the apparel was made in sweatshops where workers earned poverty wages and toiled in horrible conditions, they began to challenge their universities to examine and change the way they do business. In 1998, students at Duke University convinced their school to pass a code of conduct, becoming the first university to do so. The code forbids apparel companies from using the school's name on items produced in sweatshops. That same year, U.S. college students created a national network called United Students Against Sweatshops that now has chapters at more than 200 colleges and universities.

In 1999, as a result of student activism, Nike disclosed the names and addresses of some of the factories that make clothes for several universities, an important step in holding the company accountable. USAS is demanding university codes of conduct requiring manufacturers to meet minimum labor standards, including a living wage, independent monitoring, and full public disclosure of factory locations. It argues that if full public disclosure becomes a reality, companies will no longer be able to hide sweatshop abuses. Companies counter that disclosing detailed information on their supply chains would put them at a competitive disadvantage. It is unlikely, however, that disclosing the names and addresses of suppliers would reveal many trade or production secrets. In the sports shoe industry, for instance, Nike runners are often made in the very same factories as Adidas and Reebok running shoes. Companies are probably more concerned about the possibility that unions and labor rights advocates will gain access to this information, than they are about sharing it with their competitors.[53]

Form and Development of Codes of Conduct

As has been noted, a code of conduct is a formal statement of the values and business practices of a corporation. A code may be a short mission statement, or it may be a sophisticated document that requires compliance with articulated standards and have a complicated enforcement mechanism. The forms that firms' policies take, and how they were developed, vary widely from company to company:

- Some companies have developed special documents (which they typically refer to as "codes of conduct") outlining their values, principles, and guidelines in a variety of areas, including child labor. These documents are a means for companies to clearly and publicly state to their suppliers, customers, consumers, and shareholders the way in which they intend to do business. Some are intended for wide distribution, including posting in workplaces.
- Other companies do not have a formal code of conduct, but have circulated letters stating their policies on child labor to all suppliers, contractors, and/or buying agents.
- Compliance certificates are yet another vehicle used by firms to state their policies regarding child labor. These certificates generally require suppliers, buying agents, or contractors to certify in writing that they abide by the company's stated standards prohibiting the employment of children.
- Still others state their child labor policies in formal documents such as purchase orders or letters of credit, making compliance with the policy a contractual obligation for suppliers.
- Some companies have both formal codes of conduct and contractual clauses or a certification form. Others' policies on child labor are exclusively contained in contracts or certification forms rather than in a formal code of conduct.

There are also differences among companies in how they have created their codes of conduct Some of the pioneer companies in establishing codes of conduct designed their own codes independently, based on their needs and experiences and sometimes drawing on existing models, such as multilateral codes of conduct (e.g., the International Labor Organization [ILO] and the Organization for Economic Cooperation and Development [OECD]), private sector initiatives (e.g., the *maquiladora* standards), and internationally recognized labor standards set by the ILO. U.S. corporations that have adopted codes more recently have benefited from the experience of firms that took this path earlier. In other cases, companies utilize the code of conduct or policy of a trade association or buying agent, either in lieu of, or in addition to, their own.[54]

Implementation Challenges Posed by Production Organization

The challenges of implementing a child labor policy for a given company in the apparel industry differ greatly and depend on how production is organized. Generally, the closer the relationship between the importer and the company actually producing the items, the greater the ability to influence labor conditions, including prohibitions on child labor, in the production facilities. Conversely, the longer the chain of production, and the more levels of contractors, subcontractors, and buying agents used, the more complex and challenging is the implementation. If, however, there is commitment to effective implementation, this can be accomplished under any organization of production.

To illustrate, a manufacturing company that produces most of its imports in wholly owned facilities abroad has more control over production conditions and can more easily implement its child labor policy than can a firm whose productions take place in the facilities of hundreds or even thousands of contractors and subcontractors. Some manufacturers have different policies for wholly owned plants and contractors. A manufacturer or retailer with an ongoing relationship with a contractor that accounts for a large percentage, if not all, of that contractor's orders can more easily ensure its child labor policy is being respected by that contractor than can a manufacturer or retailer that only uses that contractor for an occasional order.

Retailers are often, but not always, more removed from the production process than manufacturers. However, the large retailers, because of the enormous bargaining power they wield over suppliers, also have the ability to require vendor compliance with any child labor standard they develop. In addition, retailers that directly contract out the manufacture of private-label merchandise overseas can directly influence the labor conditions in the contractors' facilities.

Often, entities all along the garment production chain—retailers, domestic-based manufacturers, buying agents, and foreign manufacturers—have their own policies regarding child labor. Nevertheless, the proliferation of codes creates growing opportunities for cooperation among the various actors along the supply chain in developing and implementing standards on child labor and other working condition issues.

By subcontracting portions of the production process, particularly labor-intensive manufacturing and assembly, to smaller firms, multinational firms try to distance themselves from the most exploitative aspects of global production. When confronted with gross violations of basic rights by their subcontractors, multinationals commonly claim that they have no knowledge and no control over these conditions. But consumer and worker groups point out that multinationals routinely send representatives to subcontracting firms to monitor the quality of their production processes. If these companies do quality checks over the products produced by workers in subcontracted firms, they should not turn a blind eye to the labor and environmental abuses of those subcontractors.

A global network of sweatshops has propelled multinational growth. More than two million workers are currently employed in overseas assembly plants that produce goods for firms like Disney Company, Nike, The Gap, and J.C. Penney. The National Labor Committee found that Disney contracts with a Haitian company that pays its workers 28 cents an hour to make Pocahontas and Mickey Mouse pajamas. Subcontractor employees producing Nike shoes in Southeast Asia complain that they are forced to work sixty hours per week, are paid $2.20 a day, and sometimes suffer physical torture.[55]

Specific Examples of Codes: Levi Strauss and Reebok

Most available information on codes of conduct is on large corporations. For example, U.S. companies in such diverse industries as footwear (Nike, Reebok), personal care products (Gillette), photographic equipment and supplies (Polaroid), stationery products (Hallmark), hardware products (Home Depot), restaurants (Starbucks), and electronics and computers (Honeywell) are known to have corporate codes of conduct. In addition, several business organizations have issued codes of conduct designed to be used by medium- and small-sized member companies whose corporate structures may not be sufficiently large to develop their own code of conduct.[56]

Levi Strauss

As a privately held company, free from the burden of shareholder control, Levi Strauss has done more in less time with corporate social responsibility than many other firms in overseas business. In creating its code of conduct, Levi Strauss evaluated the United Nations' Universal Declaration of Human Rights, in addition to other international human rights documents. In March, 1992, the Levi Strauss Executive Management Committee approved the two-part code of conduct, the Business Partner Terms of Engagement and Guidelines for Country Selection. The first part, "terms of engagement," covers environmental requirements, ethical standards, health and safety, legal requirements, and employment practices to the extent they are issues that are substantially controllable by individual business partners. The employment practices section specifically addresses six types of employment conditions: wages and benefits, working hours, child labor, prison labor/forced labor, and discrimination and disciplinary practices. The second part, guidelines for country selection, deals with issues Levi Strauss believes are beyond the scope of individual partners. They include brand image, health and safety, human rights, legal requirements, and political and social stability. In addition to Levi Strauss's advisory use of its code of conduct, the company has created a detailed internal monitoring and enforcement system. It begins with a questionnaire on employment practices in foreign supplier plants that deals with every element of the terms of engagement. Additionally, the internal enforcement mechanism permits audits, including surprise visits, intensive review by company personnel, and a cutoff of contractors for violators. In 1993, a year after adopting these policies, Levi Strauss had terminated contracts with thirty suppliers worldwide and had forced employment practice reforms in more than one hundred others.[57]

Reebok

Reebok's Code of Conduct for its commitment to human and labor rights, known as the Reebok Human Rights Production Standards, addresses seven areas of labor rights: working hours/overtime, forced or compulsory labor, fair wages, child labor, freedom of association, and a safe and healthy work environment. The Reebok Code differs from the Levi Strauss Code in a number of material ways. First, Reebok recognizes the right of its workers to organize and bargain collectively, whereas Levi Strauss does not acknowledge the right of its foreign workers to form trade unions or bargain collectively. Second, Reebok, unlike Levi Strauss or Nike, uses joint-venture factories (i.e., joint ownership between Reebok and local business entities), rather than contract with a government or third-party, investor-owned facility. This method enables the company to manage the workplace environment more effectively, implement its codes of conduct, and assure the quality of its product. Third, the Reebok Code, compared to the Levi Strauss Code, is a less defined instrument for auditing, evaluating, and enforcing the terms of its code.[58]

Three Key Attributes

Credibility is the critical element for codes of conduct. Without it, the promises contained in a code are hollow and the credibility of the company falters. Companies' success in assuring the public that their policies on labor practices abroad are indeed being followed will depend on the three key elements of implementation: (1) transparency, (2) monitoring, and (3) enforcement.[59]

An important issue regarding the implementation of corporate codes is their transparency, or the extent to which foreign contractors and subcontractors, workers, the public, nongovernmental organizations, and governments are aware of their existence and meaning. Contractors, subcontractors, workers, and other interested parties who are familiar with codes can enhance their implementation and effectiveness. Transparency reinforces the message of codes and leads to more credible implementation. When transparency is absent, interested parties cannot benefit from a code of conduct. There are several concrete ways by which U.S. companies add transparency to the implementation of their codes of conduct:

- Some American corporations hold training sessions with foreign suppliers (contractors or subcontractors) to make them aware of their code of conduct and implementation expectations. Some companies require foreign suppliers to sign a statement indicating that they have received the code of conduct and understand its meaning and implementation expectations, including possible penalties for lack of implementation.
- Some companies also train their own employees or buying agents on their code of conduct to ensure that individuals at all stages of the purchasing process are aware of its provisions.
- A small number of U.S. corporations require that the contents of their code of conduct be posted in production facilities at a location that is accessible to workers (e.g., a

lunch room or entrance to locker room). In some cases, the U.S. company translates the code into the local language.

- A small number of companies solicit input from outside groups in developing and implementing their code.

Unfortunately, codes of conduct conceived in the headquarters of U.S. apparel importers are not necessarily well known in the overseas facilities that produce their garments.[60]

Companies utilize a variety of means to monitor that their codes of conduct or policies on child labor are respected by their suppliers:

- Some companies use a form of active monitoring, which involves site visits and inspections, by company staff, buyer agents, or other parties, to verify that suppliers are actually implementing the importing company's policy on child labor.
- Some use contractual monitoring, whereby they rely on the guarantees made by suppliers, usually through contractual agreements or certification, that they are respecting a company's policy and not using any child labor in production. This may be seen as self-certification by contractors or suppliers. Companies that use contractual monitoring in some cases have no mechanism for compliance.
- Some firms use a combination of active and contractual monitoring.

Active monitoring may be done through regular checks, formal audits or evaluations, or special visits by corporate staff. The frequency and intensity of visits vary greatly from company to company. For example, some companies may focus their site visits on their larger suppliers or suppliers where there have been alleged problems or may only monitor those facilities from which they import directly or which manufacture their private-label merchandise.

Contractual monitoring shifts at least part of the burden of responsibility for ensuring compliance with codes of conduct onto the foreign manufacturer, the supplier, or the buying agent. Even when monitoring is primarily contractual, there are instances in which the U.S. corporation requires documentary proof of compliance or reserves the right to carry out on-site inspections.

While technically not a monitoring activity, evaluation of prospective contractors with regard to labor standards has become an important aspect of code implementation. On-site evaluations or inspections have long been made primarily to verify whether the facilities have the physical capacity to meet quality and quantity specifications. Increasingly, the working conditions and employment practices of prospective contractors are also being evaluated, screening out firms that are violators or have the potential for being so in the future.

A limited number of corporations use external monitoring. For external monitoring to be at all credible, however, monitors must: be truly independent from the enterprise; understand internationally recognized labor standards; have practical experience; a real understanding of labor relations; and special knowledge of how labor standards are applied in the workplace. Corporations who do external monitoring sometimes use monitors who have little or no experience with labor standards. For example, auditing firms are often used for monitoring purposes. Although auditors may be able to apply a set of pre-developed questions as a way of monitoring, monitoring requires more skills than simply filling in blanks on a questionnaire. It requires a working knowledge of labor standards and labor experience, which is not something that many auditors are familiar with. In addition to lacking significant experience in applying fundamental rights in the workplace, many auditing firms will also have previous relationships with the corporation they are monitoring. This, in itself, detracts from the necessary credibility that is required in order for any monitoring program to be a success.[61]

While a credible system of monitoring to verify that a code is indeed being followed in practice is essential, there is no agreement on the best way to conduct monitoring. The most effective type of monitoring may vary according to the characteristics of the importing company, such as whether it has a strong presence abroad or whether it is vertically integrated. It appears that the closer a company is to the production, the more leverage it has to ensure that the conditions at manufacturing facilities comply with its policies. There also appears to be some dispute among retailers, manufacturers, overseas contractors, and other parties as to who has the ultimate responsibility for monitoring. Moreover, many companies find themselves in a Catch-22 position. Refusing to publicly disclose audit findings calls into questions a firm's commitment to fix what's wrong. "Until we are able to see what they're doing, it's hard to know what is really going on. We have to open the lid and look inside," says Massachusetts Institute of Technology Professor Dana O'Rourke, who has observed inspections at more than 100 factories as part of his academic research. "Independent monitoring can play a positive role in improving factory conditions, but only if it is much more transparent and can be verified by workers and local nongovernmental organizations."[62]

Superficial Monitoring: Nike and Andrew Young

In the summer of 1997, Andrew Young, the civil rights leader and former United Nations ambassador, completed a carefully guided tour of Nike factories in the Far East and declared that all is well. "What we saw overwhelmingly was good," said Young. This comment and Young's findings in his report drew widespread and severe criticism. While Nike's much-touted report by Young claims to take a hard look at its Asian factories and labor practices, finding generally favorable conditions, human rights groups say the report is misleading and is riddled with methodological problems. The director of Vietnam Labor Watch, Thuyen Nguyen, assailed Young for failing to address such issues as poverty-level wages, excessive overtime, minimum-wage violations, corporal punishment, and a militaristic management style to control workers. The head of Global Exchange maintained, "If Young's report weren't so attractive from a public relations point of view, I'd say it was a big joke. The methodology is totally flawed."[63] An editorial by Anita Chan of the Contemporary China Centre at Australian National University in Canberra also criticized Young's methodology. She says Young failed to investigate labor practices in many Chinese footwear factories that require workers, most of whom are poor migrants from rural areas, to pay an illegal deposit, which is supposedly returned to them at termination of employment. Wellco, a Korean Nike subcontractor with a factory in south China, demands a deposit equivalent to one month's wage. Chan contended that those workers who quit short of a year have to forfeit their deposit, no matter how much they dislike the working conditions.[64]

Monitoring is critical to the success of a code of conduct; it also gives the code credibility. Yet, most of the codes do not contain detailed provisions for monitoring and implementation, and many companies do not have a reliable monitoring system in place.

Enforcement

Enforcement of codes of conduct refers to how U.S. companies respond to violations of their codes of conduct. Child-labor violations of their codes are less common than other types of violations, such as safety and health. Factories that have passed the screening process and have become contractors of U.S. apparel importers may face a range of corrective measures should they fall short in complying with codes of conduct. Examples of corrective measures include changes to the physical plant (improvement of bathrooms, eating facilities, lighting, ventilation), monetary penalties, immediate dismissal of young workers, and termination of contracts. Continued access to the U.S. market is a very large incentive for overseas garment producers to meet quality/timeliness requirements and comply with codes of conduct.

Enforcing a code of conduct becomes more difficult when offshore vendors and subcontractors are involved. Although some firms have tried to export their code of conduct to international vendors and subcontractors, apparel manufacturers can find it extremely difficult to identify and effectively react to labor abuses occurring on the other side of the globe. A long-distance relationship complicates matters: not only do the code of conduct documents have to be translated, but they must be explained and enforced in cultures different from that of the United States. Subcontractors in impoverished nations often will sign anything to obtain a major contract. Once the contract is signed, subcontractors continue operating as they always have, altering their operating standards only if they know that complete monitoring will often follow.

However, spot checks, that is, audits and on-site monitoring, of vendors and subcontractors, are costly and labor-intensive. Many apparel companies are not even aware that such compliance/monitoring programs exist because there are so few players domestically, and even fewer with international capabilities.[65]

One method for increasing the effectiveness of enforcement is through the monitoring of all workers who are covered by the code. Corporations will either conduct monitoring internally or externally. Internal monitoring is most common and, by its very nature, raises serious questions regarding its legitimacy. Understandably, internal monitors often have very strong ties to the company itself, thus raising immediate doubts regarding their objectivity. In addition, questions remain regarding internal monitors' expertise in terms of understanding and applying internationally recognized labor standards.[66]

Despite the growing number of voluntary corporate codes of conduct, few, if any, of them adequately incorporate adequate safeguards ensuring full compliance. Accordingly, it should not be surprising that serious questions are being asked regarding the commitment of certain corporations to adopt meaningful codes. In view of the aforementioned, corporations must seriously ask themselves whether they are truly interested in empowering their workers through the introduction of corporate codes of conduct. If they are not, then they should admit it and not try to fool themselves, the public, and their workers into believing otherwise. If, on the other hand, corporations are truly interested in empowering workers, then they should develop codes that do not contain the flaws that have been highlighted. If a company discovers child workers in a facility, the quickest and perhaps easiest way to resolve the problem, codes notwithstanding, is to require their immediate dismissal.[67]

NOTES

1. Wayne Barrett and Tracie McMillan, "Geraldine Ferraro: Sweatshop Landlord," *The Village Voice,* 10 March 1998, 41.

2. U.S. House of Representatives, Committee on Manufactures, *Report on the Sweating System,* 1898, IV.

3. This was the number of shops registered under a New York law designed primarily to safeguard the health of those using the manufactured items, as reported in Thomas Sewell Adams and Helen L. Sumner, *Labor Problems,* (London: Macmillan, 1985), 128–129.

4. John A. Garraty, *The American Nation: A History of the United States,* (New York: Harper & Row, 1975), 653.

5. U.S. General Accounting Office, *"Sweatshops" in the U.S.: Opinions on Their Extent and Possible Enforcement Options,* (Washington, DC: USGPO, August 1988), 9.

6. Kenneth C. Crowe, "Student Briefing Page On The News: Children Toil In Sweatshops," *Newsday,* 9 September 1998, A20.

7. New York State Department of Labor, *How to Identify Garment Sweatshops: A Business Guide For Manufacturers and Retailers,* n.d.

8. Bruce Frankel, "A New Wave of 'Expendables': Factories Feeding Off Immigrants," *USA Today* 17 June 1993, 3A.

9. Bureau of National Affairs, "Garment Industry Sweatshop Conditions Persist Despite More Coordinated Enforcement, GAO Says," *Daily Labor Report,* 17 November 1994, D-5.

10. Farhan Haq, "United States: Critics Link Immigration Laws to Sweatshops," *Inter Press Service,* 26 March 1996.

11. Paula L. Green, "New York Keeps Pressure on its Apparel Sweatshops," *Journal of Commerce* 26 March 1997, 5A.

12. UNITE Research Department, "How Many Sweatshops Are There in the United States Today?" *Sweatshop Information Sheet,* n.d., 2.

13. "California Adopts Toughest Sweatshop Law of its Kind in the Country," *Sweatshop Watch,* 5(2) (Fall 1999): 1.

14. Fang-Lian Liao, "Illegal Immigrants In Garment Sweatshops: The Universal Declaration of Human Rights and The International Covenant on Civil and Political Rights," *Southwestern Journal of Law and Trade in the Americas,* 3 (Fall 1996): 487.

15. "Labor: Unemployment," *Migration News,* 8(11) (November 2001): 2.

16. "Get Involved: What is a Sweatshop?" *In Our Sanctum,* 30 March 2002.

17. Robert Collier, "U.S. Firms Reducing Sweatshop Abuses," *San Francisco Chronicle,* 17 April 1999, Al.

18. John F. Hudacs, "Homework Can Be Bad for Kids," *Newsday,* 1 October 1992, 46.

19. Linda N. Edwards and Elizabeth Field-Hendrey, "Home-Based Workers: Data from the 1990 Census of Population," *Monthly Labor Review,* (November 1996): 26, 33.

20. Hilary Silver, "Work at Home Invites the Exploiter to Come In: Sweating the Worker," *The New York Times,* 2 December 1986, A34.

21. Del Jones, "Home-Sewing Sweatshops Thrive in USA." *USA Today,* 4 June 1996, 18.

22. "Industrial Homework Investigation in LA Garment Industry Continues," *DIR NEWS,* 15 August 1996.

23. Elaine D' Aurizio, "Garment Labor Abuse Cited; Bill Would Outlaw Homework," *The Record* (Bergen, NJ), 3 October 1990, B05.

24. Testimony by Richard Trumka, Secretary-Treasurer, AFL-CIO, on Labor-HHS Appropriations before the House Appropriations Committee, Subcommittee on Labor, Health and Human Services, and Education, 22 May 2001.

25. K. Oanh Ha, "Worker Settles Lawsuit with Contract Employer over Piecework," *San Jose Mercury News,* 15 November 2000.

26. The Associated Press, "Legal Curb on Sewing Draws Ire," *New York Times,* 15 June 1989, C9.

27. Verena Dobnik and Ted Anthony, "From Fields and Factories, Children's Voices Emerge," The Associated Press, 9 December 1997.

28. Steven Greenhouse, "Farm Work by Children Tests Labor Laws," *The New York Times,* 6 August 2000, 12.

29. Testimony by the Farmworker Justice Fund, Inc. on "Environmental Toxins and Children: Exploring the Risks," before the Select Committee on Children, Youth, and Families, (Washington, DC: USGPO, 1990), 178.

30. James Rainey, "Opposite Views Arise on Farm Labor Fines; Agriculture: To Workers, Data Show Lax Enforcement. Growers Say Drop in Sanctions Marks Better Compliance," *Los Angeles Times* 19 April 2000, A1.

31. Ron Nixon, "Caution: Children at Work; Child Agricultural Laborers," *The Progressive,* 60(8) (August 1996): 30.

32. Caroline Cox, "Working with Poisons on the Farm," *Journal of Pesticide Reform,* 14(3) (Fall 1994): 2–5.

33. National Resources Defense Council, "Pesticides Threaten Farm Children's Health," 22 November 1998.

34. U.S. Environmental Protection Agency, *Basic Principles of the Worker Protection Standard,* 6 July 1999.

35. Valerie A. Wilk, *The Occupational Health of Migrant and Seasonal Farmworkers in the United States* (2d ed.) (Washington, DC: Farmworker Justice Fund, Inc., 1986), 99.

36. National Resources Defense Council, "Trouble on the Farm: Growing Up with Pesticides in Agricultural Communities," October 1998, 4.

37. Lisa J. Gold, *Pesticide Laws and Michigan Migrant Farmworkers: Are They Protected?,* JSRI Research Report" # 12 (East Lansing, MI: The Julian Samora Research Institute, Michigan State University, 1996) 10.

38. "Farm Worker Illness Following Exposure to Carbofuran and Other Pesticides—Fresno County, California, 1998," *Morbidity and Mortality Weekly Report,* 48(6) (19 February 1999): 113–116.

39. Penelope A. Fenner-Crisp, "Pesticides—The NAS Report: How Can the Recommendations Be Implemented?" *Environmental Health Perspectives,* 103 (Suppl. 6) (1995): 159–152.

40. Bert McMeen, "Groups Petition For Protection of Children Living on Farms, Citing Exposure Studies," *Toxics Law Reporter,* 13(24) (November 11, 1998): 752.

41. Don Villarego and Celia Prado, "WPS Unknown To Farmworkers," *On-Line News,* (Davis, CA: University of California Agricultural Health and Safety Center, Winter 1997), 4.

42. Kenneth Rosenman, "Reports of Pesticide Related Toxicity in Michigan," *Pesticide Notes,* 8(3) (May–June 1995): 2.

43. *May 1999 Meetings of the Education and Practice Workgroups,* (Washington, DC: Environmental Protection Agency, Office of Pesticide Programs).

44. U.S. General Accounting Office, *Pesticides: Improvements Needed to Ensure the Safety of Farmworkers and Their Children* (March 2000) 11–12.

45. "GAO Says EPA Needs to Act on Farm Pesticides, Children," *Toxic Chemicals Litigation Reporter,* 18(1) (2 June 2000): 8.

46. "Officials Want To Improve Farmer Medical Care," *BC Cycle,* (30 May 1990).

47. *Recent Developments in the Clothing Industry* (Geneva: International Labor Organization, 1995) 7.

48. "The Anti-Sweatshop Movement and Corporate Codes of Conduct," *Perspectives on Work,* 5(1): 15–16.

49. "Apparel: Administration Plan To Combat Sweatshops Called Deeply Flawed," *Daily Labor Report,* (58) (26 March 1999): A-10.

50. "Apparel: Former White Counsel Named Head of Entity Monitoring Labor Standards," *Daily Labor Report,* (175) 10 September 1999, A-14.

51. "Nearly 1000 Companies Announce Intention To Join The FLA: Universities Urge Licensees To Join," *Fair Labor Association Press Release,* (12 June 2001).

52. Saurav Sarkar, "Charlie Ruff, FLA and Sweatshops," *Yale Daily News* (20 September 1999).

53. MSN Resource Centre, *Codes Primer* (Toronto, Canada, n.d.)

54. U.S. Department of Labor, Bureau of International Affairs, *The Apparel Industry and Codes of Conduct: A Solution to the International Child Labor Problem,* (Washington, DC: USGPO, 1996) 31.

55. Ibid., 41–43.

56. Robert D. Haas, "Ethics—A Global Business Challenge: Character and Courage," Speech to the Conference Board, New York City (4 May 1994), *Vital Speeches of the Day,* 506, 507 (on file with the International Child Labor Study).

57. Lance Compa and Tashia Hinchcliffe-Darricarrere, "Enforcing International Labor Rights Through Corporate Codes of Conduct," *Columbia Journal of Transnational Law,* 33 (1995): 663.

58. Ibid.

59. DOL, Bureau of International Labor Affairs, *The Apparel Industry Codes of Conduct,* 41–43.

60. Ibid.

61. Owen E. Herrnstadt, "Voluntary Corporate Codes of Conduct: What's Missing?" *The Labor Lawyer,* 16 (Winter/Spring 2001): 349.

62. Tim Vickery, "Who's Watching the Shop Floor?" *The Christian Science Monitor,* 30 April 2001, 11.

63. Boaz Herzog, "Reports Disagree on Nike Factories," *Oregonian* (May 16, 2001): D01.

64. Bob Herbert, "Mr. Young Gets It Wrong," *Chattanooga Times,* 1 July 1997, A4.

65. Jorge Perez-Lopez, "Promoting International Respect for Worker Rights Through Business Codes of Conduct," *Fordham International Law Journal,* (17)(1) (1993): 9–12.

66. Compa and Hinchcliffe-Darricarrere, "Enforcing International Labor Rights," 674–675.

67. Steven Greenhouse, "Students Urge Colleges to Join a New Anti-Sweatshop Group," *New York Times,* 20 October 1999, A-23.

7
The Impact of Child Labor upon Education and Development

Employment during high school is increasingly common among youth and recent government policies, notably school-to-work programs, are further promoting employment for high school students. What are the advantages and drawbacks for youth who are working while in school? Should we be encouraging it? How does it affect individuals' decisions regarding investments in education? Do effects persist for the long term? Does employment affect all youth similarly?[1]

YOUTH EMPLOYMENT AND EDUCATION

In their comments, two researchers lead us into a discussion of the linkage between youthful employment and the educational process, with both positive and negative consequences, which will be explored in this chapter.

Overview

Teens have always worked, helping out on family farms and filling the factories of the Industrial Revolution. In the first half of the twentieth century, however, the percentage of teens in the labor force dropped rapidly. Youths spent more time in school as the demand for cheap, unskilled labor declined and child labor laws went into effect. By 1940, fewer than 3 percent of U.S. high school students were working while in school. But after World War II, the number of working teens soared in the United States.[2] In today's American society, it has become common for adolescents to hold part-time jobs during non-school hours. Reasons for the increasing rates of youth entering the workforce in recent decades include the rise in the retail and service sectors of the economy and the increasing cost of living.

It has been estimated that 85 percent of American teenagers have or have had a part-time job while in high school. This figure shows that more than half of high school students are taking on more than the responsibility of academics. This raises the questions: How much work is too much? And what are the effects of this work? Research has attempted to answer these questions. Studies show that varying the amount of work hours have different positive and negative effects on adolescents. A common theme is that it is not necessarily whether you do or do not work that poses problems, but rather the duration of time worked.

It is not uncommon for adolescents today to manage school, friends, family, and work. For teens, obtaining employment outside the home is a mark of their transition into adulthood and their growing ability to become independent from their family of origin. It has been estimated that American youth, 44 percent of males and 41 percent of females, will have held jobs before leaving high school.[3] Of the 5.5 million American teenagers who are employed, 6 percent work to help their families, while the remaining 94 percent work in order to have their own spending money. Youth from middle-income families are more likely to hold jobs as compared to their low-income counterparts, 73 percent versus 60 percent. This trend may be related to the students' reason for working.[4]

The United States is the only country in the world where full-time students are encouraged to work. This American emphasis on working students contrasts with most other industrial countries, where the worlds of work and school are considered separate. A new study by the International Labor Organization (ILO) demonstrated that American teenagers work far more than teenagers in most other countries. The study found that 53 percent of American teens, from the ages of 16 to 19, work in any given week. In Japan, 18 percent of teenagers aged 15 through 19 work, while in Germany, 30.8 percent of teenagers in that age bracket are employed.[5]

Increasing Educational Requirements

Youth employment is part of the fabric of American family life today. This is even more true today than at any other time since the child labor laws were passed. This issue is significant today because the educational demands on American youth to prepare them for the competitiveness of the global workforce is at odds with declining educational achievement, skills, standards, and effort. Increasingly, part of the blame is attached to adolescent employment.

The intuitive belief that work is beneficial has, until recently, precluded any serious consideration that an early transition into work may, in fact, be detrimental for some youth. The changed attitude toward youth employment is in large part due to an increased awareness of the significance of educational attainment.

The relative importance of a high school education has changed dramatically over the last half century in the United States. When the grandparents of today's high school students entered adulthood, a high school education was an asset in the labor force, an asset held by about half of the population, ages 25 through 29 in 1950. By the early 1970s, when the parents of today's high school students entered the workforce, about 83 to 84 percent of the population, ages 18 through 24, who were not enrolled in high school had completed a high school education. At that time, a high school education still served as an entryway to a number of promising career paths. Now, a quarter of a century later, technological advances in the workplace have increased the demand for a skilled labor force to the point where a high school education serves more as a minimum requirement for entry into the labor force. Completing a high school education is now even more essential in order to access additional education and training for the labor force.[6]

Effects of Sleep Deprivation

Sleep deprivation is a problem a lot of teenagers have because a lot of part-time jobs involve working late at night. Too many hours spent working leave little time for schoolwork, and school performance may suffer. Research suggests that the normal (circadian) rhythm of adolescents would result in their rising later in the morning and going to bed later in the night. That is, puberty appears to cause a change in the mechanism that triggers when the adolescent needs to go to sleep and to arise. Forcing the adolescent to get up early does not seem to alter the cycle. The result is that the adolescent who gets "out of sync" becomes sleepy and moody.

The need for sleep may be nine hours or more per night as a person goes through adolescence. At the same time, many teens begin to show a preference for a later bedtime, which may be due to a biological change. Teens tend to stay up later but have to get up early for school, resulting in their getting much less sleep than they need.

Sleep deprivation can impair memory and inhibit creativity, making it difficult for sleep-deprived students to learn. Teenagers with chronic sleep debt are likely to fall asleep frequently in class or while studying. They are also prone to brief lapses of attention or responsiveness, creating even more problems, whether in the classroom or behind the wheel. Also, adolescents who have trouble getting out of bed in the morning and to class on time are more likely to have conflicts with parents and teachers. Those who resort to stimulants or nicotine in an effort to seem more alert only compound the problem.[7]

School schedules requiring students to attend at a time when they struggle to stay awake limit the students' motivation and interest in the educational process. In contrast, many students go to after-school jobs at a time when they are more alert. This more friendly time frame, as well as the tangible monetary reward of jobs, may contribute to many students' preferences for work over school. Sleep and circadian rhythms, therefore, have a powerful impact on their disaffection with school and their affinity for after-school jobs.[8]

The amount of sleep students get may affect their grades. In surveys, those who reported mostly A's and B's went to bed earlier on both nights and weekends than those who received D's and F's. High achievers averaged thirty-five minutes more per day than low achievers.[9]

Harmful Effects of Excessive Employment

There appears to be very little correlation between employment opportunities for youth and their educational development, given the nature of most current teen employment opportunities.

The vast majority of today's adolescent employment (predominantly retail and service industry jobs) does not measure up. The average adolescent food service worker, for example, spends about one minute of every hour on the job using school-taught skills. Moreover, the majority of teenagers have few chances to make major decisions and have little influence over the actions of others. Most work under a great deal of time pressure and are expected to repeat a limited number of highly routinized tasks quickly, efficiently, almost mechanically, without involving any meaningful thought processes.

Beginning in the mid-1980s, numerous studies on part-time student employment have concluded that excessive and late night work during the school year impact academic achievement. When part-time employment exceeds fifteen hours weekly, a decline in academic achievement normally follows. The decline is hastened dramatically when work exceeds twenty hours per week. In one of Laurence Steinberg's projects, he and his colleagues followed student employment over a two-year period. This study examined the over-time relation between school-year employment and adjustment in a heterogeneous sample of approximately 1,800 high school sophomores and juniors. The longitudinal study has some interesting results: First, many adolescents who choose employment are less engaged in school before they enter the labor force, but taking on a part-time job further exacerbates the problems of school performance and orientation. Second, compared with their counterparts who remained out of the labor force, adolescents who entered the workplace exhibited a greater occurrence of developmental dysfunctions. In particular, these dysfunctions were identified: working adolescents spend less time on homework, cut class more often, report lower educational expectations, and are more disengaged from school, even after taking into account any differences in these variables that preceded their labor force entry. Third, when minors enter the labor force, and, in particular, take on a job for more than twenty hours weekly, their investment in school diminishes, delinquency and drug use increases, and autonomy from parental control grows. Fourth, among adolescents who work moderate hours, increasing their work hours beyond twenty hours per week weakens their investment in school further, whereas leaving the labor force leads to an improvement in school performance or orientation. And finally, over one-third of the working adolescents admitted to taking easier courses to maintain decent grades. Because so many students work, some teachers are responding by demanding less in the classroom. A study within several Wisconsin schools in the early 1980s revealed that teachers shortened reading assignments, simplified lectures, and reduced out-of-class assignments to accommodate teen work schedules.[10]

While the effects of working during high school were generally negative, there were some effects of work that had positive influences on student outcomes. Specifically, working to save money for college had noticeable positive effects on students' academic and social outcomes, especially actual college attendance.[11]

Work Intensity and School Leaving

In recent years, educators have become concerned that having a part-time job may detract from academic success; in particular, it may increase the likelihood of leaving school before a certificate or diploma is earned. Research results have been contradictory. One study found that hours worked during the school year were an important predictor of dropping out, with the risk of non-completion increasing as hours work increased. However, an earlier study found that students who worked less than twenty hours per week were more likely to remain in school than students who were not employed. It would appear that a relationship exists between work involvement, school experiences, and academic performance. Working moderate hours tends to be associated with positive school experiences and academic success.[12]

It seems likely that intensive work involvement increases the risk of school leaving for many students, particularly males, either because the balance between the time demands of school and work can no longer be maintained, or because long work hours are indicative of an underlying process of disengagement from school. Long hours may then reinforce the school-leaving process by providing tangible and immediate psychic and monetary rewards that outweigh the more abstract and long-term benefits of graduation.

The lower risk of school leaving associated with moderate work involvement among both men and women may indicate that a self-selection process is operating. That is, students who perform well academically, have positive school experiences, and participate in classroom and extracurricular activities may also have the extra energy for a job and the motivation to keep part-time hours manageable. In contrast, students with lower school performance and negative school experiences may lack the necessary skills or the interest in employment, or may take on jobs with extensive time commitments as they begin to disengage in school in favor of work.[13]

Work During High School and Academic Performance

The greater the work involvement, the more likely students are to get lower grades. Students' previous grades also affect their later working behaviors; students who had higher grades in elementary and middle school are less likely to work longer hours when they reach tenth grade.[14] Students of high ability are likely to hold regular jobs that require few hours each week. But school-year employment tends to compromise academic performance overall. The largest adverse effect is among minority students, especially those who go from not working to working more than twenty hours weekly in most or all weeks of the school year. In one study, these students' averages declined about 0.20 grade points in one year. Summer employment, unlike employment during the school year, has no adverse impact on students' grade point averages.[15]

Students who worked part-time tended to modify their course selections. Part-time work intensity, or the number of hours worked, had a significant negative effect on the number of mathematics courses that these students took. The more hours that students worked, the fewer mathematics courses they completed; this, in turn, led to lower achievement in mathematics. Similarly, part-time work intensity had a negative effect on science course work; the higher the work intensity, the fewer science courses students took.[16]

There also may be a negative relationship between work intensity and school completion. Working during high school may lower the overall educational aspirations of adolescents. Researchers found that students who did not work during high school had completed an average of three quarters of a year more of schooling five years after graduation.[17] Also, more fundamental factors may cause both long work hours and low school performance. One researcher concluded that adolescents who worked longer hours were already less academically inclined and that their drop in grade point average was not necessarily the result of their work schedule.[18]

Consequences of School Leaving

One measure of the success of a country's educational system is the level of education achieved by its young adults. In this country, the primary standard of educational level has been high school graduation. Indeed, one of the oldest series of data collected by the federal government is the proportion of the population that has completed high school. These data show that there has been remarkable progress in the last half-century in high school completion rates. Rates increased from 38 percent of all 25-to-29-year-olds in 1940 to around 86 percent in the early 1980s and have remained constant since. As a consequence of this progress, during the past fifty years, high school completion became an expectation for young people in this country.[19]

In many school systems around the country, especially those in wealthy suburbs, a high percentage of students stay in school and graduate on time with a good education. However, many students, especially those living in troubled inner-city areas, attend schools where graduating on time with a solid education is more the exception than the rule. In high-poverty neighborhoods in large cities (neighborhoods with poverty rates above 20 percent) one-fifth of 16-to-19-year-olds were high school dropouts in 1999.[20]

Teens who drop out of high school will find it difficult to achieve financial success in life. The most recent data available from the Census Bureau's Survey of Income and Program Participation suggest that high school dropouts are three times as likely to slip into poverty from one year to the next as those who have finished high school.[21] A recent report from the Department of Education concludes, "In terms of employment, earnings, and family formation, dropouts from high school face difficulties in making the transition to the adult world."[22]

As America moves further into the twenty-first century, when advanced skills and technical knowledge will be required for most meaningful jobs, the prospects for those who have not completed high school will be even more dismal. Ongoing changes in the U.S. economy have increased the financial costs of dropping out of high school. Between 1973 and 1999, for example, the average hourly wage (adjusted for inflation) of high school dropouts fell 24 percent. The deterioration of wages among poorly educated workers has hit the youngest workers the hardest, and this factor often is implicated in the erosion of family formation and family stability among young adults.[23]

Researchers illustrated the complexity of the dropout dilemma using the High School and Beyond (HSB) data. A key finding was that most of the dropouts reported they regretted their decisions to leave school early. Within a two-year period after dropping out, the participants in one study reported unemployment in addition to poor job satisfaction because of being trapped in low-paying jobs.[24] In another research project utilizing the HSB data furnished by the National Center of Educational Statistics, more consequences of dropping out of school were identified. Specifically, salary for current job, work satisfaction, extent of unemployment, and number of jobs held were examined. Almost 600 dropouts participated as well as more than 1,300 high school graduates. Analysis revealed that dropouts reported lower work satisfaction, changed jobs more often, and experienced longer periods of unemployment as compared to graduates.[25] Dropping out carries a high price. Nationally, 18 percent of workers with less than a year of high school live below the poverty level, compared to 13 percent of those who dropped out later in high school and 7 percent who graduated, according to a 1999 survey. And while elementary school dropouts were 7 percent of the 1997 U.S. adult population, they were 13 percent of local and county jail inmates and 14 percent of state prison inmates, according to the Department of Justice.[26]

Recent Dropout and Completion Rates

While progress was made during the 1970s and 1980s in reducing high school dropout rates and increasing high school completion rates, these rates remained comparatively stable during the 1990s. To help provide a clear picture of high school dropouts, three statistical measures are used by the Department of Education: event dropout rates, status dropout rates, and high school completion rates. *Dropout Rates in the United States: 2000* discusses these measures, as well as examines the characteristics of high school dropout and high school completers in 2000.[27]

Event Dropout Rates

Event dropout rates for 2000 describe the proportion of youth ages 15–24 who dropped out of grades 10–12 in the twelve months preceding October 2000:

- Five out of every 100 15-through-24-year-olds who had been enrolled in high school in October 1999 left school before October 2000 without successfully completing high school. The percentage that left school each year decreased from 1972 through 1987. Despite year-to-year fluctuations, the percentage of students dropping out of school each year has stayed relatively unchanged since 1987.
- In 2000, the event dropout rate for Hispanics was 7.4 percent, 6.1 percent for blacks, 4.1 percent for whites, and 3.5 percent for Asians/Pacific islanders.
- In 2000, the dropout rate for students from the lowest 20 percent of all family incomes was six times that of their peers from families in the highest 20 percent.
- In 2000, about three-fourths (76 percent) of the current-year dropouts were ages 15 through 18; moreover, about two-fifths (42 percent) of the dropouts were ages 15 through 17.

The Status Rate

The status dropout rates represent the proportion of young people ages 16 through 24 who are out of school and who have not earned a high school credential. Status rates are higher than event rates because they include all dropouts in this age range, regardless of when they last attended school. According to the status rate, over the last decade, between 347,000 and 544,000 tenth-through-twelfth-grade students left school each year without successfully completing a high school program. Other statistics include:

- In October 2000, some 3.8 million 16-through-24-year-olds were not enrolled in a high school program and had not completed high school. These youths accounted for 11 percent of the 34.6 million 16-through-24-year-olds in the United States in 2000. As noted with event rates, status rates have declined from the early 1970s into the late 1980s, but since then, have remained stable.
- In 2000, the status dropout rate for Asian/Pacific islander youth was lower than for youth from all other racial/ethnic groups. The status rate for Asian/Pacific islanders was 4 percent compared with 28 percent for Hispanics, 13 percent for blacks, and 7 percent for whites.
- In 2000, 44 percent of Hispanic youth born outside the United States were high school dropouts. Hispanics born within the United States were much less likely to be drop-

outs than foreign-born Hispanics, but had higher rates than youth from other racial/ ethnic groups born within the United States.

High School Completion Rates

High school completion rates represent the proportion of 18-through-24-year-olds, not currently enrolled in high school or below, who have earned a high school diploma or an equivalent credential, including a General Educational Development (GED) credential. The completion rate is distinguished from a high school graduation rate, which includes only high school diplomas. High school completion rates increased for white and black young adults between the early 1970s and late 1980s, but remained relatively constant during the last decade. In 2000, 92 percent of white and 84 percent of black 18-through-24-year-olds had completed high school.[28]

The Plight of Adolescent Farmworkers

Three images of teen farmworkers come to mind. A small portion of teen farmworkers continue to be local rural youths whose parents are not farmworkers. These youths fit the traditional American image of students who work in the fields during school holidays. One example would be middle-class teens detasseling corn in Midwestern farm communities. However, while most teen farmworkers were born in the United States, the majority of them have characteristics that are very different from those of the aforementioned group. Overall, teen farmworkers are very poor; more than half live in households below the federal poverty threshold. Most are from poor, often migrant, households, with incomes under $25,000 annually.

These less-advantaged teen farmworkers consist of two groups. One group works along with their parents in the fields. Almost one-fourth of these school-age children of farmworkers are behind in grade or have dropped out of school. Few children of farm laborers attend school on a regular basis, and few school boards enforce compulsory attendance laws. The result is a very low rate of graduation from high school. Only 62 percent of children who did farm work were learning at a grade level compared with 78 percent who did not perform farm labor. Twenty-two percent of the adolescents working on farms were behind in grade and 16 percent had dropped out.[29]

In addition, there is a new and growing group of adolescents who are de facto emancipated minors. These teenagers live and work on their own, away from their families. According to the National Agricultural Workers Survey (NAWS), four in five migrant teens were de facto emancipated minors, not living with any other family member. The vast majority (91 percent) of minor migrant teens were foreign-born. These farmworker teens were falling behind academically. Nearly two-fifths worked in agriculture for more than thirteen weeks in a year, indicating that they probably did some farm work during the school year. These youths were at a high risk of never completing high school. Fewer than half (47 percent) were attending school at a grade level corresponding to their age. Fifteen percent were in school but behind in grade and 37 percent were dropouts who did not have a high school diploma and had not attended school within the last year.[30] (This information on the characteristics and work patterns of hired laborers who perform crop work in the United States was obtained from interviews with 4,199 workers in eighty-five counties between 1 October 1996 and 20 September 1998.)

Children of migrant farm laborers, more than other children, confront a number of risk factors for school failure. Some of these factors, including mobility, poverty, and lack of access to schooling, were recognized and described as early as the 1940s. Estimates of the number of adolescent farmworkers working in agriculture range from the General Accounting Office GAO)'s 300,000 15-to-17-year-olds who are employed each year to the 800,000 child farmworkers of the United Farm Workers union. The GAO acknowledges that its numbers most likely are an undercount due to so-called methodological problems largely resulting from the exclusion of children under 14 years of age. In fact, children under 14 are not included in any nationally based surveys of farmworkers.[31]

The truth is that one group of students from culturally and linguistically diverse backgrounds whose special education needs have not been adequately addressed is that of the children of migrant farmworkers. They face the dilemma of attending school or working in the fields to help support their families. It is estimated that a significant number of migrant children work the harvest, resulting in high rates of absence from school.[32] Although a number of federal programs target children with educational and economic disadvantages, the extent to which children involved in migrant and seasonal farm work participate in, or are helped by, these programs is generally unknown. Except for the programs that target only migrant and seasonal farmworkers and their children, program information does not classify participants by occupational status. Even those few programs that target children working in agriculture or children whose parents work in migrant and seasonal agriculture have limited data. For these children, the difficulties associated with poverty, limited English ability, and rural and social isolation place them at considerable risk of academic failure. Their school enrollment rates and high school completion rates are among the lowest in the nation. For example, according to one source, 45 percent of migrant youths had dropped out of school, entering the full-time workforce without the credentials and skills needed to compete for any but the lowest paying jobs.[33]

Mobility Considerations

Although migrant workers may take into account factors such as the availability of schools or the presence of friends and relatives when moving, ultimately, decisions about where and when to move are based primarily on economic necessity. They consider such factors as the length of seasons, changes in crop conditions, wages, and housing availability. Since the family's migration is not patterned around the traditional school year, migrant students experience considerable disruptions in the continuity of their education. Although migrant summer programs enable many students to make up missed instructional time, it is often difficult for migrant students to accrue enough academic credit to stay at grade level with their non-migrant peers. Frequent moves, adjusting to differing school systems, curricula, and social conditions, late starts or early exit during the school year, problems with records and credit transfers are migration-related problems that contribute to lower academic achievement and high dropout rates among migrant students.[34] Migrant children experience two types of mobility that compound the other social problems they face. For low-income children, particularly those who are migrant workers or children of migrant workers, schooling is frequently interrupted, and school days are lost, because of moves among school districts and states. Migrant children move, on average, 1.2 times a year.

Such moves not only disrupt schooling but also often prevent the development of social and community ties that can facilitate school attendance and educational achievement. The second type of mobility concerns movement in and out of schools. Children who have changed schools frequently are more likely to be low achievers in both reading and math and to repeat a grade. Changing schools four or more times often results in students dropping out of school in comparison to students who remained at the same school. Studies have shown that mobility rates are high for students in primary grades and then level off and begin to increase at the eighth grade.[35] Children who move often are two and a half times more likely to need to repeat a grade than children who do not move. The average migrant child may be in three different schools in one year. Five times as many migrant students are enrolled in the second grade as in the twelfth grade.[36]

There is a constant need for children to work in the fields in order to contribute to the family's income. By the time a migrant child is 12, he or she may be working between sixteen and eighteen hours per week. As one Guatemalan youth in Morgantown, North Carolina, said, "If we don't work, we don't eat. That's why we don't go to school."[37] The years between ages 14 to 17 are key because during these years youths are most likely to drop out of school. Beginning around age 14, these youths become legally and competitively employable for farm work, and in some cases, they will attempt to achieve economic independence as hired farmworkers. Meanwhile, some of these youths, particularly those who are older and over-aged for their grade, may associate school experiences with failure and the opportunity for them to be graduated might appear remote. For example, according to the National Agricultural Workers Survey (NAWS), more than 90 percent of farm workers' children aged 13 or younger who were in school were "on grade level," that is, had completed a grade appropriate to their age, but this measure dropped to about 80 percent for 14- to 16-year-old students and to 71 percent for 17-year-old students.[38]

Transition from school to work normally occurs following the completion of at least a high school education for most students in the United States. For migrant workers, this transition often precedes the completion of formal education. Schedules of parents and children also interfere with education, as some migrant children begin their school year in October or November and leave before the semester is finished. For children whose families return to Mexico during the year, the disruption may be even more severe, because school systems on both sides of the border generally have not recognized the progress students make outside of their own systems.[39]

Youth Employment and Discretionary Spending

The old image of child labor calls to mind images of small children working in the sweatshops and mines, or the poor migrant children, deprived of school and playtime, helping out so that their families wouldn't starve. While such conditions may still exist for some adolescents, most American teenagers employed in after-school or part-time jobs earn money not for family survival basics, but for their own personal spending money. Such disposable income is spent on highly advertised consumer goods and entertainment.

Most adolescents secure employment not to pay the rent, utility bills, insurance, or medical care, but to buy CDs and videos, to go to movies and concerts, to get more clothes, or to make car payments. Such are the luxuries of an affluent society that advertising has led children to assume and to expect as necessities. Are they simply spoiled children? Most would probably not view themselves in that manner.

But, many youths have not reflected about this issue, nor have they considered that perhaps they are "spending their youth" on the wrong things. An after-school or part-time job may take up hours better spent in developing both their intellectual and physical skills. Adolescent earnings are a symbol of the transition to adulthood and can promote maturity. In cases where adolescents' earnings contribute to the family's budget, relationships with parents can be strengthened. On the other hand, adolescent earnings can also encourage unrealistic financial values.[40]

Premature Affluence

The economic power of teenagers has raised concerns about premature affluence. Teenage spending continues to be on themselves for mostly discretionary, nonessential items and is an amount young adults living independently of parents often cannot duplicate. Their consumption level and style is beyond their productive capacity in an independent adult world. The inability to replicate the lifestyle experienced as a teenager has resulted for many in a lower level of satisfaction with life as a young adult.[41]

Do these earning and spending patterns among high school students represent problems worth worrying over? There may be two broad areas of concern: 1) the impacts of these experiences during the high school years and 2) the longer-range impacts of the spending habits and tastes developed during the high school years. As to what happens during the high school (and junior high school) years, concerns have been expressed that working fairly long hours at part-time jobs may interfere with some of the primary developmental tasks of adolescents, by reducing their involvement with family and with the academic and extracurricular activities that go on in school. Additionally, it has been argued that the large amounts of discretionary income in the hands of adolescents had led to a sort of separate youth culture reflected in all sorts of products, including designer jeans, movies targeted at youth audiences, and records, tapes, and high-powered stereo systems, which may systematically damage the hearing of a whole generation. And, of course, the ready availability of cash makes it easier for young people to acquire alcohol, marijuana, and other drugs, as well as automobiles, which increase mobility, relative isolation from adults, and accompanying risks. In sum, it can be argued that earning and spending patterns during high school can involve physical risks (e.g., drug abuse, death or injury on highways) and may also interfere with important developmental processes.

Developmental Deficiencies

Work is assumed to provide positive opportunities to improve and practice cognitive skills developed in school and to offer valuable training. However, many of the service-sector jobs held by teens have minimal training associated with them, and the skill requirements are bare minimum. The hope that jobs would allow adolescents to interact with adults in an adult fashion often does not occur. Most of the teenage jobs are located in sites where even the supervisors are in their late teens or early twenties and the other workers tend to be teenagers.

Also of concern is what the job replaces. Teenagers with excessive workplace involvement may lack opportunities to experiment with other nonemployment roles and to explore their identities, both important developmental tasks in adolescence. For example, holding a job may preclude a teenager volunteering in the community, and, thus, the long-term effect to the community is loss of that value in a new generation of adults. In one study on teenage employment, the benefits cited were skill development, practical knowledge increase, an opportunity for financial responsibility, and a contributing factor to improved relationships. On the other hand, however, the costs of employment cited were some physical risk, lower grades, less time spent with family, and fewer extracurricular activities.[42]

Whereas working may contribute to the development of personal responsibility, it does not appear to enhance, and in some regards may even undermine, social responsibility, broadly defined. Contrary to claims made by advocates of earlier work experience, youngsters who work do not become more committed to the welfare of others or more tolerant of individual and cultural differences. Moreover, many adolescents become more accepting of unethical business practices. This overall pattern may be related to the nature of the work open to adolescents in our society. Although their jobs may teach them such things as the importance of coming to work punctually, some workers also learn to do only the amount of work that is necessary—a sample cynical remark is, "Anyone who works harder that he or she has to is a bit crazy"—and to violate the law if it is expedient to do so.[43]

Impact on Family Life

The longer the hours a teenager works, the less likely he or she is to share dinner with the family. This is, no doubt, in large part due to the particular days and times of day and evening that teenagers are likely to be at work. Similarly, there is a trend toward less frequent outings with the family among teenagers who work long hours. For girls, working long hours leads to diminished feelings of closeness to their family. And finally, working youngsters help out less at home than they did before they secured employment.

The eminent developmental psychologist Urie Bronfenbrenner has noted that, "[w]hile the family still has the primary moral and legal responsibility for the character development of children, it often lacks the power or opportunity to do the job, primarily because parents and children no longer spend enough time together in those situations in which training is possible."[44]

A study of 10-to-11-year-olds in Oakland, California, demonstrated that the average youngster spent less than an hour and a half per day with his or her parents, including time spent together in front of the television set. It is likely that the comparable figure for 14- and 15-year-olds would be even lower.[45] Clearly, longer hours of work for adolescents are not likely to lead to more family contact. The child who works more than twenty hours per week when school is in session will probably work on weekends and weeknight evenings, exactly the times that parents are most likely to be available.

Parental Monitoring

When teens have less time to spend with their families, parental monitoring is difficult. Parents often assume that teens who work many hours can function more autonomously and should be permitted to have more independence.[46] The negative outcomes of working longer hours are interrelated. For example, students who spend less time with their families and receive less parental monitoring tend to get involved in high-risk behaviors more often than children who spend a lot of time with their families do. Researchers disagree about the direction of the negative effects of youth employment. Some argue that students who work long hours are less interested in school and more inclined to experiment with drugs and alcohol before they join the workforce, which explains their interest in working longer hours.[47] Of course, the other side of the coin concerns the amount of time parents have for interaction with their children. Unfortunately, there is a time deficit that surrounds many of the children of the United States: the increasing scarcity of time that parents have for their children, driven largely by workforce pressures. Compared with 1960, children in the United States have lost, on average, ten to twelve hours per week of parental time.[48]

Parents are their children's first and most influential teachers. What parents do to help their children learn is more important to academic success than how well-off the family is. Parents can do many things at home to help their children succeed in school. Unfortunately, there is evidence indicating that many parents are doing much less than they might. For instance, American mothers on average spend less than half an hour a day talking, explaining, or reading to their children. Fathers spend less than fifteen minutes. They can create a home curriculum that teaches their children what matters. They do this through their daily conversations, household routines, attention to school matters, and affectionate concern for their children's progress. Parents stay aware of their children's lives at school when they discuss school events, help children meet deadlines, and talk with their children about school problems and successes. Research on both gifted and disadvantaged children shows that home efforts can greatly improve student achievement. For example, when parents of disadvantaged children take the steps listed above, their children can do as well at school as the children of more affluent families. The research is overwhelmingly clear: When parents play a positive role in their children's education, children do better in school. This is true whether parents are college-educated or grade-school graduates and regardless of the family income, race, or ethnic background. What counts is that parents have a positive attitude about the importance of a good education and that they express confidence their children will succeed. Major benefits of parental involvement include higher grades and test scores, positive attitudes and behavior, more successful academic programs, and more effective schools.[49]

Any proposal that encourages young teenagers to work longer hours is likely to diminish children's family life. The quantity and quality of American family life are already matters of national concern.

However, the most influential factor determining educational attainment remains family income, and the news is not good, as the gap widens along an income fault-line. Families with the lowest 25 percent of incomes have a high school graduation rate of 67 percent, compared to 94 percent among students with families in the top 25 percent of earners. The latter are also as much as ten times more likely to earn a college degree than are those in the bottom 25 percent. The proposition that, "In America, everybody goes to college" is a myth.[50]

School Dropouts and Peer Relationships

While early childhood positive familial relationships are often a good predictor of early adolescence and a youth's socially positive peer association, patterns of poor parent-child relationships can intensify the potential risk of peer rejection and antisocial behavior during adolescence. In fact, the weaker a youth's links to his or her family, the greater the importance of association with other groups that play a central role in his or her daily life. When young people cannot find what they need within their own family, they turn to other groups to have their needs met.[51]

The nature of the bonds that a young person establishes at school is of the utmost importance for peer association and exercises an important influence on a young person's school achievements.[52]

It is now demonstrated that youth who are at risk of dropping out usually establish stronger bonds with school dropouts and other at-risk youth than most students. Dropping out of school, in return, increases the risk of getting involved with the law.[53] It is believed that having a network of friends where school and prosocial behavior are not valued contributes to and accelerates the development of problematic behavior that can lead to criminal involvement.[54]

Behavioral Changes

In addition to affecting academic performance, work sometimes changes behavior. In one study, students who worked while attending school experienced higher rates of such problem behaviors as alcohol and other drug use and minor delinquency in comparison with their nonworking peers.[55] Another study supported the finding that work-intensity variables were significant predictors of alcohol use among students.[56]

An analysis of the psychosocial aspects of work experience for high school students in Orange County, California, concluded that it "may make them economically rich, but may also make them psychologically poor." Many working youth expressed a cynical attitude toward work; spent most of their pay on personal luxuries, or on alcohol, marijuana, and, for males, gambling; and admitted to illegal or immoral conduct, such as stealing merchandise or falsely calling in sick. These developments occurred more than fifteen years ago, commanding widespread attention, and beginning a more serious debate about the supposed benefits of work experience.[57]

Study after study has found that teenagers who work longer hours are more likely to drink alcohol or use illicit drugs than peers who work fewer hours. Jerald G. Bachman, who surveyed 70,000 high school seniors between 1985 and 1989 for the Institute of Social Research at the University of Michigan, found, for example, that twelfth-grade boys working more than thirty hours a week were twice as likely to use cocaine as counterparts who worked five or fewer hours a week.[58] But, as was the case with academic achievement, the link between long hours of after-school work and substance abuse presents researchers with a chicken-or-the-egg kind of problem. Are students who take drugs and drink illegally the kind of students who are more likely to work long hours? Or does working too many hours instill dangerous habits? The evidence is unclear. If keeping youth busy helps reduce delinquency, activities besides employment may better serve this goal.

There is another interesting explanation of why work might increase delinquent behavior: Parental control over a child's behavior depends in part on the resources available to the parents relative to the resources available to the child and upon the child's aspirations. If working provides enough money to meet the child's needs, and if the child does not seek parental support for continuing education, dependence on the parent and the ability of the family to control behavior is diminished.[59] Another variable to be considered is the age at which the unwise behavior begins. The former commissioner of the Food and Drug Administration, Dr. David Kessler, contends that "[a] person who hasn't started smoking by age 19 is unlikely to ever become a smoker. Nicotine addiction begins when most tobacco users are teenagers, so let's call this what it really is, a pediatric disease."[60]

As already noted, high school dropouts are also at special risk. One nationwide survey found that respondents who left school before graduating were more than twice as likely to report smoking in the past week as were those who currently attended or had graduated from high school. Several frightening statistics should be noted: Smoking causes more deaths every year than fires, automobile accidents, alcohol, cocaine, heroin, AIDS, murders, and suicides combined.[61]

Also, according to a Surgeon General's report, if current smoking prevalence rates remain unchanged, 20 million children of the 70 million children in the United States will become smokers. At least 5 million of them would then die of smoking-related diseases.[62]

Early use of alcohol, tobacco, or illicit drugs is often a strong risk factor for addiction. Substance abuse by young people under age 20, and particularly by those under 15, increases the likelihood of substance abuse problems later in life. People with more education are more likely to drink, but those with less education are more likely to drink heavily. Rates of heavy alcohol use are highest among those with less than a college degree. Among people with less education, smoking is more common, and smoking cessation less likely. In addition, heavy smoking is higher among those without a high school diploma. Similarly, current illicit drug use is twice as high among those aged 26 to 34 who have not completed high school than those in the same age group with a college degree. Use of multiple drugs, including alcohol and tobacco, is common among substance abusers, particularly among the economically disadvantaged.[63]

Schooling and Delinquency

Delinquent behavior is also associated with school behaviors according to one study. First, truancy was significantly related to delinquency for all adolescents. Students who frequently skipped classes reported higher levels of serious and more minor delinquent behaviors relative to those rarely absent from class. Second, white students who dropped out of school were no more likely to be involved in criminal activity than were white adolescents who were current students or high school graduates. For African-American males, however, students who had dropped out of school had higher rates of delinquency compared to those who graduated or remained in school.[64]

Society pays a high price for children's school failure. Growth in the U.S. penal system over the last twenty-five years has produced extraordinarily high incarceration rates among unskilled men. In 1996 more than 7 percent of young, white, male, high school dropouts and 36 percent of young male dropouts were in prison or jail.[65] Each year's class of dropouts costs the nation more than $240 billion in lost earnings and foregone taxes over their lifetimes. Billions more will be spent on crime control, including law enforcement and prison programs, welfare, health care, and other social services. The staggering economic and social costs of providing for the increasing population of youth who are at risk of leaving or who have left the education mainstream are an intolerable drain on the resources of federal, state, and local governments and the private sector.[66]

Almost one in three (32 percent) young, black males in the 20–29 age group is under some type of correctional control (incarceration, probation, or parole) as is one in fifteen young, white males and one in eight young, Hispanic males. Sixty-five percent of state prison inmates in 1991 had not completed high school. Thirty-three percent of jail inmates in 1991 were unemployed prior to entering jail. Thirty-two percent of jail inmates in 1991 who had been free for at least one year prior to their arrest had annual incomes of under $5,000.[67]

Gender and Racial Differences in Work Histories

The U.S. Department of Labor has reported recently that nearly half of all 12-year-olds in this country have some employment experience, but right from the start, boys and girls go into different lines of work. The American work ethic starts at an early age. Half of 12-year-olds do baby-sitting or lawn work, and the numbers go up from there: 57 percent of 14-year-olds and 64 percent of 15-year-olds have jobs. For the most part, these are informal jobs that don't interfere with their schoolwork. At 14, both girls and boys are working in food service and entertainment, but boys are cooks and cleaners while girls are waitresses and cashiers; From ages 12 to 15, both boys and girls move from freelance to employee jobs, both during the school year and in the summer; however, 14- and 15-year-old males are more likely than females to have employee jobs.

Employed 15-to-17-year-olds worked an average of about seventeen hours a week during the school months and twenty-three hours during the summer; boys work more hours than girls. White youth are more likely to have jobs than black or Hispanic youth; teens from two-parent households are more likely to have jobs than those from single-parent households; and teens from middle-class families are more likely to have jobs than those from poor families. Teens who work may fare better later: there is some correlation between working in the teen years and employment success later, but this may simply be because of personal characteristics of the young workers.[68]

The Link between Education and Labor Market Experiences

Data from the National Longitudinal Survey of Youth allow for fairly precise determination of measures of labor market activity not available from any other data source. These data indicate that work experience between the ages of 18 and 27 varies substantially by sex, race, and educational level, and reveal patterns of work behavior that are somewhat surprising. For example, by age 27, individuals with one to three years of college education have, on average, worked more weeks than have high school graduates. Also, college graduates average more total weeks worked than do high school dropouts at all ages, even between the ages of 18 to 22, when many college graduates are attending school full time. This finding reflects the fact that young, female high school dropouts acquire very little work experience. In addition, the data indicate that education accounts for much of the sex and race differentials in labor market activity. Gender and race differentials are particularly conspicuous among high school dropouts. However, with increased educational attainment, most of these differentials become smaller, and are particularly small or nonexistent among college graduates. For example, college-educated women have more jobs and workweeks from age 18 to 27 than do college-educated men, whereas female high school dropouts hold approximately one-and-a-half fewer jobs and work only about half as many weeks as do their male counterparts. Also, by age 27, there is very little difference among college-educated whites, blacks, and Hispanics in the number of weeks worked. In general, the data indicate that greater educational attainment allows young workers to spend more time employed, and thus to acquire work experience more readily.[69]

Job Retention

Young adults who are less skilled exhibit less attachment to the employed workforce than other workers, maintaining this pattern as they mature. This lack of attachment appears to be a barrier to future employment and the acquisition of productivity/wage-enhancing training that most people receive on the job. For example, researchers found that individuals with low levels of education were noticeably more likely to leave employment for nonemployment. A high school dropout was 63 percent more likely to move from employment to nonemployment.[70]

Less-educated workers are less likely to jump jobs and are more likely to be pushed out. One study in particular has pointed out that this group of workers is more likely to have new jobs than the most educated (22.7 of high school dropouts were in jobs with less than one year's tenure in 1996 compared with 16.6 percent of college graduates) and are also less likely to be offered health insurance when they change jobs (15.4 percent are offered coverage on new jobs, compared with 45.2 percent of college graduates), and this likelihood has declined dramatically in the past twenty years. Thus, those workers who have moved a lot continue to move a lot, and if there are intervening spells of joblessness, those workers have fewer weeks worked in the year. There are consequences other than lost earnings capacity. In 1996, almost one in four workers with less than a high school education was in a job lasting less than a year, compared with only one in six college-educated workers. This is important, because predicted job tenure is an important determinant of the training decision, and training is very closely related to wage growth. Workers who are likely to leave the job for nonemployment are 17 percent less likely to receive training.[71]

The picture for high school dropouts becomes even grimmer when we consider trends for young people entering the labor market after the early 1980s. The trends were relatively stable for young men with at least a high school diploma. In contrast, dropouts have become even less likely to be working full time and more likely to be neither working nor in school, and more of them are taking longer to get stable jobs. If these trends are drawn out to the year 2015, the results are even more devastating. Male workers with only a high school education will have lost 38 percent of what comparable male workers earned in 1976. And those without a high school diploma will have lost 52 percent in real earnings over the same period. If the U.S. economy continues to place a high value on a college-educated workforce, then only college graduates will be able to hold their own economically out to 2015.[72]

What Employers Want

A major role for policy makers is to improve training, both prior to and during employment. The results of every study point directly to the importance of education—high school dropouts are much more likely to be churned through the labor market than college graduates. Since it is clearly not feasible to turn all dropouts into graduates, it may be more useful to look directly at what employers want. This would reduce turnover by making the employees more valuable and more costly to fire. A study using matched surveys of employers and employees suggests that employers want workers to be able to read, do arithmetic, deal with customers, possess motivation, and be polite.[73]

Labor Market Volatility

Two important labor market developments have merited attention in recent years. First, the transition to permanent employment has lengthened. Young workers who do not go on to college are more likely to be intermittently unemployed and to rely on part-time jobs for a greater number of years. This is especially marked among high school dropouts. Those who do go on to college are more likely to work while enrolled and to significantly draw out that period of enrollment. For both groups, it takes longer to find a full-year job than it has in the past. Second, not only has the transition become longer, it has become more volatile. Youthful workers are less likely to make a single and clean transition to the labor market. Instead, these young workers are more likely to move back and forth between work, unemployment, enrollment, and nonparticipation. The frequency of these interruptions has increased as well. Workers at all levels of education have experienced this greater volatility, but it has been most pronounced among those with less education.

Positive Effects of School Employment

Although we have pointed out the disadvantages of intensive work during adolescence, there are several advantages accruing to youth employment during school. For instance, employment during high school holds a number of potential advantages for facilitating school-to- work transitions over the usual alternatives, such as vocational education. While these advantages would affect all students they may be especially important for at-risk students.

One clear advantage of high school work is that it helps youths establish connections with future employers. One possibility, of course, is that the employer of a high school student would offer the youth later employment. But even if a particular employer has no openings, the connection might open doors to other employers. Apart from any skills gained through high school work, just having worked might itself signal to employers that the youth is a reliable worker. Such a signal may be particularly important for at-risk youth whose other characteristics may leave employers uncertain about their value. Certainly, having a recommendation from a former employer can carry considerable weight when one is looking for a job, since former employers, unlike teachers, have observed the youth in real work situations. In the case of at-risk youth, alternative linkages to employers such as through family connections—the way a large fraction of youths find jobs—are likely weak. And most high schools are generally more geared to providing connections to post-secondary educational institutions than directly to employers.

Employment also has an advantage because it pays youth and thereby may promote a taste for earning income, which could motivate interest in a continued connection to the labor market. In addition, immediate monetary rewards might better focus youth on productive activity than classes that typically rely on the prospect of future rewards. For at-risk youth, many of whom may face the temptation of turning to crime for economic reasons, establishing these tastes early may be particularly important.

There could also be a number of efficiency advantages to high school employment. Success in the work world, for example, requires disciplined work habits. It is possible that these habits are transmitted more effectively in the workplace rather than schools. High school employment may also be more efficient, since work habits learned on the job are a relatively costless byproduct of doing one's work. In addition, employers generally have a clear monetary incentive to see that youth exhibit productive and appropriate work behaviors. Incentives in schools are less clear.[74]

One key to making after-school jobs pay off in the long run may be the quality of those jobs. Were young employees, in other words, given opportunities to advance, to learn something new, or to discuss problems with caring adult supervisors? Were their work schedules flexible enough to avoid conflicts with school responsibilities?[75] A good job can help a student discover what she or he is good at and interested in. Some jobs help students develop skills and knowledge about occupations that they might pursue in the future. Many jobs to which teens are attracted also offer fairly flexible scheduling. Baby-sitting, yard work, and golf caddying are examples of jobs that offer students a good deal of schedule flexibility.[76]

Education, Employment, and Earnings

There is a definite link between educational attainment and earning capability. Wage data show that school dropouts who obtain jobs earn extremely low wages. Only 36.1 percent of white high school dropouts who are employed full-time earn a salary above the poverty line. More troubling is that only 6.8 percent of black high school dropouts, working full-time, reach this level of income. Such wage problems are not limited to out-of-school youth; the median weekly earnings of all male employees ages 17 to 24 dropped from 74 percent of the wages of workers 25 and older in 1967 (93.7 percent for women) to 51.2 percent in 1996 (64.2 percent for women). This resulted in a 31 percent overall decline in real weekly earnings of young men since 1975 (a 17.2 percent decline for women). Even in a booming economy, full- and part-time employment rates among students without a college degree were actually lower in 1997 than in 1989. And for minority youth, full-time employment is 20 to 30 percent lower than that of their white counterparts. Overall, inflation-adjusted earnings for 20-to-24-year-old male workers fell by one-third, while young women were earning 16.5 percent less. In 1997, more than one-fourth of out-of-school young adults who were working full-time were earning less than the poverty line income standard of just over $16,000 annually for a family of four.[77]

Data further show that employment rates and wages increase significantly with each additional level of educational attainment. In 1997, the full-time employment rate of white high school graduates ages 17 to 24 was 62.9 percent (53.1 percent for blacks), much higher than the rate for dropouts. For college graduates, the full-time employment rates increased to 83.2 percent—more than twice the rate for high school dropouts. Similarly, 51.4 percent of high school graduates, aged 17 to 24, earned a salary above the poverty line (28.2 percent for blacks), well above the rate for high school dropouts. Again, college graduates are most successful, with 74.2 percent of full-time workers earning a salary above the poverty line—also more than two times the rate for high school dropouts.[78]

Four out of five 16-to-24-year-olds not enrolled in school in October 2000 were in the labor force. Among young persons not enrolled in school, a greater percentage of whites were in the labor force (84.6 percent) than were Hispanics (77.0 percent) and blacks (73.2 percent). Labor force participation rates were notably higher for men (88.7 percent) than for women (78.3 percent); however, the unemployment rates were similar—9.3 percent for men and 9.0 percent for women. The disparity in labor force participation between young men and young women is largest among those who have not completed high school and nearly disappears among college graduates.

Higher levels of education generally corresponded to lower unemployment rates. The unemployment rate for those who had graduated from college was 5.6 percent for men and 3.1 percent for women. In contrast, those with less than a high school diploma experienced the highest unemployment rates—16.3 percent for men and 20.3 percent for women.

Between October 1999 and October 2000, slightly more than half a million youths dropped out of high school. Among these high school dropouts, more than two-thirds were in the labor force in October 2000. However, 28.1 percent of these young labor force participants were unemployed—a full 15 percentage points higher than the unemployment rate for recent high school graduates who were not enrolled in college. Among high school dropouts, men were more likely than women to participate in the labor force (74.4 percent versus 59.4 percent). The unemployment rate was higher for these young women (34.2 percent) than for young men (24.5 percent).[79]

Change of economic status is not the only consequence of unemployment. Loss of structured activity, of social contacts, and of a sense of identity and purpose go hand-in-hand with economic hardship. Young school-leavers are unlikely to experience significant loss of income as a result of not being able to find employment, yet their distress may be as great as any adults faced with job loss.[80]

The traditional and most widely accepted sequence for an American education is continuous schooling from kindergarten through graduation after twelfth grade, after which students often continue on to college. Yet this is not possible for everyone and does not work for all adolescents. In fact, 75 percent of children in the United States start work without a college degree.[81]

An important consideration for young people regarding their career choice is the monetary outcome of that decision. Here are a number of examples from the U.S. Department of Commerce from 1998. Men over age 25 in a full-time job make an average of:

- $23,958 without a high school diploma.
- $31,477 with a high school diploma.
- $36,934 with some college education but no degree.
- $40,274 with an Associate's degree.
- $51,405 with a Bachelor's degree.
- $62,244 with a Master's degree.
- $75,078 with a Doctorate.

Women over age 25 in a full-time job make an average of:

- $16,482 without a high school diploma.
- $22,780 with a high school diploma.
- $27,420 with some college education but no degree.
- $29,924 if they had an Associate's degree.
- $36,559 with a Bachelor's degree.
- $45,283 with a Master's degree.
- $57,796 with a Doctorate.[82]

Clearly, there is a correlation between higher levels of education and increased income. According to U.S. Census data, a person with a professional degree on average, in his or her lifetime income, earns more than five times the amount of someone who did not graduate from high school.[83]

Final Thoughts

Clearly, academic performance, school experiences, and school completion are closely related. Dropouts are less likely than graduates to have had a high grade point average in their final high school term. Dropouts are far more likely than graduates to have had negative school experiences, such as a lack of enjoyment or interest. Given the complex set of factors involved in determining the likelihood of school leaving, questions understandably have arisen about the effect of work on the risk of dropping out.

In agriculture, the federal government provides millions of dollars for state-run programs to fund summer school, interstate coordination, high school equivalency programs, and other special services to help migrant children complete their education. Despite these special programs, school enrollment for migrant children is lower than that of any other population group, and their high school dropout rate is twice the national average. For nearly sixty years, most children in the United States have been protected from the hazards of the workplace and from economic forces that once compelled them to contribute to the family income. However, to this day, migrant farmworkers' children are exposed to many work-related conditions that threaten their health and their long-term prospects for participating as educated Americans in the mainstream economy.

Young people are under so much pressure to spend that most of them are eager to earn. Certainly, teenagers should have an opportunity to learn from a working experience. They should arrive at adulthood with an appreciation for work and with the experience of meeting work situations responsibly. Yet, some limits must be set on the amount of work a teenager can do if he or she is to make the most of other learning opportunities. The high school student who works long hours to support a car may have little time or energy left for study, school activities, or other important developmental social experiences.

Since school dropouts generally make the transition from school to work during the adolescent years, the range of physical, emotional, and social problems they have to deal with as part of their maturation may compound with the stresses of unemployment to make the whole experience more confusing than for the older person. This combination of factors could have added potential for long-term psychological impact.

A practice that is firmly fixed in the national work ethic may be more problematic than it was in the past because the changing economy greatly rewards those who stay in school longer, making early work experiences ultimately less valuable than additional education.

NOTES

1. Duncan Chaplin and Jane Hannaway, *High School Employment: Meaningful Connections for At-Risk Youth.* A paper presented at the 1996 annual meeting of the American Educational Research Association, New York City, 12 April 1996.

2. Ellen Greenberger and Laurence Steinberg, *When Teenagers Work: The Psychological and Social Costs of Adolescent Employment* (New York: Basic Books, 1986), 81–82.

3. B.N. Kablaoui and A.J. Pautler, "The Effects of Part Time Work Experience on High School Students," *Journal of Career Development,* 17(3) (1995): 195–209.

4. M. Bensimhon, "The Exhausting Days and Sleepless Nights of a Working Teenager," *Life* 16 (1993): 74–83.

5. Steven Greenhouse, "Problems Seen For Teenagers Who Hold Jobs," *New York Times,* 29 January 2001, A22.

6. U.S. Department of Education, National Center for Education Statistics, *Digest of Economic Statistics, 1999* (Washington, DC: USGPO, 2000), 9.

7. M.A. Carskadon, "When Worlds Collide: Adolescent Need for Sleep versus Societal Demands," *Phi Delta Kappan,* 80(5) (January 1999): 348–349.

8. Gordon D. Wrobel, "The Impact of School Starting Time on Family Life," *Phi Delta Kappan,* 80(5) (January 1999): 360–364.

9. M.A. Carskadon, "Patterns of Sleep and Sleepiness in Adolescents," *Pediatrician* 17(1) (1990): 5–12.

10. S. Lamborn, N. Mounts, B. Brown, and L. Steinberg, "Putting School in Perspective: The Influence of Family, Peers, Extracurricular Participation, and Part-time Work on Academic Engagement." In F. Newmann (ed.), *Student Engagement and Achievement in American Secondary Schools* (New York: Teachers College Press, 1992) 153–181.

11. J.G. Oltanji, "The Effects of High School Curriculum on Education and Labor Market Outcomes," *Journal of Human Resources,* 30 (3) (1995): 409–438.

12. Herbert W. Marsh, "Employment During High School: Character Building or a Subversion of Academic Goals?," *Sociology of Education,* 57 (July 1984): 172–189.

13. Ronald D'Amico, "Does Employment During School Impair Academic Progress?" *Sociology of Education,* 57 (July 1984): 157–164.

14. K. Singh, "Part-time Employment in High School and Its Effect on Academic Achievement," *Journal of Educational Research,* 91(3) (1998): 131–139.

15. G. Oettinger, "Does High School Employment Affect High School Academic Performance?" *Industrial and Labor Relations Review,* 53(1) (1999): 136–151.

16. K. Singh and M. Ozturk, "Effect of Part-time Work on High School Mathematics and Science Course Taking," *Journal of Educational Research,* 91(2) (2000): 67–74.

17. J.T. Mortimer and M.D. Finch, "The Effects of Part-time Work on Adolescent Self-concept and Achievement." In K.M. Borman and J. Reisman (eds.) *Becoming a Worker* (Norwood, NJ: Ablex, 1986) 66–89.

18. Karen Kelly, "Working Teenagers: Do After-School Jobs Hurt?" *Harvard Education Letter Research,* 30 April 2001, 18.

19. U.S. Department of Education, *Digest of Education Statistics: 1999* (Washington, DC: U.S. Department of Education, Office of Educational Research and Improvement, National Center for Education Statistics, 2000), 2.

20. Frank F. Furstenberg, Jr., Thomas D. Cook, Jacuelynne Eccles, Glen H. Elder, Jr., and Arnold Sameroff, *Managing to Make It: Urban Families and Adolescent Success* (Chicago: University of Chicago Press, 1999), 3.

21. U.S. General Accounting Office, *Child Abuse Prevention Programs.* (Washington, DC: U.S. General Accounting Office, 1992), 13.

22. Sari Siegel, *Access to Primary Health Care: Tracking the States.* (Washington, DC: National Conferences of State Legislatures, 1998).

23. U.S. General Accounting Office, *Welfare Reform: Implications of Increased Work Participation for Child Care* (Washington, DC: U.S. General Accounting Office, 1997), 75.

24. S.S. Peng and R.T. Takai, *High School Dropouts: Descriptive Information from High School and Beyond."* A paper presented at the annual meeting of the American Educational Research Association (Washington, DC: National Center for Educational Statistics, Report No. NCES-83–221b, 1983).

25. E.J. McCaul, *Personal and Social Consequences of Dropping Out of School: Findings from High School and Beyond.* Paper presented at the annual meeting of the American Educational Research Association, San Francisco, CA (ERIC Document Reproduction Service No. ED 236 366, 1989).

26. "Thousands of Troubled Students Drop Out Before High School," *The Chicago Reporter,* (June 2001), part 3, l.

27. U.S. Department of Education, "New Report Shows Dropout Rates Remain Stable over Last Decade," Press Release, Office of Public Relations, 15 November 2001.

28. Ibid.

29. U.S. Department of Labor, *Report on the Youth Labor Force* (November 2000), 55–57.

30. Kala Mehta, et al., *Findings from the National Agricultural Workers Survey (NAWS) 1997–1998: A Demographic and Employment Profile of United States Farmworkers* (U.S. Department of Labor: Research Report No. 8, 2000).

31. U.S. General Accounting Office, *Child Labor in Agriculture: Characteristics and Legality of Work* (Washington, DC: USGPO, 1998), 2.

32. S. Gabbard., Richard Mines, and B. Boccalandro, *Migrant Farmworkers: Pursuing Security in an Unstable Labor Market* (Washington, DC: U.S. Department of Labor, Office of the Assistant Secretary for Policy, Research Report No. 5, 1994).

33. Lynda Diane Mull, "Broken Covenant: The Future of Migrant Farmworker Children and Families in the United States," *Protecting Children,* 12(1) (1996): 18–21.

34. Sandra Kirkpatrick and Andrea Lash, "A Classroom Perspective on Student Mobility," *The Elementary School Journal,* 91(2) (November 1990): 171–191.

35. U.S. General Accounting Office, *Elementary School Children: Many Change Schools Frequently, Harming their Education* (Gaithersburg, MD: U.S. General Accounting Office, 1994), 45.

36. Yolanda G. Martinez and Jose A. Velazquez, "Involving Migrant Families in Education, *ERIC Digest* (December 2000), 1.

37. Ibid.

38. U.S. Accounting Office, *Child Labor In Agriculture: Changes Needed to Better Protect Health and Educational Opportunities* (Washington, DC: U.S. General Accounting Office, August 1998), 51.

39. L.C. Velazquez, "Voices from the Fields: Community-Based Migrant Education." In P.A. Sissel (ed.), *A Community-Based Approach to Literacy Programs: Taking Learners' Lives into Account.* (San Francisco: Jossey-Bass, Summer, 1996) 27–36.

40. Michael J. Shanahan, Glen H. Elder, Margaret Burchinal, and Rand D. Conger. "Adolescent Paid Labor and Relationships with Parents: Early Work-family Linkages," *Child Development,* 67(5) (1996): 2183–2200.

41. Jerald G. Bachman, "Premature Affluence: Do High School Students Earn Too Much?" *Economic Outlook USA* (Summer 1983) 64–67.

42. Greenberger and Steinberg, *When Teenagers Work,* 115–120.

43. Laurence D. Steinberg, Ellen Greenberger, Laurie Garduque, and Mary Ruggieri, "Effects of Working on Adolescent Development," *Developmental Psychology,* 18(3) (1982): 385–395.

44. Urie Bronfenbrenner, *Two Worlds of Childhood.* (New York: Russell Sage Foundation, 1970), 95–119.

45. E. Medrich, J. Roizen, V. Rubin, and S. Buckley, *The Serious Business of Growing Up.* (Berkeley: University of California Press, 1982), 94–111.

46. Shanahan, et al., "Adolescent Paid Labor," 2183–2200.

47. Laurence Steinberg, Suzanne Fegley, and Sanford M. Dornbusch, "Negative Impact of Part-time Work on Adolescent Adjustment: Evidence from a Longitudinal Study." *Developmental Psychology,* 29(2) (1993): 171–180.

48. V. Fuchs and D. Reklis, "The Status of American Children," *Science*, 255 (1992): 41–46.

49. M.E. Graue, T. Weinstein, and H.J. Walberg, "School-based Home Instruction and Learning: A Quantitative Synthesis," *Journal of Educational Research*, 76 (1983): 351–360.

50. Samuel Halperin, ed., *The Forgotten Half Revisited: American Youth and Young Families, 1988–2008* (Washington, D.C.: American Youth Policy Forum, 1998).

51. Catherine Bagwell, et al., "Preadolescent Friendship and Peer Rejection as Predictors of Adult Adjustment," *Child Development*, 69(1) (February 1998): 140–153.

52. Kathryn R. Wentzel and Kathryn Caldwell, "Friendships, Peer Acceptance, and Group Membership: Relations to Academic Achievement in Middle School," *Child Development*, 68(6) (December 1997): 1198–1209.

53. Clyde A. Winters, "Learning Disabilities, Crime, Delinquency and Special Education Placement," *Adolescence*, 32(126) (Summer 1997): 451–462.

54. Adrian Raine, *The Psychopathology of Crime: Criminal Behavior as a Clinical Disorder*. (New York: Academic Press, 1993), 268–286.

55. National Research Council and Institute of Medicine, Committee on Health and Safety Implications of Child Labor, *Protecting Youth at Work: Health, Safety, and Development of Working Children and Adolescents in the United States*. (Washington, DC: National Academy Press, 1998), 3–4.

56. J. Mortimer, M. Finch, S. Ryu, M. Shanahan, and K. Call. "The Effects on Adolescent Mental Health, Achievement, and Behavioral Adjustment: New Evidence from a Prospective Study, *Child Development*, 67 (1996): 1243–1261.

57. Greenberger and Steinberg, *When Teenagers Work*, 129–135.

58. Jerald G. Bachman and John Schulenberg, " How Part-Time Work Intensity Relates to Drug Use, Problem Behavior, Time Use, and Satisfaction Among High School Seniors: Are These Consequences or Merely Correlates?" *Developmental Psychology*, 29(2) (1983): 220–235.

59. Travis Hirschi and Michael Gottfredson, "Age and the Explanation of Crime," *American Journal of Sociology*, 89(3) (1983): 181–221.

60. *Smoking: A Pediatric Disease*. A speech by Food and Drug Administration Commissioner David Kessler at the Columbia University School of Law, 8 March 1995.

61. U.S. Department of Health and Human Services, HHS Fact Sheet, *Deaths from Smoking*. (Washington, DC: FDA Press Office, August 1995).

62. Centers for Disease Control and Prevention, Office on Smoking and Health, *Controlling Tobacco Use by Youth: A Community Issue*. (Atlanta: Information Resource and Referral Guide, August 1995) A-4.

63. "New Report Calls Substance Abuse Number-One Health Problem in U.S." (Princeton, NJ: The Robert Wood Johnson Foundation, 9 March 2001).

64. Kristin E. Voelkl, John W. Welte, and William F. Wieczorek, "Schooling and Delinquency Among White and African American Adolescents," *Urban Education*, 34 (1999): 69–88.

65. Bruce Western and Becky Pettit, "Incarceration and Racial Inequality in Men's Employment," *Industrial and Labor Relations Review*, 54 (2000): 3–16.

66. A. Beck et al., *Survey of State Prison Inmates* (Washington, DC: Bureau of Justice Statistics, U.S. Department of Justice, March 1993), 3.

67. Corrections Compendium, and the Sentencing Project, *Facts About Prisons And Prisoners*. (Washington, DC: U.S. Department of Justice, April 2000).

68. Office of Public Affairs, U.S. Department of Labor, "Work Experiences Differ Between Girls, Boys," press release in Labor Department Report: *Half of American Youngsters Have Work History.* (Washington, DC: U.S. Department of Labor, 7 July 2000).

69. Jonathan R. Veum and Andrea B. Weiss, "Education and the Work Histories of Young Adults," *Monthly Labor Review,* 116(4) (April, 1993): 11–20.

70. Robert Topel and Michael Ward, "Job Mobility and the Careers of Young Men," *Quarterly Journal of Economics.* 107(2) (May 1992): 439–479.

71. Henry Farber, "The Changing Face of Job Loss in the United States, 1981–1995," *Brookings Papers on Economic Activity,* (1997): 55–142.

72. J.A. Klerman, and L.A. Karoly, "Young Men and the Transition to Stable Employment," *Monthly Labor Review,* 117 (1994): 31–48.

73. Harley Frazis, Maury Gittleman, Michael Horrigan, and Mary Joyce, "Results from the 1995 Survey of Employer Provided Training," *Monthly Labor Review,* 121(6) (1998): 3–13.

74. M. Sanford, D. Offord, K. McLeod, M. Boyle, C. Byrne, and B. Hall, "Pathways into the Work Force: Antecedents of School and Work Force Status," *Journal of the American Academy of Child and Adolescent Psychiatry,* 33(7) (1994): 1036–1045.

75. Constance Stevens, Laura A. Puchtell, Songryeol Ryu, and Jeylon T. Mortimer, "Adolescent Work and Boys' and Girls' Orientations to the Future," *Sociological Quarterly,* 33 (May 1992): 153–169.

76. Laurence Steinberg and Ann Levine. *You and Your Adolescent* (New York: Harper-Collins, 1997) 365–367.

77. Thomas Bailey and Annette Bernhardt, "In Search of the High Road in A Low-Wage Industry," *Politics & Society,* 25(2) (1997): 179–201.

78. Vince Spera, *What's Really Happening with America's Out-of-School Youth?* A brief based on an American Youth Policy Forum, Washington, DC, 18 April 1997.

79. *College Enrollment And Work Activity Of Year 2000 High School Graduates.* Press Release. (Washington, DC: U.S. Department of Labor, 23 April 2001).

80. Ross M. Gurney, "The Effects of Unemployment on the Psycho-social Development of School-leavers," *Journal of Occupational Psychology,* 53 (1980): 205–213.

81. Barbara J. Hopkins, Darl Naumann, and Frederick C. Wendel, "Building the School-to-Work System." *Phi Delta Kappan* 446 (1999): 9–49.

82. U.S. Department of Commerce, *Outcomes of Education* (Washington, DC: Bureau of the Census, Current Population Reports, Series P 60), 436.

83. Richard W. Riley, "You Spell Out Several Routes to Success—For Yourselves and Those Less Fortunate," *Money* (July 1995), 13.

8

Remedies and Reflections

EMPLOYMENT RISKS FOR YOUTH

Millions of children work in this country, and many are exposed to hazardous conditions despite federal and state laws prohibiting their employment in these areas. Work-related injuries to children and adolescents often involve the use of machinery for which they have been poorly trained and result in at least temporary disability. Many of these injuries result in hospital emergency room visits.

Young workers may be at particular risk because of inexperience, absence of meaningful safety training, lack of appropriate supervision, desire to show their independence and ability to get the job done without going to the supervisor or older co-workers, learning unsafe work practices from co-workers, and failure to let parents, employers, or educators recognize hazardous or prohibited work tasks.

The Key Actors

Many interested parties can play a part in young worker safety. Employers should know the child and safety laws and provide safe employment and appropriate supervision. Parents should take an active role in their children's employment decisions. Educators should consider safety as a primary concern when signing work permits and preparing young people for work. Medical providers should take work histories, note employment information on medical records, and provide young workers with safety information.

Improving Preventive Measures

Many injuries and illnesses in the workplace are preventable if proper work practices are followed and only proper equipment is utilized. Neither young workers nor employers want injuries and illnesses to occur, but often they simply do not know how to prevent them. In some instances, medical personnel do not know how to perform certain procedures, which limits proper reporting and correct treatment and prevention. Medical personnel and providers are often unaware of work-related reporting requirements. This results in underreporting that hinders and delays prompt prevention action.

The occurrence of work-related injuries in persons less than 18 years old represents a failure of prevention and suggests inadequacies in the protection of working children and adolescents. More specific studies of occupational injuries in the young are needed to evaluate thoroughly whether accidents occur in proscribed industries and to determine if new hazardous occupations should be added to the proscribed list. Active surveillance of occupational injuries in minors should be instituted at federal and state levels. A serious or fatal work-related injury should be viewed as an occupational sentinel health event, that is, a preventable disease, disability, or untimely death whose occurrence serves as a warning signal that the quality of preventive health measures may need to be improved. Workers' compensation claims, hospital visits, school absences, physicians' reports, and other sources of information about occupational injuries could be used to identify serious and fatal injuries in working children and adolescents. Follow-up investigations of these cases could identify areas where preventive strategies could be improved.

Health and Safety in Agriculture

There are multiple dangers inherent in almost all aspects of agricultural production: the operation of complex and powerful machinery, the use of toxic chemicals, being in close proximity to unpredictable animals, and facing the awesome power of the weather and ungrounded electricity.

In general, little research has been conducted on children's work. Research is needed to learn the values parents are trying to teach their children through work, the parents' motivations behind asking children to work, and the importance of children's work in preparing them for adult roles.

The teaching of farm chores to children at an early physical and cognitive age is socially acceptable in farm families. Parents believe this teaching has many benefits in addition to getting the work done. Children become more responsible. It builds their self-confidence. However, the teaching of responsibility by assigning chores is not unique to farm families. Urban parents have reported that character building and responsibility are primary reasons for assigning chores.

It is clear that one develops expectations based upon the observed experiences of others. Imitation is an important means of learning behaviors. Reductions in childhood farm injuries will only be achieved once farmers themselves adopt safer work procedures. Those who are in the position to influence the safety practices of farm youth must take into consideration the effect they have as role models. Parents should acknowledge that levels of maturity, skills, and competencies, and to a lesser degree, chronological age, are viable criteria when recommending tasks for children and youth.

The Ingrained Farm Culture Vis-à-Vis Safety

Although farmers recognize the hazards they face, the "nothing can happen to me" attitude prevails as the primary motivation for neglecting the need for safety. Most farmers strive to produce and supply in order to make a reasonable profit. To achieve this objective, many operate in the most economical way. Unfortunately, such an approach may mean that safety receives a low priority. Consequently, safe practices are often overshadowed by issues of cost and customer demand. Yet, in response to calls for stricter legislation or policies, farmers stress that safety is adequately addressed, that they know safety is in their best interest, and that the government need not remind them of that fact. In other words, farmers believe that new legislation would merely hinder their business, not increase their concern for safety.

The reluctance to stiffen federal legal enforcement seems to be endemic. No less prestigious a group than the National Committee for Childhood Agricultural Injury Prevention called for changes in federal law only as a last resort and asked for only $5 million annually from the government. The committee concluded, "A last resort for protecting children from agricultural hazards is the enforcement of laws and use of penalties."[1] Nothing fits better here than the old adage, "Penny wise and pound foolish."

Farmers' Perceptions of Health and Safety Issues

A substantial proportion of farmers either grow up on a farm or are introduced to farming by family members. It is reasonable to infer, therefore, that primary socialization to farming occurs within the family. Based, in part, on their own farm family experiences, farmers come to create for themselves a unique life setting wherein they develop their own perceptions about, and expectations of, what has to be done for them to stay safe. These perceptions, perspectives, and expectations influence how they approach their work and their safety on the farm. For example, farm tractor owners/operators tend to neglect the maintenance of tractor safety devices as the age of the tractor increases. In the most general way, a lack of safety consciousness on the part of tractor owners/operators is apparent. Fatalities could be prevented by adherence to standard safety practices applicable to workers of all ages, such as the proper usage of ROPS and seat belts, properly securing attachments, and operating at safe speeds.

One of the questions to ask when planning safety education programs is whether or not the participants realize a problem exists. Farmers' perceptions of health and safety issues, accident causes, and methods of accident prevention indicate farm families are aware that farming is a hazardous occupation and that safety is important even when this factor is ranked alongside such matters as price and the environment. Farm families are receptive to receiving constant reminders and literature about safe working practices, especially when these practices can be put to use by all ages. Unfortunately, farm operators and family members, in times of stress, may make decisions that, under more ideal conditions, would have been considered dangerous and unwise. For instance, a farmer may throw aside a bent power take-off shield so that grain unloading can go forward, rather than wait until the shield can be repaired. In this example, the operator is unconsciously making the economic decision that the value of the time required to repair the shield is greater than the potential loss that might result from an injury. But, under identical conditions, this same operator would probably not forget to check the tractor's oil level or to lubricate the moving parts as required.

Farmers' access to safer machinery must be increased, as they preferentially use it when their children are involved. Approaches to increasing the number of safer tractors include financial and insurance incentives for ROPS and further research into additional safety features on new tractors and into retrofitting older tractors with rollover protective structures.

Data Deficiencies and Needs

There is a need for continued and improved injury surveillance. A major barrier to progress in the prevention of agricultural injuries has been not only a lack of knowledge about the magnitude of the problem but also a deficiency in knowledge about the specific causes or risk factors due to the lack of analytical studies. The status of injuries and illnesses includes information about the victim, the agent that caused the injury or illness, the task being performed when the illness or injury occurred, and other information that will describe the event. The issue of children's exposure to farm machinery could be better served by getting more precise data on the specific tasks and situations in which parents allow their children to participate, and on the particular types of farm machinery involved.

Studies should be undertaken to obtain a fuller understanding of farmers' and their families' perspectives and perceptions of the occupational and environmental health and safety risks they face and to gain their insights about actual and potential preventative measures, including prevention programs. We must develop a better understanding of injury circumstances and identify effective prevention strategies for all children exposed to agriculture production hazards, not just those who are doing what is traditionally considered work, but also those who are exposed to agriculture production hazards in their living environments or when they accompany their parents to work. The populations of principal interest are children of farm families, youths who work on farms, and children of migrant and seasonal farmworkers.

Agriculture, perennially, has one of the highest work death rate of industries. However, because of the lack of reporting requirements for such accidents, there is no primary, up-to-date source of farm accident data to guide prevention efforts. Workers' compensation data for agriculture are not consistent—or even widely available—owing to numerous exclusions, exemptions, and loopholes in state laws. Also, agriculture is physically dispersed so that collecting data about injuries requires substantial time and money. Moreover, migrant and seasonal farm labor is not treated as a separate occupational category; therefore, national agricultural accident statistics include both farmer and farmworkers in the same category. Other data systems collect farm accident data in various forms, but selection criteria such as age, relationship of farm work to the person's occupation, or number of employees on the farm result in limitations in the data collected.

There is a need for consistency in the definition of a farm accident and for classifying farm accidents as work-related, recreational, home-related, or other.

An Important Caveat

More than anything else, accident reduction depends on changing behavior. In the years to come, technological advances probably will give us farm machinery that is more powerful and more efficient, but not necessarily any safer unless efforts are made to see that it is. Safer equipment plays a role, to be sure. Awareness of the presence and nature of hazards is also very important. However, prevention of injury and death on the farm ultimately depends on each individual's ability and willingness to modify work habits, and thereby minimize exposure to risks.

The greatest contribution to safety on American farms will result from the ongoing processes of education, training, and promotion. Habitual behavior patterns tend to be established early in life. There is an urgent need to deliver safety education programs to young people. It is reasonable to assume that safety lessons learned at an early age continue to be applied every day in farm operations. The most successful education efforts to improve farm safety will involve farmers, farm family members, farmworkers, educators, researchers, farm equipment design engineers, and political policy leaders. All of these groups have a stake in farm safety.

Sweatshops in the Fields

Today, hundreds of thousands of young children work long, hard hours in agriculture, many in migrant and seasonal work, under conditions that threaten their health, safety, and well-being. Under current federal law, children working in agriculture receive less protection than children working in any other industry. Many farmworker families feel they have no choice but to bring their children to the fields. Because farmworker adults cannot earn a living wage working in agriculture and do not typically collect public assistance, parents are forced to bring their children to the fields in order to put food on the table. It becomes an economic necessity for their children to work so that the family can survive.

What is the federal government doing to ensure that farm-working adults earn enough and have access to child care and educational facilities for their children so that children are not forced to work for their family's survival under degrading conditions? Unfortunately, child labor laws in agriculture have remained basically the same as they were when enacted many decades ago. Part of the problem is that our child labor laws do not adequately protect these children. Consider these facts. Children as young as 10 years of age may work in field labor, while the minimum age for work in other occupations is 14. A child farmworker at the age of 16 may work more than forty hours a week (even during the school term) while no other child can. A migrant farmworker child can work unlimited hours before school. No other child can.

The few legal protections that are supposed to shield these children in the fields from harm are sparsely enforced, and the educational opportunities that could help them better their lives are sadly inadequate. What is the impact on the lives of farmworker children? The rate of school enrollment for farmworker children is lower than for any other group in the United States. The school dropout rate for migrant children is 45 percent, the highest of any group in the nation. Much of youth employment negatively impacts the education of minors. It is not so much that work is conducted during school hours, as it is that work is so excessive that education suffers.

The experiences growing up in a migrant farmworker family provide little exposure to the alternative opportunities that may expand the young person's outlook for the possibility of a different life and improved standard of living. As a result, these children may not learn as early as their peers about the range of occupational options available to them and they may fail to develop an appreciation of their potential for capitalizing on the connection that exists between good jobs and educational achievement. Migrant farmworker youth also perform farm work during scheduled school sessions or in lieu of summer school attendance that is needed for completing a grade advancement. This practice establishes a pattern of reduced primary school participation that leads to reduced high school completion rates for the children of farmworkers.

The Pesticide Problem

Another area involving farmworker children and adolescents, and one that has received inadequate attention, concerns pesticide usage. During the past decade, the public has grown increasingly concerned about agriculture pesticide use. Exposure to pesticides, even at low doses, is associated with a wide variety of health effects, and these compounds are now commonly found throughout our environment. Despite some important advances, federal pesticide regulatory programs have failed to prevent an overall increase in pesticide use, risks, and reliance. This not only threatens public health and the environment, but it puts farmers' livelihood in jeopardy. Farmers purchase materials that are legal and that they believe can be used safely and effectively for crop production, only to later be denied the use of some of these chemicals because they are discovered to be hazardous.

Government regulations have so far done little to protect farmworkers from the hazards of pesticides. The common cliché, "Too little, too late," seems to apply well to these regulations. Hundreds of different pesticides are applied in thousands of different settings, posing different risks of acute poisoning, reproductive and nervous system damage, and cancer. Farmworkers frequently lack the training to fully understand the risks they face and the political influence to successfully combat them. The farm economy is seasonal, reliant on contractors to manage labor, and exempt from much of the basic social legislation that protects workers' interests in other sectors.

Pesticide companies are able to exploit the regulatory system in their favor. They know how to play the toxicology game and have decades of experience in protecting chemicals from legislative mandates. They can manipulate these new requirements by tying up inordinate amounts of time, money, and effort to delay regulatory action, while also seeking waivers to exempt their products from the new standards.

The reason pesticides are used so widely today is that short-run costs of alternative production techniques remain higher than for pesticide-based approaches. The only way to achieve lasting toxics-use reduction is by developing economically as well as environmentally sustainable practices. The only solution is to move toward a completely new paradigm, one that emphasizes the reduction of pesticide use and substitution of less toxic alternatives. For farmers and the agricultural industry, this requires a transitional phase of pesticide-use reduction through what is known as "integrated pest management," with a clear goal of eliminating pesticide uses and relying on natural predators, crop rotation, judicious matching of crops with local ecosystem attributes, and other components of a sustainable agriculture.

The public and state and federal governments should investigate the ecology, economics, and ethics of pesticide reduction. A careful assessment must be made to evaluate the benefits and risk of pesticides and nonchemical alternatives for society. Expanded integrated pest management programs and organic farming will ultimately help most in reducing pesticide exposures for our children and grandchildren. We can no longer simply talk about substituting toxic chemicals with chemicals of lower toxicity. We must talk about replacing toxic materials with pest management approaches that are not reliant on poisons.

If farm children are not protected from pesticides, then the U.S. Environmental Protection Agency is failing to implement the law, and our society is failing to protect its future. The food on our tables comes at a cost that remains hidden from many people. Although farm children are on the front lines, bearing the brunt of pesticide exposures, other children are not far behind. If we adequately protect farm children, the most exposed children in our society, then we will better protect all children.

Recommendations to Physicians

Physicians can make important contributions to safety and health issues involving children. They need to recognize that many children and adolescents work, and to become knowledgeable about the industries in their area and about the hazards associated with working in those industries. Industries that engage in illegal employment practices are especially hazardous for working youth.

The physician who learns that the patient's job duties or hours violate wage or hour rules should be alerted to the additional possibility of health and safety violations. At a minimum, the physician should advise the patients that the work is illegal and may be dangerous, understanding that the young workers may nevertheless need the job and that other options may be scarce. With the teenager's consent, the physician should include parents or legal guardians in this discussion.

Traumatic injuries to a child or adolescent may be work-related. Other conditions such as carpal tunnel syndrome or pesticide poisoning also may be work-related. A brief occupational history needs to be obtained on every injured child when the cause is not validated. Moreover, a child may be reluctant to reveal that work was the source of the trauma because of fear of losing a job, receiving a reprimand, or even undergoing deportation. Physicians may wish to conduct surveys of medical records of trauma patients in their practice to assess the possible frequency and patterns of work-related injury.

Deaths from diseases other than those that are respiratory in nature are difficult to attribute to the workplace for several reasons, For example, many diseases appear the same with or without occupational exposures; and some have latency periods of many years between exposure and disease development.

Physicians have the opportunity to contribute to the prevention of occupational disease and injury in young workers. Job applicants under age 18 generally must have parental permission as well as permission from a school authority. A physical examination is also routinely required under many state laws. Physicians in this role are acting in the field of occupational medicine and should use information about hazards and demands of particular jobs in evaluating whether job applicants are fit for employment. Even legally permitted work may pose potential hazards, and the physician should counsel the young worker accordingly.

Physicians are extraordinarily well positioned to speak out against the abuses of child labor, to urge strengthening of regulation and legislation, and to insist on the need for mandated occupational health and safety training of children and adolescents who propose to enter the workforce. Work-related injuries and illnesses are largely preventable. Family physicians can help their adolescent patients avoid these occupational hazards through appropriate office-based intervention. Most importantly, physicians need to serve as advocates for working children.

Garment Industry Sweatshops

Child labor and sweatshops are two things that most Americans believe no longer exist. Very few are aware of the facts, that tens of thousands of young people are working at young ages in hazardous jobs for long, illegal hours. They are slicing meat in fast-food restaurants, operating paper-baling machines and trash compactors, selling candy door to door, driving forklifts and pizza delivery cars, and working in garment industry sweatshops.

In the case of garment industry sweatshops, the problem of abusive conditions that illegal immigrants must endure has been documented in the media. Nonetheless, these abuses will continue to exist as long as illegal immigration is not stopped and as long as the garment industry does nothing to prevent the proliferation of sweatshops.

U.S. retail and clothing manufacturers benefit by hiding their connection to thousands of small factory owners, who must shave their prices to win sewing contracts from these giants. The foreign factory owner may be the official employer, but what Nike, Reebok, or Liz Claiborne decides to pay for the goods fixes the wages for the children and young women who work there.

The major retail chains and big-name apparel companies call the shots in the clothing industry. By constantly driving down the price they will pay for goods, they force sweatshop conditions on sewing factories. That means higher profits for the retail and apparel giants, not lower prices for consumers. Five department store chains account for nearly two-thirds of all department store sales in the United States. These retail chains have tremendous power over the companies that make the clothing the stores sell. Most of the garment factories, here and around the world, couldn't stay in business if they lost the business of the retail giants. That's why the big retailers could stop sweatshops if they wanted to, or if they had to. When these retailers demand quality merchandise and on-time delivery, they get them. If they also demanded that every garment had to be made under decent conditions, there is no question that things would improve fast.[2]

However, there are complications and obstacles in the way of an anti-sweatshop consensus. For one thing, the global production process is diffuse and complex. For example, the running shoes that are for sale in an American sports store may very well have been designed in the United States and manufactured by a Taiwanese subcontractor operating in Vietnam. There has been difficulty in reaching a consensus about the issues to be included in any corporate code of conduct for it to be credible. Issues such as child labor and a living wage do not yield to simple solutions. There is controversy about methods to be used to ensure that corporate codes are being faithfully implemented. Skeptics contend that many corporations are not committed to real improvements but adopt codes merely as a marketing tool.

Corporate Codes of Conduct

For implementation to be effective, codes of conduct must be administered through cooperative efforts with workers and their representatives. Corporate codes of conduct cannot be unilaterally established and implemented in isolation from the workers who are affected by them. Unfortunately, this aspect of implementation appears to be seriously deficient in most voluntary corporate codes of conduct. If a code is to be effective, it must be understood by the workers it targets. That means that it must be widely and freely distributed to everyone concerned in an understandable language. In addition, knowledge must also be extended to all levels of management and all departments within the enterprise. It does little to advance a corporate code of conduct if only the human resources or personnel departments are aware of these international standards and have the requisite knowledge to apply them to the workplace. For example, if marketing is basing its costs on nonunionized workforces and/or situations in which fundamental rights are not recognized or honored, the transaction they engage in may have an impact on what human resources or personnel would have accomplished had everyone in the enterprise been familiar with these fundamental human rights. Corporate-sponsored monitoring systems seem almost designed to miss the most critical issues in the factories they inspect. Auditors often act as if they are on the side of management rather than on that of the workers. Problems may also develop if the knowledge of codes is not extended beyond the corporation to enterprises with which the corporation has a relationship. Firms that have complex supply chains could easily avoid a corporate code simply by outsourcing. In addition to being covered by the corporate code, subcontractors and suppliers must also have full knowledge of the code itself.

Perhaps most important, workers must be informed about all aspects of the code. Workers who don't understand the corporate code and who don't understand the basic concepts the fundamental rights encompass can hardly enjoy the rights conveyed to them by such codes. While many companies have adopted codes to prevent, or in response to, adverse publicity, having a code of conduct can, ironically, make companies more vulnerable to criticism if conditions are found that violate the code. Indeed, this may explain why some corporations still consider it safer to avoid any public declaration of their standards through a code of conduct. For that matter, corporations that have developed codes may have done so without being aware of possible significant limitations that may hinder their efforts; that is to say, codes are not without limitations. These shortcomings are two-fold. First, they typically do not contain mechanisms for enforcement. Second, they usually do not contain provisions regarding monitoring of foreign business partners. Also, when a code does require or recommend monitoring, such monitoring is generally not conducted by an independent party. All too often, these firms are branches of the manufacturer's accounting firm and have no training in oversight and investigation of work practices. Most of these private firms do not interview workers in private, or at off-site locations, for example, where they can speak candidly. Without that sort of attention to detail, it is easy to overlook a host of abuses, such as overly long work hours, piece rates that violate minimum wage laws, and child labor abuses. Workers need access to monitors they trust and who will transmit the workers' reports back to U.S. manufacturers accurately. Otherwise, on the basis of these monitoring deficiencies, companies will be able to sew a "100% Sweat Free" label into all their garments.

These are the harsh realities of self-monitoring in the apparel industry. Contractors use every trick in the book to hide violations. Can a manufacturer's relatively untrained inspectors ferret out the problems? Can professional compliance inspectors, whose credentials are not checked by anyone, do any better? Meanwhile, the manufacturer's only real sanction is to stop sending work, an action that ends up further victimizing the workers by leaving them without jobs. The Department of Labor, whose efforts to get manufacturers to take responsibility for conditions in their contractors' shops were well intentioned, doesn't have the staff to monitor the monitoring. And the workers, who have everything to lose by blowing the whistle, for the most part, dare not complain. As a result, these codes may be more bark than bite. While serving well as public relations facades for corporations, they have done little for those for whom they were created. No code of conduct is worth the paper it is printed on without strict enforcement of its requirements.

For the most part, work on corporate accountability has emphasized voluntary approaches, systems of self-regulation based on ethical principles, rather than on forms of legal accountability supported by mechanisms to enforce them. This is true of company-sponsored codes of conduct.

Where commitments are voluntary, more enlightened companies can lose out to competitors who do not make similar commitments or are not serious about compliance. Where clear minimum standards exist, companies that do more can rightly claim to be more socially responsible. As things stand, however, the most inadequate voluntary code can be hyped by the company concerned, while even excellent ones are difficult to defend against critics.

It is clearly not enough to expose one company at a time, nor to count on industry-paid consulting firms to monitor labor conditions. Immigrants often provide the labor for sweatshops. Illegal immigrants are especially vulnerable to exploitation because of the implicit or explicit threat of being reported to the Immigration and Naturalization Service if they object to wages or working conditions. Even legal immigrants are vulnerable to the extent that language barriers and other obstacles limit their work options.

Illegal immigration could be reduced or stopped by making jobs that illegal immigrants usually hold more attractive to U.S. workers in terms of wages and working conditions. However, the problem is that employers will not increase wages or improve working conditions unless labor laws are enforced. In addition, the consumers' consciences must be raised to the realities of sweatshops, so that manufacturers and contractors will be put on notice that consumers might not purchase clothing made in sweatshops.

Thus, it would take the concerted effort of workers, manufacturers, and employers, consumers, and government agencies to stop and prevent the enslavement of illegal immigrant workers in garment industry sweatshops. Sweatshops will not be cleaned up until garment manufacturers and retailers are held accountable for the conditions of workers who sew their clothes. Consumers must keep up the call to action, but it is only the corporations that can make exploitative labor practices truly a thing of the past. The truth is that the only effective monitor is a worker who can report violations without fear of retaliation, namely one protected by a union contract. Unionization would enable garment workers to gain power. It is their powerlessness and exploitability that lie at the root of the sweatshop problem.

Student Employment, Education, and Development

Injury and illness are not the only risks to teenage workers. Working students juggle class time, homework, and family, social, religious, and civic activities with demands of their jobs. The typical after-school job fails to teach new skills. Adolescents programmed to make coffee every eight minutes or flip a burger every ninety seconds learn to think of work as a boring, hateful task. Job stresses can lead to drug abuse and heavy drinking, financed in part by the teenager's paycheck. Some parents, though, cling to the Protestant work ethic. "My son," one irate mother argued, "learned more at Burger King than he ever did in high school."[3]

Employment can provide opportunities for youth to learn specific job skills, save money for college, develop trusting and healthy relationships with non-family adults, and experience feelings of reward and intellectual stimulation. The determining factors are the type of job an adolescent takes and the number of hours worked. The job should be meaningful to the teen in some genuine way, and it should not interfere with time needed for schoolwork or family interaction. Teenagers' needs for adequate nutrition, exercise, and rest should not be compromised by a job.

Faced with a fast-changing job market through which there seems to be no discernible pathway to economic survival, many non-college-bound students fall through the cracks and find there is no safety net. The reasons: (1) These students often are poorly prepared, or not prepared at all, for the jobs that exist. (2) There is no consistent policy framework nor are there programs that effectively facilitate their transition from school to work. As a result, most are left to their own devices. The effect on the individual is devastating, and the economic results for society are inescapable. The situation is much worse when the student is poor, a minority, or a school dropout. Since completing a high school education without interruption is the best foundation for realizing the dreams of youth, it is crucial that both educators and families find ways to make it possible for all students, the pregnant and parenting, the ones who need to hold jobs, the failing, and even the most problematic student, to stay in school.

The Downside of Higher Educational Standards

Since the 1983 report of the National Commission on Excellence in Education, *A Nation at Risk*, and later President George Bush's call for raising high school graduation requirements, known as Goals 2000, many states have raised graduation requirements, but found that by raising the standards, by requiring 2.5 more courses spread over the four years of high school, an additional 26,000 to 65,000 students will drop out. There is hard evidence that more marginal students will drop out if standards are raised. The proof comes after an analysis of state-level data on dropout rates from the 1980 and 1990 U.S. Census and data on public school attrition rates from 1980 to 1994.[4] Since higher standards can put more students at risk of dropping out, states should look for more ways to identify students at risk and consider instituting or adapting existing programs to support students before they drop out. Policy makers need to be aware of these potential factors when they decide to raise standards.

Recent Developments

The federal education bill Congress passed in December 2001 requires states to keep track of dropouts and report that data to the federal government. However, the new law does not force states to standardize or improve dropout accounting. That means schools that try to hide their dropout rates can continue to do so. And even schools that truly care about their dropouts can't do much about them. Only a handful of states have tracking systems to see whether dropouts enroll in other schools.

Keeping accurate track of dropouts is probably the most ignored and serious problem of school reform. In many urban school districts, dropout rates run as high as 50 percent. Yet, because the counts are so suspect, the underlying problems causing the high dropout rates are not addressed. One way to expose the problem is to agree on a standard way of calculating dropout rates. That, however, is fraught with problems. For example, should students who eventually earn a GED (general equivalency diploma) count as high school graduates? If so, national graduation rates would improve considerably. But GED students generally fare no better in life than dropouts, suggesting they should not be counted in the same category as graduates. That's just one question that must be settled before states can arrive at a solution for tracking dropouts. Yet, there is little progress on a common formula and even less success building accurate tracking systems. Without those solutions, thousands of students will continue to slip away unnoticed.

Data Deficiencies

Our ability to survey and assess the state of occupational safety and health has improved over time. However, occupational safety and health surveillance data remain fragmented, collected for different purposes by different organizations using different definitions. We continue to have substantial gaps in surveillance information. Each surveillance system has limitations, particularly those that attempt to quantify occupational illness. While accident prevention is the stated objective of compiling statistics, many users are not aware as to how the statistics can be used.

Mechanisms for collecting these statistics more efficiently and for accessing other data sets that are potentially useful but currently only minimally available, are badly needed. There is a compelling need to improve, expand, and coordinate occupational safety and health surveillance activities to develop and augment the data necessary to guide illness and injury prevention efforts.

The problem of inaccurate and misleading data was highlighted by the large number of errors and uncertain cases in the 2000 Census, where approximately 6.4 million people were missed altogether, on the one hand, and 3.1 million individuals, on the other hand, were counted twice, resulting in a net undercount of 3.3 million. The 2000 Census missed Blacks, Hispanics, Asian Americans, American Indians and most notably, for our purposes, children.

We cannot account for all children who work illegally because available data are limited. For example, census-takers, like labor enforcement agents, have trouble finding the very children who are among the most easily exploited: children of migrant workers, illegal immigrants, and the very young. Data from the 2000 Census were not available as this book was being written, but children under 18 constituted 25 percent of the U.S. population in 1990 and accounted for 52 percent of the census undercount that year. Half of the uncounted children were poor. The traditional enumeration in 2000 was considered a success relative to 1990, generally considered a disaster. Still, as preliminary results became clearer, there is little doubt that the so-called factual enumeration in 2000 included millions of errors and did not provide a complete picture of the American population.[5]

We have discussed the data-gathering problems related to the numbers of working children and adolescents. The 2000 Census undercount of children means that thousands, and perhaps tens of thousands, of child laborers will remain invisible statistics, ineligible for legal protection, occupational safety and health programs, and educational support.

Lax Legal Enforcement

Businesses aren't overly concerned about the child labor violations that they commit because the laws are rarely enforced. Even when companies are inspected and violations are found, the maximum penalty of $10,000 per violation is rarely enforced. One report found that the average business could expect to be inspected once every fifty years or so. Inspectors spend only about 5 percent of their time looking into child labor problems.[6] Nearly half the employers caught breaking child labor laws have fines reduced by hundreds or even thousands of dollars, raising fears that lax enforcement has put children at risk. A 1998 investigation revealed:

- The average amount of the penalty reduction was 43 percent.
- The United States waived nearly $1 million in fines for 1998.
- Just 5,588 children were found to be working in violation of the law in 1998, compared with nearly 40,000 in 1990.
- Even in cases when a child has died, fines were reduced by thousands of dollars.[7]

Declining inspections by the federal agencies and inadequate record-keeping methods that do not detect or identify child workers have made it easier for unscrupulous employers to conceal the number of children working illegally, to get away with egregious minimum wage violations, and to expose child workers to harsh and dangerous working conditions. When the federal government falls short in its responsibility to protect the nation's working children, advocates look to the states. But in many cases, they don't find much. Some state laws governing child labor are vague and difficult to enforce; other states lack resources or commitment to pursue reports of children working illegally. The variations can be dizzying. Some state child labor laws are more stringent than federal laws, others more lenient.

Required Measures

Enforcement of the Fair Labor Standards Act (FLSA) and state child labor laws need to be strengthened. If policy makers are interested in the full extent of children's involvement in violations, the only way to do this is through adequately staffed enforcement agencies which devote more time and personnel to the child labor area. Exemptions in the FLSA that allow young children in agriculture to work with pesticides and heavy machinery need to be stricken from the law. More field inspectors are needed. Hazardous jobs, such as farm labor, lawn care, and fast-food delivery services, need to receive special attention by inspectors. The federal initiative to relax certain labor regulations that protect children at work, particularly the regulations limiting industrial homework, needs to be reversed.

The differential treatment of children working in agriculture as opposed to children working in other occupations is indefensible and discriminatory. Legislation is required that would raise the levels of protections for children working in non-family agriculture to be equivalent with that for children in other industries. It is a myth that Occupational Health and Safety Administration (OSHA) regulations do not apply to agriculture. It is true that farms with fewer than eleven employees are exempt from inspections and some record-keeping requirements, but, in general, OSHA regulations apply to any operation that has one or more employees. Presently, immediate family members who work are not considered employees. This distinction between small, family farms and giant agribusinesses should be eliminated.

Child farm workers are twice denied. The poverty their families suffer, and which forces them to work, denies them the joys of childhood. The opportunities for education and learning denied them during childhood also rob them of a future in which they can fully realize their potentials as human beings.

The depressing domino effect is easy to imagine: increased child labor means less education, which means less skills, which leads to lower compensation and a depressed economy. And the proliferation of child labor only feeds the cycle as employers, successfully exploiting the vulnerable with impunity, see no incentive to reform their practices. Government regulations are being reviewed. Congress is proposing laws to shorten work hours, tighten work permit requirements, and update the list of hazardous occupations. The Labor Department is seeking to strengthen regulations, but so far the Office of Management and Budget has caused delays. Employers believe tougher enforcement and more stringent laws will drive up labor costs and stifle the initiative of young people looking for work.

The solutions are as complex as the problem, but a generation of child workers will remain at risk until something is accomplished. As Jonah Edelman, executive director of Stand for Children, stated, "Take one step and stand with us to create fairness and justice for children, which in the end is the most important way to ensure our security and protect our quality of life."[8]

The time is late. The clock is running.

NOTES

1. Jim Luther, "Group Working To Reduce Injuries To Farm Children," *Chattanooga Free Press,* 7 July 1996, 5.

2. Union of Needletrades, Industrial & Textile Employees, AFL-CIO, "What Is a Sweatshop?" 2000.

3. "The Latest Worry for Parents of Teens," *Fortune,* 2 February 1987, 8.

4. Susan S. Lang, "As Graduation Standards Get Tougher High School Dropout Rate Rises, Economists Find," *Cornell University News,* 14 March 2000, 1.

5. Janny Scott, "Study Puts Census Errors At $4 Billion," *The New York Times.* 8 August 2001, B5.

6. Ron Nixon, "Working in Harm's Way," *Southern Exposure,* Fall/Winter 1995, 16–26.

7. Stephanie Armour, "Child Labor Violators' Fines Often Slashed," *USA Today,* 23 December 1998, 1A.

8. Jonah Edelman, (a message presented at the Heuther Workshop, Chicago, 15–17 November 2001).

Selected Bibliography

BOOKS

American Industrial Hygiene Association. *Hazardous Harvests: Exploring Occupational and Environmental Health and Safety Hazards of U.S. Farmworkers.* (Fairfax, VA: AIHA Press, 2001).

Atkin, S. Beth. *Voices from the Fields: Children of Migrant Farmworkers Tell Their Stories.* (Boston, MA: Little, Brown, 1993).

Beyer, Dorianne. *Child Labor Laws and Youth Employment: A Compendium, An Analysis and a Design for Change.* (New York: National Child Labor Committee, 1986).

Coles, Robert. *Migrants, Sharecroppers, Mountaineers* (Volume II of *Children of Crisis*). (Boston, MA: Little, Brown, 1971).

Coles, Robert. *Uprooted Children: The Early Life of Migrant Farm Workers.* (Pittsburgh: University of Pittsburgh Press, 1970).

Holzer, Harry. *What Employers Want: Job Prospects for Less-Educated Workers.* (New York: Russell Sage Foundation, 1996).

Lumpkin, Katherine and Dorothy Wolff Douglass. *Child Workers in America.* (New York: Robert M. McBride and Company, 1939).

Meltzer, Milton. *Cheap Raw Material.* (New York: Penguin Books, 1994).

National Research Council, Institute of Medicine. *Protecting Youth at Work.* (Washington, DC: National Academy Press, 1998).

Rothenburg, Daniel. *With These Hands: The Hidden World of Migrant Farmworkers Today.* (New York: Harcourt Brace, 1998).

Stephens, William. *Our Children Should Be Working.* (Springfield, IL: Charles C. Thomas, 1979).

Taylor, Ronald. *Sweatshops in the Sun: Child Labor on the Farm.* (Boston: Beacon Press, 1973).

JOURNAL ARTICLES

Bailey, A. "Teenagers' Employment, Earnings, and Spending." *Journal of Home Economics* 84 (1992): 20–24.

Baker, Mark B. "Private Codes of Corporate Conduct: Should the Fox Guard the Henhouse?" 24 *University of Miami Inter-American Law Review* 399 (1993).

Bazzano, Matthew C. "Current Public Law and Policy Issue; Child Labor: What the United States and Its Corporations Can Do To Eliminate Its Uses." 18 *Hamline Journal of Public Law and Policy* 200 (1996).

Beyer, Dorianne. "Current Trends in State Child Labor Legislation and Enforcement." *American Journal of Industrial Medicine* 24 (1993): 347–350.

Brennan, S.H., and H. Peterson Rhodes. "Infection after Farm Machine-related Injuries in Children. and Adolescents." *American Journal of Diseases of Children* 144 (1990): 710–713.

Brewster, Claudia R. "Note and Comment, Restoring Childhood: Saving the World's Children from Toiling in Textile Sweatshops." 16 *Journal of Law and Commerce* 191 (1997).

Brown, Martin, Jens Christiansen, and Peter Philips. "The Decline of Child Labor in the U.S. Fruit and Vegetable Canning Industry: Law or Economics?" *Business History Review* 66(4) (Winter, 1992): 723–770.

Byard, R, J. Gilbert, and James R. Lipsett. "Pathologic Features of Farm and Tractor-Related Fatalities in Children." *American Journal of Forensic and Medical Pathology* 20 (1999): 73–77.

Castillo, D.N., and B.D. Malit. "Occupational Injury Deaths of 16- and 17-year-olds in the United States: Trends and Comparisons to Older Workers." *Injury Prevention* 3 (1997): 277–281.

Centers for Disease Control and Prevention. "Occupational Burns among Restaurant Workers—Colorado and Minnesota." *Morbidity and Mortality Weekly Report* 42 (1993): 713–716.

Centers for Disease Control and Prevention. "Work-Related Injuries and Illnesses Associated With Child Labor," *Morbidity and Mortality Weekly Report* 45(22) (June 7 1996): 464–468.

Centers for Disease Control and Prevention, "Youth Agricultural Work-Related Injuries Treated in Emergency Departments–United States." *Morbidity and Mortality Weekly Report* 47(35) (1998): 733–737.

Centers for Disease Control and Prevention. "Fatal Occupational Injuries—United States, 1980–1994." *Morbidity and Mortality Weekly Report* 47 (1998): 297–302.

Chen, G.X, and D.E. Fosbroke. "Work-Related Fatal-Injury Risk of Construction Workers by Occupation and Cause of Death." *Human and Ecological Risk Assessment* 4(6) (1998): 1371–1390.

Clark, Charles S. "Child Labor and Sweatshops." *CQ Researcher* 16 August 1996, 723–730.

Crispell, D. "Why Teens Get into Trouble." *American Demographics* 17 (1995): 19–20.

Darrah, C. "Skill Requirements at Work: Rhetoric Versus Reality." *Work and Occupations* 21 (1): 64–84.

Debarr, Kathy A., Dale O. Ritzel, W. Russell Wright, and Mark J. Kittleson. "Friends and Family: Implications for Youth Tractor Safety." *Journal of Safety Research* 29(2) (1998): 87–95.

Ekstrom, R.B., M.E. Goertz, J.M. Pollack, and D.A. Rock. "Who Drops Out of High School and Why? Findings from a National Study." *Teachers College Record* 87 (1986): 356–373.

Greenberger, Ellen, and Laurence Steinberg. "The Workplace as a Context for the Socialization of Youth." *Journal of Youth and Adolescence* 10 (1981): 185–210.

Hawk, Cheryl., Kelley J. Donham, and Jane Gay. "Pediatric Exposure to Agricultural Machinery: Implications for Primary Prevention." *Journal of Agromedicine* 1(1) (1994): 72.

Hayes-Lundy, C., R.S. Ward, J.R.Saffle, R. Reddy, G.D. Warden, and W.A. Schnebly. "Grease Burns at Fast-Food Restaurants: Adolescents at Risk." *Journal of Burn Care & Rehabilitation* 12 (1991): 203–208.

Kablaoui, B.N. and A.J. Pautler. "The Effects of Part-Time Work Experience on High School Students." *Journal of Career Development* 17(3) (1991): 195–209.

Kisner, S.M., and D.E. Forsbroke: "Injury Hazards in the Construction Industry." *Journal of Occupational Medicine* 356(2) (1994): 137–143.

Landrigan, P.J. "Child labor: A Re-emergent Threat." *American Journal of Industrial Medicine* 24 (1993): 267–268.

Landrigan , P.J., and R. Belville "The Dangers of Illegal Child Labor." *American Journal of Diseases of Children* 147 (1993): 1029–1030.

Landrigan, P.J., and D.B. Baker. "The Recognition and Control of Occupational Disease." *Journal of the American Medical Association* 266 (1991): 676–680.

Lemen, R., L. Layne, D. Castillo, and J.H. Lancashire. "Children at Work: Prevention of Occupational Injury and Disease." *American Journal of Industrial Medicine* 24 (1993): 325–330.

Markey, James P. "The Labor Market Problems of Today's High School Dropouts." *Monthly Labor Review* 111(6) (June 1988): 36–43.

McNeal, R.B. "Are Students Being Pulled Out of High School? The Effect of Adolescent Employment on Dropping Out." *Sociology of Education* 70 (1997): 206–220.

Mort, Jo-Ann. "Return of the Sweatshop." *Dissent* 35 (Summer 1988): 363–366.

Mortimer, J.T., M.J. Shanahan, and K.T. Call. "The Effects of Work Intensity on Adolescent Mental Health, Achievement, and Behavioral Adjustment: New Evidence from a Prospective Study." *Child Development* (1996): 1243–1261.

Murray, Jill. *Corporate Codes of Conduct.* (Geneva: ILO, Working Paper, 1996).

Ore, T., and N.A. Stout. "Risk Differences in Fatal Occupational Injuries among Construction Laborers in the United States." *Journal of Occupational and Environmental Medicine* 39(9) (1997): 832–843.

Perry, M., & F. Bloom. "Perceptions of Pesticide Associated Cancer Risks among Farmers: A Qualitative Assessment." *Human Organization* 57(3) (1998): 342–349.

Peters, J. "Youth, Family, and Employment." *Adolescence* 22 (1987): 465–473.

Peterson, L., B. Ewigman, and C. Kivlahan. "Judgments Regarding Appropriate Child Supervision To Prevent Injury: The Role of Environmental Risk and Child Age." *Child Development* 64 (1993): 934–950.

Pitt, Harvey L., and Karl. A. Groskaufmanis. "Minimizing Corporate Civil and Criminal Liability: A Second Look at Corporate Codes of Conduct." 75 *Georgetown Law Journal* 1559 (1990).

Pittman, R.B. "Social Factors, Enrollment in Vocational/Technical Courses, and High School Dropout Rates." *The Journal of Educational Research* 84 (1991): 288–295.

Quandt, S., T. Arcury, C. Austin, and R. Saavedra. "Farmworker and Farmer Perceptions of Farmworker Agricultural Chemical Exposure in North Carolina." *Human Organization* 57(3) (1998): 359–368.

Rubenstein, Harriet, and Marna R. Sternbach. "Protecting the Health and Safety of Working Teenagers." *American Family Physician* 60 (August 1999): 575–587.

Richter, E.D., & J. Jacobs. "Work Injuries and Exposures in Children and Young Adults: Review and Recommendations for Action." *American Journal of Industrial Medicine* 19 (1991): 747–769.

Rumberger, R. "Dropping Out: A Complex Phenomenon." *American Educational Research Journal.* 32(3) (1995): 583–625.

Runyan, C.W., and E.A. Gerken. "Epidemiology and Prevention of Adolescent Injury: A Review and Research Agenda." *Journal of the American Medical Association* 262 (1989): 2273–2279.

Sanford, M., D. Offord, K. McLeod, M.Boyle, C. Byrne, and B. Hall. "Pathways into the Work Force: Antecedents of School and Work Force Status." *Journal of the American Academy of Child and Adolescent Psychiatry* 33(7) (1994): 1036–1045.

Schill, W.J., R. McCartin, and K. Meyer. "Youth Employment: Its Relationship to Academic and Family Variables." *Journal of Vocational Behavior* 26 (1985): 155–163.

Schober, S.E., J.L. Handke, and W.E. Halperin. "Work-Related Injuries in Minors." *American Journal of Industrial Medicine* 14 (1998): 585–595.

Shaver, C.S., and T. Tong. "Chemical Hazards to Agricultural Workers." *Occupational Medicine* 6(3) (1991): 391–413.

Simonson, J.R. "Congressional Approaches Toward Remedies to Problems of Child Labor." *American Journal of Industrial Medicine* 24 (1993): 339–345.

Smith, S.L. "In Harm's Way: Child Labor in the 90s." *Occupational Hazards* 57(11) (1995): 23–26.

Stern, D., J.R. Stone III, C. Hopkins, and M. McMillion. "Quality of Students' Work Experience and Orientation toward Work." *Youth and Society* 22(2) (1990): 263–282.

Stout, N.A., E.L. Jenkins, and T.J. Pizzatella. "Occupational Injury Mortality Rates in the United States." *American Journal of Public Health* 86 (1996): 73–77.

Suruda, A.W. Halperin. "Work-Related Deaths in Children." *American Journal of Industrial Medicine* 19 (1991): 739–745,

"Sweatshops: What You Can Do To Stop Them." *Co-Op America Quarterly* (Summer 1997): No. 42.

"Sweatshops: Solutions to a Global Problem." *Co-Op America Quarterly* (Fall 1998): No. 46.

Tevis, Cheryl. "Helping Kids Do the Job Safely." *Successful Farming* 97(7) (1999): 17–31,

Wolfson, A., and M. Carskadon. "Early School Start Times Affect Sleep and Daytime Functioning in Adolescents." *Sleep Research* 25 (1996): 117.

Woodruff, R.J., A.D. Kyle, and F.Y. Bois. "Evaluating Health Risks from Occupational Exposures to Pesticides and the Regulatory Response." *Environmental Health Perspectives* 102(2) (1994): 1088–1096.

GOVERNMENT REPORTS

Bureau of Labor Statistics. *Fatal Workplace Injuries in 1997: A Collection of Data and Analysis* (Washington, DC: U.S. Department of Labor, Report No. 34, 1999).

Fraser, B.S., I. Charner, K.L. Rose, S. Hubbard, and S. Menzel. *Minor Laws of Major Importance: A Guide to Federal and State Child Labor Laws.* (Washington, DC: National Institute for Work and Learning, Academy for Educational Development, 1994).

Hartnett, T.F. *Children in the Workforce: Setting Our Priorities.* (Albany: New York State Department of Labor, 1989).

Jenkins, E.L., S.M. Kisner, D.E. Fosbroke, et al. *Fatal Injuries to Workers in the United States, 1980–1989: A Decade of Surveillance: National and State Profiles.* (Washington, DC: U.S. Government Printing Office, DHHS [NIOSH] Publication Number 93–108S.) 1993).

National Institute for Occupational Safety and Health. *Request for assistance in preventing deaths and injuries of adolescent workers.* (Cincinnati, OH: U.S. Department of Health and Human Services, Public Health Service, [DHHS] publication no. [NIOSH] 95–125, 1995).

National Institute for Occupational Safety and Health. *Special Hazard Review: Child Labor Research Needs.* (Washington, DC: U.S. Department of Health and Human Services, August 1997).

U.S. Department of Labor, Bureau of Labor Statistics. *Occupational Injuries and Illnesses in the United States by Industry, Bulletin 2366* (Washington, DC: General Accounting Office/HRD-91–83BR, June 1991).

U.S. General Accounting Office. *Child Labor—Characteristics of Working Children: Briefing Report to Congressional Requesters.* (Washington, DC: GAO/HRD-91–83BR, June 1991).

U.S. General Accounting Office. *Child Labor—Increases in Detected Child Labor Violations Throughout the United States.* (Washington, DC: GAO/HRD-90–116, April 1990).

U.S. General Accounting Office. *Child Labor—Work Permit and Death and Injury Reporting Systems in Selected States: Fact Sheet for Congressional Requesters.* (Washington, D.C.: GAO/HRD-92–44FS, March 1992).

U.S. General Accounting Office. *Sweatshops in New York City—A Local Example of a Nationwide Problem.* (Washington, DC: GAO/HRD-89–101BR, June 1089).

U.S. General Accounting Office. *Sweatshops in the U.S.—Opinions on Their Extent and Possible Enforcement Options.* (Washington, DC: GAO/HRD-88–130BR, August 1988).

Washington State Department of Labor and Industries. *Protecting Children in the Workplace.* (Olympia: WA: Employment Standards, Apprenticeship and Crime Victims Compensation Division, Washington Department of Labor and Industries, 1990).

NEWSPAPER ARTICLES

Cooper, Richard T. "Jobs Outside High School Can Be Costly, Report Finds; Study Confirms That for Students Who Also Work Long Hours, There Are Troubling Trade-Offs." *Los Angeles Times,* 6 November 1998, A1.

"U.S. Says 64,000 Teen-Agers a Year Are Injured on the Job." *New York Times,* 22 April 1994, A28.

Warshaw, Robin. "Is Your Teenager Safe At Work?" *Woman's Day,* 17 May 1994, 41–44.

OTHER RESOURCES

AFL-CIO Human Resources Development Institute in cooperation with the U.S. Department of Labor. *It's Your Job . . . These Are Your Rights.* (Washington, DC: AFL-CIO, 1994).

Anderka, M., S.S. Gallagher, and C. Azzara. *Adolescent work-related injuries.* Paper presented at the annual meeting of the American Public Health Association. Washington, DC, November 1985.

Lee, B., and P. Gunderson (Eds). *Childhood Agricultural Injury Prevention: Issues and Interventions from Multiple Perspectives.* Proceedings from the Childhood Agricultural Injury Prevention Symposium, Marshfield, WI, April 1–3, 1993.

Schwab, C.V., J. Shutske, and L. Miller. *Match Age and Abilities to Farm Chores.* (Ames, IA: Iowa State University of Science and Technology, 1993).

Index

About the Author

MARVIN J. LEVINE is Professor of Industrial Relations, Robert H. Smith School of Business, University of Maryland. He is the author or coauthor of ten earlier books, including *Worker's Rights and Labor Standards in Asia's Four New Tigers.*